# THE SOVIET IMAGE OF UTOPIA

This book has been brought to publication with the generous assistance of the Andrew W. Mellon Foundation.

Manufactured in the United States of America.

The Johns Hopkins University Press, Baltimore, Maryland 21218
The Johns Hopkins University Press Ltd., London

Library of Congress Catalog Card Number 74-24388
ISBN 0-8018-1696-3

Library of Congress Cataloging in Publication data will be found on the last printed page of this book.

# THE
# SOVIET IMAGE
# OF UTOPIA

JEROME M. GILISON

THE JOHNS HOPKINS UNIVERSITY PRESS
BALTIMORE AND LONDON

FOR MARGOT

# CONTENTS

# CHAPTER I PATHWAYS TO COMMUNISM

> And where do you fly to, Russia? Answer me! . . . She doesn't answer. The carriage bells break into an enchanted twinkling, the air is torn to shreds and turns into wind; everything on earth flashes past, and, casting worried, sidelong glances, other nations and countries step out of her way.[1]

Thus, over a century ago, Nikolai Gogol closed his novel *Dead Souls*. He was not alone in believing that his Russia had a special messianic mission to perform for humanity. The theme is an old one in Russia, and while it once had the overtones of Orthodox Christianity, it now is phrased in the lexicon of Marxism-Leninism. Gogol pictured a worried world standing aside, puzzled over the destination of the magnificent Russian carriage. And today—revolution, famine, industrialization, and two world wars having been added to Russian history—the destination is hardly any clearer to a world that remains bemused by the phenomenon that is Russia.

This book is a study of recent attempts by Soviet writers to answer the question "Whither goest thou, Russia?" that has peculiarly plagued the Russian intelligentsia for centuries. The messianic tradition has not completely died, although the emphasis has shifted from mystical, pan-Slavist, and religious visions to a "scientific" framework, ostensibly derived from the teachings of Marx, Engels, and Lenin. Perhaps some advance in clarity has been made over this time, for we at least now know the name of this destination. Leonid Brezhnev, in celebrating the fiftieth anniversary of the USSR, repeated the phrase heard so often in recent decades: "Now the Soviet Union is marching onward. The Soviet Union is moving toward communism."[2] And what will this "communism" be? Brezhnev, typically, paints with broad strokes. Despite all the obstacles, the Soviet

---

[1] Nikolai Gogol, *Dead Souls*, trans. Andrew R. MacAndrew (New York: New American Library, 1961), p. 278.

[2] *Pravda* and *Izvestiia*, December 22, 1972 (*Current Digest of the Soviet Press* [hereafter *CDSP*], vol. 24, no. 51, p. 19).

Union, he says, is "the herald of a new era in the history of mankind" and is building "a new, truly just and free society . . . and an indestructible fraternal union of many peoples."[3] So we know that the old dream of Russia uniting the world in a common understanding of its destiny is still alive within the new concept of communism, but we know little else.

The contemporary Soviet vision of a perfect society called communism can be seen as an outgrowth of a deeply rooted Russian tradition. But this vision can be seen from two other perspectives as well. One is the tradition of Marxist-Leninist thought to which we have already alluded; the other is the tradition of utopian thought which can be traced back at least to Plato. We shall attempt to relate each of these traditions to contemporary Soviet thinking later in this chapter, but it should be mentioned here that all three—Marxist, Russian, and utopian thought—have contributed a dimension to the thinking of present-day Soviet futurists.

Before placing the contemporary Soviet ideas on communism in the perspective of intellectual history, it is necessary to outline the circumstances which led to the recent Soviet emphasis on communism, and the historical context in which those ideas were developed.

### Khrushchev and Communism

The very process by which Nikita Khrushchev came to power cost the Soviet Union its previously undisputed ideological leadership in the world communist movement. During Stalin's lifetime, all communist parties the world over, in or out of power, looked to Moscow for ideological guidance in addition to material and spiritual support. While it was possible for the Chinese to disregard Stalin's instructions and eventually develop their own doctrines, they made no open show of their differences, and in fact paid Stalin all due ceremonial fealty on the appropriate occasions. In the days of Stalin, there was only one Rome and one spiritual father for the world communist movement.

The death of Stalin created a spiritual vacuum, for he had been given credit for a series of "ingenious" developments of the doctrine, and, consequently, Marxism-Leninism had become Marxism-Leninism-Stalinism. In the struggle for power which ensued in the Kremlin, none of the contestants had established a reputation for especially brilliant contributions to the "treasurehouse" of Marxist-Leninist-Stalinist thought. They all, in fact, had contented themselves with servile praise of Stalin's views and tedious repetitions of his phrases. Indeed, the absolute dominance of Stalin over this sphere actually prevented any of them from developing any independent reputation for ideological innovation.

[3] *Ibid.*

In the course of Khrushchev's struggle with his colleagues, he eventually came into conflict with a group that had been more closely identified with Stalin in the past than had Khrushchev. This group, which included Malenkov, Molotov, and Kaganovich, could be particularly embarrassed by public disclosure and denunciation of Stalin's crimes against the Party leadership and his violation of so-called "Leninist norms of Party guidance." Then too, Khrushchev was fighting a desperate battle and had some personal interest in preventing a repetition of Stalin's merciless annihilation of all his fallen foes. Of course, Khrushchev was implicated in the terrible tale of Stalin's crimes, and directly involved in the execution of Beria which followed Stalin's death, but Khrushchev could also leap on the shoulders of his Politburo enemies by demolishing the Stalin "personality cult." By seizing the initiative, he could force the other Party leaders to join—however unwillingly—in the chorus of denunciation, which in this case would be a form of self-criticism. Thus one need look no further than Khrushchev's personal ambitions to find a source of the de-Stalinization campaign.

Perhaps we can also give Khrushchev some credit for personal honesty, for genuine indignation and frustration over his helpless complicity in some of the more sordid and sanguinary episodes in Stalin's career. He had, possibly, become convinced that Stalinism leads, in the long run, to the demoralization of honest people and hypocrisy for the rest. Certainly his whole career was marked by a search for methods of revitalizing Soviet society, which had sunk into the doldrums after years of strenuous efforts under Stalin. The zeal with which he pursued de-Stalinization through his career indicates that there were other motives than the power struggle alone.

Whatever complex of motives stirred this ebullient, energetic, and shrewd man, the results were not all that he had expected. De-Stalinization led to demoralization of the Party leadership, emboldened anti-Stalinist factions in Poland and Hungary, and revived unrealizable hopes among the non-party Soviet intelligentsia. Khrushchev had unintentionally released forces which had to be controlled in the interests of party hegemony, as the Polish and Hungarian uprisings had clearly shown. De-Stalinization had also contributed to increased friction with the Chinese, who still (at least publicly) held Stalin in high esteem despite his earlier mistakes in China.

It is difficult to overestimate the shock of de-Stalinization within the Party. Men who had learned from childhood to revere Stalin as a demigod, and who had in their public and private lives molded themselves in his image, were now told to regard him as having been a psychopath, at least during the last decades of his life. The disorientation of Party bureaucrats following Khrushchev's secret speech denouncing Stalin in

February 1956 tended to weaken the Party's control over forces in society that were already emboldened by the implications of a more liberal policy. In addition, the Party leadership wavered indecisively because of the increasingly bitter struggle between Khrushchev and the Stalinist faction. When Khrushchev finally defeated this group—which he later labeled the "anti-Party group"—in June 1957, the Party was in great need of a new sense of purpose, a new mission behind which it could mobilize its disheartened cadres.

The Party has always been at its best when challenged by heroic missions. It was originally designed by Lenin as a combat organization, its centralization of command and dedication of lower echelons justified by the sanctity of the appointed mission. In the late 1950s, however, the Party seemed to be an army without a battle in sight, a flaccid corps of middle-aged bureaucrats whose *élan* was weakened by the threat of prolonged peace. Still self-righteous, but increasingly self-contented, the Party bureaucracy (the so-called *apparat*) needed revitalization if it were to meet the challenges of the 1960s, particularly the challenge of remaining a vital directing force in an increasingly mature and industrial society.

Nikita Khrushchev, an authentic product of the Party *apparat*, sensed this need, and after his defeat of the "anti-Party group" he had the power to impose a new sense of purpose on the Party. At the same time, the increasingly troublesome Chinese gave Khrushchev the inspiration which ultimately brought the nature of the Party's new mission into sharp focus. In 1958 the Chinese embarked on a program of rapid economic and social development, using native resources. This program, whose major theme was self-reliance (and learning to do without Soviet economic aid), was intended to be not only a "great leap forward" in production but also a qualitative leap forward into a new era of social relations, and in fact into the cherished goal of Marxism: the communist society. The Chinese press unabashedly proclaimed that communism was imminent in a society that was still basically agrarian. Reports such as the following appeared with increasing frequency during 1958:

> What will become of our future? A few years from now China will become a Communist society. In that society, each and every person will be able to take up his position in the general division of labor—he will be able to farm, to work, to carry out several specialized fields of work, to participate in scientific research, and to write. In other words, each and every one of us will be an "all-round hand."[4]

---

[4] *Jih Pao* (Peking), July 29, 1958 (*Survey of the China Mainland Press*, no. 1835, p. 2).

The reaction in Moscow to these Chinese claims can only be understood in the context of the theories which then held the various parts of the world communist movement loosely together. It was generally acknowledged, even by the Chinese (but not by the Yugoslavs), that the Soviet Union represented the vanguard of the world movement. The Soviet cadres, having had a longer period to develop socialism, were conceded the primacy due experience, even though it was no longer said (as under Stalin) that Soviet experience was directly applicable to all other countries. In terms of historical theory, the Soviet Union was pictured as leading the way down the "road to socialism" and thence, eventually, to the higher stage of communism. Although Khrushchev had already conceded to the Yugoslavs that there could be different roads to socialism, it was generally assumed that these paths converged in the progression toward communism and that the Soviet people would be the first to tread its hallowed ground.

It was this assumption that the Chinese implicitly attacked in their "great leap forward" propaganda. The Soviet Union in 1958 had no program for entering communism in the immediate, or even foreseeable, future. The topic had not been seriously discussed for years. Communism had become a concept almost drained of meaning by years of repetition in slogans sewn into ceremonial banners. Its main features were learned like a catechism by all school children, but the concept had long ceased to stir any excitement in young people, primarily because its appearance had been tacitly postponed to the remote future.

The Chinese thus caught their Soviet comrades in an embarrassing position. If the Chinese were to enter communism in the immediate future, they would presumably have overtaken and passed the Soviet "vanguard" slowly plodding down the road. By clear implication, this was a challenge to the leading role of the Soviet Union in the communist bloc, and it could not go unchallenged. Khrushchev's subsequent decision to write a new Party Program including an explicit timetable for Soviet entry into the stage of communism was both a direct response to this Chinese challenge and an attempted remedy for the psychological malaise within the Soviet Party resulting from de-Stalinization and the Party's changing role in managing society.

The choice of this idealistic goal as the restored motive power for Soviet society was also highly indicative of Khrushchev's leadership style, which was chiefly characterized by perpetual, undaunted optimism, a deep faith in the destiny of the system he led, and the certainty that any goal could be reached if only people could be sensibly organized to overcome minor, insignificant obstacles. His optimism was the product of his belief that socialism and communism were inevitable and that the Soviet Union and its allies (the "peace forces" of the world) had already demonstrated their inherent superiority over the imperialist forces and would continue to do so. Nothing could sway him from his conviction. He continually challenged his Western adversaries and promised to outproduce the United States in both guns and butter—and to do it quickly. He once described himself with typical candor: "You know, comrades, that I am an optimist, and I believe that we can overtake the United States in these five years in per capita output of farm products. The whole question is how to organize the work."[5]

To say that there was an idealistic side to Khrushchev's personality is not to deny that there was a shrewd, level-headed, practical core. He was by no means a utopian dreamer. His statements about communism were interlaced with cautionary reminders that many practical tasks must be accomplished before communism could become a reality. He could not permit the chiliastic vision of communism to divert the energies of the people. If communism lay just around the corner, the corner still had to be turned by hard efforts before the new society could be seen and enjoyed. Khrushchev was able to combine an insistence on practical managerial efficiency with a vision of the future that embodied many utopian features—a recipe for communism exemplified by a passage in his report to the Twenty-first Party Congress (in 1959):

> Communist society has always been the cherished dream of the men and women of labor. But to make this dream a reality one must not seal oneself off from life, one cannot forget that the chief thing in building communism is the production of material values to improve life. The communist ideals can be achieved only when society has an abundance of material and cultural benefits. That is why, when we speak of the great plans of building communism, we emphasize the prime importance of expanding production of metal, machinery, oil, electric power, grain, meat, butter, clothing and footwear, and the construction of housing.[6]

Clearly, Khrushchev's response to the Chinese challenge was a very un-Chinese notion of communism. The Chinese road to communism, from a Soviet perspective, was an illegal shortcut to a society that would proclaim itself communist without possessing the material prerequisites for true communism. The Chinese model was based on an agrarian society in which the peasants would be organized communally, and fundamental to it was a change in the psychology of people brought about by ideological "remolding" in small "study" groups. This would lead to communist relations among people, reinforced by the social institutions of the commune. Technological and industrial development

---

[5] *Pravda*, January 22, 1961.
[6] *Pravda*, January 28, 1959 (*CDSP*, vol. 11, no. 5, p. 19).

was not neglected, but it was not considered essential to the formation of a communist society.

For Khrushchev, on the other hand, the new society had to be grounded in material conditions which would obviate competition for scarce goods. He called this "material superabundance," meaning a superfluity of all desired material goods, which would leave a surplus after each individual had achieved satiety (assuming "normal healthy" appetites). He once stated: "The cup of communism is the cup of abundance, and it must always be filled to the brim. Everyone must make his contribution to it and everyone must drink from it."[7] Khrushchev's approach, unlike that of the Chinese, was that people could not be conditioned to behave in a communist (i.e., cooperative, collaborative, mutually supportive, and altruistic) manner unless all societal sources of conflict were eradicated in advance. As Khrushchev put it: "If we stated that we were introducing communism at a time when the cup was not yet full, it would not be possible to drink from it according to need."[8] From this it is clear he denied the possibility that even the future communist man could satisfy his *needs* by subjectively *wanting* only the relatively small portions that would come from a partially empty cup.

While Khrushchev's insistence on superabundance raises some fundamental theoretical questions (to be discussed later), it does establish a criterion for communism that is closer to the grasp of the USSR than to that of the People's Republic of China. Superabundance is obviously not a characteristic of Soviet present reality, but if the term has any practical meaning at all (which, as we shall see, is questionable) it is certainly easier to picture it in a Soviet setting than in a Chinese. By insisting on superabundance and ridiculing "pants-less" Chinese versions of communism, Khrushchev could point up a significant and, for the Chinese, embarrassing difference in standards of living between the two countries. On this basis, Soviet claims to the leadership of the world movement could be maintained on the basis of its more advanced economy, and its precedence in the eventual passage through the gates of communism was restored.

In surveying Khrushchev's comments on communism during the last three years of his leadership, another theme emerges with some regularity: the idea that the successful building of communism in the Soviet Union will prove the superiority of the USSR over the West (which has always putatively heaped contempt on Russia) and will stir the working classes in the West to overthrow capitalism and build communism

---

[7] *Pravda* and *Izvestiia*, October 19, 1961 (*CDSP*, vol. 13, no. 44, p. 9).
[8] *Ibid.*

themselves. The well-known Russian ambivalence toward the West, the inferiority-superiority complex so noticeable even in prerevolutionary times, is easily detected in Khrushchev's speeches. It is fair to say that in virtually every respect his single measure of Soviet success was the ability to surpass the United States in the production or accomplishment of one thing or another. He seemed never to reflect on the possibility that by attempting to catch up to the United States in every respect— even to the growing of American corn in unsuitable Soviet soil—he was running along an American track, implicitly accepting American priorities as his model. But Khrushchev's attitude toward the West was ambivalent. Like so many of his compatriots, he both admired the West and resented its historical superiority, and he was not one to hide such feelings:

> Remember the time when our country was economically backward, how many capitalist figures of the West scoffed at us, saying that the Russians were clodhoppers who slurped up cabbage soup with their shoes. How they jeered at our cultural backwardness, considering us the last of the civilized countries in economic and cultural development! And suddenly those who were considered clodhoppers, about whom it was said that they slurped up cabbage soup with their shoes, so developed the economy and science that they reached space before those who called themselves civilized![9]

What better way to create envy out of Western scorn than to build the world's first perfect society, a society whose fundamental moral principles have long been the cherished goal of Western civilization! Additionally, in the course of his polemics with the Chinese, Khrushchev was at pains to point out that socialism could be attained in the West by nonviolent means, and that the Soviet Union did not believe in "export of revolution," or military intervention in capitalist countries to support a proletarian revolution. How then would socialism come about in these capitalist countries? One of Khrushchev's chief ideologists gave an interesting answer:

> The time will come, and our Party foresees that time, when many hundreds of thousands of people from the capitalist countries will visit our land, and see with their own eyes what the movement to communism is and how it manifests itself materially and spiritually. They will see a high living standard and strong, bold and happy people of the new society; they, our guests, will understand then the full rottenness and falsehood of the idle chatter by various Lords and American monopolists about so-called "communist tyranny" and "the communist menace." . . .
>
> The strength of example of the socialist countries will awaken the

[9] *Pravda*, April 16, 1964 (*CDSP*, vol. 16, no. 16, p. 12).

peoples of the capitalist countries to an active struggle to change society and liberate themselves from hired capitalist slavery. But this will be their own decision. The socialist countries will never force this decision on them.[10]

Although the controversy over Chinese priority in reaching communism faded somewhat after 1960 due to the combination of Soviet pressures and admitted Chinese failures in the "great leap forward" campaign, it had a lasting effect. By that time, Khrushchev's campaign to revive the spirit of impending communism had its own momentum and required no further outside stimulus. The goal of communism within one generation had become a fixed part of Khrushchev's policy, and it remained a centerpiece of Khrushchevism until October 1964, when Khrushchev was forcibly retired.

Indeed, the great extent to which Khrushchev personally became identified with this theme may have been a major factor in the apparent decision of the post-Khrushchev leadership to drop the idea of imminent communism in favor of the old ceremonial and rhetorical use of the word in traditional slogans. The utopian aspirations which Khrushchev's campaign inspired were seemingly incompatible with the more mundane goals of the new leadership team. While the businesslike, efficiency-oriented stance of Khrushchevism was retained, the glorious goal that gave a purpose to efficiency was pushed aside. Whether it will (or can) ever again be brought to center stage is a question we will consider at the end of this study.

### The Ideology Machine

The almost volcanic erupting and subsiding of enthusiasm for utopian goals in the period from 1958 through 1964 is directly connected to the nature of the Soviet ideology-production machine. In the production of ideology, as in the manufacture of machine tools, the top leadership makes the decision to emphasize one or another product and to divert resources from alternate production to the target item. In the beginning, it was necessary for Khrushchev himself to sponsor and endorse the idea of imminent communism. In his public statements, he provided authoritative cues to the minions of the agitation and propaganda ("agitprop") machine, from the Ideological Commission of the CPSU Central Committee down to the editorial boards of local newspapers, periodicals, and the philosophy departments of educational institutions.

---

[10] P. N. Pospelov, "Leninism Is the Invincible Banner of Struggle for the Triumph of Communism," *Pravda* and *Izvestiia*, April 12, 1958 (*CDSP*, vol. 10, no. 16, p. 19).

In the familiar pattern, these authoritative cues become the basis for lower level exegesis, as the ideological professionals energetically enlarge the commentary around the authorized nucleus. Because of the vast bureaucratic chains that link together the ideology machine and the gestation period required for unimpeachable dilations of the original cues, there is a considerable time lag until the theme is widely disseminated. Once the theme has overcome initial starting inertia, however, it rapidly gathers momentum and dominates the media output for a time even after the authoritative cues have declined in number or been discontinued. Without further cue-input, the theme may slowly decline and linger on at some low level for a considerable period. If new cues are presented which in some way contradict the old theme, it will be more quickly extinguished. The whole process is remarkably similar to a stimulus-response pattern familiar from Pavlovian psychology.

The generation of lower level exegesis is accomplished through a combination of formal and informal mechanisms. Publishing houses and university presses receive and distribute quotas for works on the approved theme. Publishing plans and output are carefully scrutinized by Party officials and insufficient production may be punished by published warnings and reprimands. Not only quantity but quality of theme exegesis is surveyed. The great majority of works produced display an unmistakable (and tedious) timidity in their expansion of the seminal cues. This is entirely understandable, if not excusable, because of the ready sanctions that can be imposed against a too adventurous or imaginative extension of a cue. Minute, mainly semantic, deviations from the accepted interpretations can produce wrathful commentary from other ideologists. Thus, just as in any other group of specialists, but to a much greater extent, there is an internal self-policing mechanism among Soviet ideologists which tends to define and enforce a narrow orthodoxy. The result is most often a mind-numbing avalanche of essentially trivial, repetitious formulations that provide hardly more than a photographic enlargement of the original cues.

The ideology-production system also fosters the "tempest in a teapot" phenomenon: the tendency of Soviet ideologists to engage in ferocious battles over virtually meaningless verbal quibbles. Some of these skirmishes over terminology will be discussed in later chapters, but it should be pointed out here that these verbal distinctions do in fact appear more crucial to the mind long-trained in the refinement of Soviet doctrine than they do to the outsider. For example, the seemingly trivial distinction between "personal" and "private" property assumes great significance within the limited confines of Soviet doctrine, where in fact it becomes a kind of linchpin holding together a whole series of arguments defending contemporary Soviet property arrangements. Difficult and exasperating though it may be, it is necessary to remain sensitive to the peculiar and specific contextual meaning of key words used as a kind of special "inner language" by Soviet ideologists in their work.

The ideology machine also has another unfortunate effect on its product: the routinization of cues into formulas. The cautious, derivative approach is indirectly encouraged because it maximizes the writer's benefits while requiring a minimum of his efforts. Accepted formulas, particularly quotations or paraphrases of the authoritative cues, are adopted wholesale by the ideologists on the basis of their elementary "cost-benefit" analysis of their professional situation. Why stir up a potentially harmful controversy by the substitution of even a single novel argument (or, indeed, even a new word) when the system is far more likely to punish such evidence of originality than to reward it? Certainly more successful careers in the ideology machine are made by sedulous mimicry than by clever originality. A minor mistake subtracts more from a reputation than a major innovation is likely to add. Thus the inherent careerism of an ideological bureaucracy leads to the routinization of ideas into formulas.

The theme-quota system inevitably tends to reduce even further the chances of originality in the exegesis. Professional ideologists have long experience in tailoring their views to fit the current authoritative themes, but the assigned theme may not always be the most congenial to the taste of individual ideologists. Write to order they must, but must they also write with deep inner conviction? The system does not really ask them to do the latter. To return to the example of Khrushchev's "imminent communism," the official patronage of an unusually idealistic theme produced a kind of knee-jerk response from the great majority of professionals. Having nothing particularly fresh to say on the subject of communist society, they culled what they could from the authorized texts and from the well-received works of their colleagues. For many of them, the call to write "something on communism" was converted into an opportunity to write something on their pet topic. This is also presumably a safety-optimizing technique, because the author is protected by an established reputation and putative expertise if he wraps the new theme in his old specialty. For this reason, many articles and books that appeared during the years of the Khrushchev-inspired renaissance of communism, with titles like "Communism and the Communist Party's Educational Role," "Communism and the Further Improvement of the Public Health System," "Communism and the Party's Guiding Role in Agriculture," turned out to be essentially restatements of earlier works by the same author with the addition of quotations from authoritative cues on the communist society theme. Thus it can safely be inferred that a large proportion of the ostensible interest in communism was artificially induced; it was the trained, conditioned response of the ideology machine to the stimulus of its master's voice.

## Utopia and Reality

The question of the relevance of ideology to Soviet life is still often debated among Western observers. Those who focus their attention on policy-making have often found it possible to ignore or give slight attention to ideological factors in their assessment of Soviet motivations. On the other hand, those who emphasize the social setting in which policies are made generally find some evidence of the importance of ideology in the fabric of Soviet society. Judging from the literature of the past, it would seem that the general question of the relevance of Soviet ideology to Soviet politics and society is just too complex to be answered on such a high level of generality, and that satisfactory answers can be given only in specific cases, if at all.

One of the obvious but crucial difficulties in dealing with the problem is the scarcity of data on the effect of ideology. Ideally, one would want a comprehensive set of carefully constructed and administered opinion polls that would enable the investigator to probe for continuities between the official doctrines and respondent attitudes. In a society such as the Soviet, where everyone is reasonably familiar with the attitudes one *should* have, special care would be required to avoid automatic responses in the presence of presumably authoritative investigators. Under present circumstances, such a prospect would have to be regarded as somewhat more utopian than the successful building of communist society in the Soviet Union. Those Soviet polls which have been published do provide some interesting (though highly questionable) information on limited topics such as job satisfaction, occupational and educational aspirations, and the like, but they do not probe into forbidden territory and are unlikely to do so in the future.

In the absence of such polls, is it possible to say anything meaningful about the influence of ideology on the pattern of attitudes and actions in the Soviet Union? Observations of Soviet life do tend to show a congruity between theory and practice, although Russians are no less likely to bend an inconvenient precept to fit an immediate purpose than others in similar circumstances. The analogy to religious belief, so often used (and misused), seems particularly apt in this case. Both the religious believer and the Marxist-Leninist believer can be assumed to have internalized a set of values which provide a generalized moral standard against which to judge daily actions and ideas. Because the beliefs are usually not specifically connected to daily occurrences, there is room for ambiguity between precept and behavior. The believer, in other words, is rarely confronted with an undeniable contradiction between his behavior and his beliefs. If the situation does occur, he will most likely attempt to resolve the contradiction (or, to use Leon Festinger's terminology, to reduce "cognitive dissonance") by altering his conception of his behavior or his belief (or both). The remoteness of these ideological values from the vicissitudes of daily life cannot be denied. But even if Marxist-Leninist values are as remote from Soviet life as the ethics of Christianity are from the operation of the American marketplace, in neither case are the values necessarily irrelevant. If Christian values do not always motivate the actions of American businessmen, they at least can provide a widely recognized standard against which those actions can be judged.

Generally, one would expect Soviet doctrines to have more impact on everyday Soviet life than Christian doctrines have on daily life in the United States. Marxism-Leninism purports to be a theory about life on earth, past, present, and future. It is sponsored by a noncompetitive political regime and is an essential part of the socialization process for each generation. The ideology machine fills the media with its messages to the point where the ideology becomes an essential ingredient of the Soviet ambience. In the Soviet Union one can neither escape its messages nor publicly reject them. One can only privately think one's own thoughts and, in selected circles, discuss them with others of like mind. And, for all the talk about "American ideology" (or the "end" thereof), there is simply no comparable situation in the United States; it has neither the mechanism for inculcating the ideas nor the ideas themselves.

Thus we should expect—although not insist—that Soviet ideology would play a larger, more pervasive role in Soviet life than any (religious or secular) sets of ideas play in American life. Can the same be said for the more utopian aspects of Marxism-Leninism that we will be examining in this study? Whatever practical guides Marxism-Leninism may provide to daily living, cannot one still safely assume that Marx's projection of a future, perfect society is entirely irrelevant to the present, imperfect Soviet society? Even if the vision of true communism stirred earlier revolutionary generations and provided them with a cause for which they could happily sacrifice everything, is it still not true that the present nonrevolutionary generations have lost their idealism and have settled down to secure lives of contented consumerism, enjoying whatever is within reach instead of stretching upward for what is still beyond their grasp?

The fact that many Western observers have drawn this conclusion does not prove it is correct, only that it is apparent. It would be impossible to deny that Soviet society is an acquisitive society with aspirations of becoming an affluent society. But the mere demonstration of these observable characteristics does not in any way prove that (a) these traits are incompatible with utopian ideals, or (b) that even if incompatible, the two sets of values cannot "peacefully coexist" in society, and indeed in individuals. It may be called "reduction of cognitive dissonance," inconsistency, rationalization, or simply hypocrisy, but it is a phenomenon that is surely not restricted to the Soviet Union.

If one looks at Soviet society for evidence that the image of communism plays a part in the life of its citizens, one finds a confusing array of contradictions. The media display the word often, but, as we have seen, "communism" has become a routine component of agitprop and has relatively little impact in its regular usage. Considerably more meaningful is the regime's use of utopian standards to pass judgment on the behavior of ordinary citizens and even on those extraordinary citizens who have become middle-level officials in the Party or state structure. The press continually discloses these failures to live up to the selfless, altruistic standards by which men would live in a communist society. The effort to make men fit to live in that future communist society is a consuming interest and major activity of the Soviet regime. The "upbringing" (*vospitanie*) of the "new socialist man" is a self-imposed project of the regime and, in a sense, is the justification for the attempt to monopolize the thoughts of Soviet citizens through the manifold activities of the ideological machine, and the exclusion of alien (i.e., contaminating) influences.

This is a highly significant point. The Soviet system tries to impose incredibly high standards of conduct on its members, and the standards are higher for those who participate actively in the system. Of course, power corrupts these standards to some extent in the Soviet Union, as it does elsewhere, but considering the absolute monopoly of power and the absolute lack of legitimate political opposition which characterizes the Soviet system, it is striking how little personal corruption exists. Not only the relative infrequency of corruption but the behavior of the corrupted, their furtive attempts to keep the matter in the "family," are evidence of the wide acceptance of the standards as appropriate for judging even men of considerable power. And it should be perfectly clear that we are not talking here of the kind of corruption that would cause arched brows and lost elections in the United States. Americans have come to expect that their leaders will live in rather staggering luxury and that they will "make money" from politics; Soviet citizens expect, and are told, that their leaders will live in a comfortable, privileged style but will not flaunt their relative affluence or use their position for accumulation of personal wealth. All luxury, even that of the very highest officials, belongs to the state, is used only as temporary compensation "according to labor performed," and will return to the state as surely as death, retirement, or demotion occurs in the life of the Soviet bureaucrat. Not even Khrushchev accumulated private wealth to any great extent. When he was let out to pasture he became a pensioner, with a very generous allotment from the regime he had led.

It would be absurd to claim that any of this represents the rigid application of utopian standards to daily life. Nevertheless, *the utopian element represents an aspiration which pulls activities and implicit norms toward it.* Daily behavior naturally falls short, since human beings collectively have never been able to rise to their ideals for any length of time. Soviet citizens are not, after all, the "new communist men" of the future society. It is fair to say that one could disprove the existence of any ideals whatever—anywhere and everywhere—if one were to judge only by actual human behavior.

If the presence of ideals cannot always be detected by observing behavior, they can sometimes be discerned by observing the psychological consequences of misbehavior, especially evidence of guilt. Only if one accepts a precept will one feel guilty for deviating from it; and in the Soviet Union, such guilt is most often betrayed by secrecy or avoidance. The contradiction between the accepted ideal and the undeniably contrary real is simply avoided, and elaborate myths are created to bridge the gap. The tremendous centralization of power is ignored, and a contrary myth of popular democracy is widely disseminated; failures in policy are ignored while books and tracts are written, all claiming new victories. Even the disgrace of Stalinism is now met with silence, and Stalin's "positive achievements" are slowly reappearing in the histories of the period. It is an embarrassed silence, perhaps even a guilty silence, and it strongly suggests that the ideals are still a "matter of socialist conscience," a small voice that chides even the power holders from time to time.

There is another strong indication of the strength of utopian ideals in the Soviet system: their use by the regime's internal critics, the dissident writers and intellectuals, to condemn the regime's practices. One might imagine dissidents to be deviants from the value consensus, men who have developed an independent, alternative set of values to those sponsored by the regime. This ability to step outside the all-enveloping framework of regime agitprop should, one would think, produce a skeptical frame of mind, a tough-minded rejection of utopian goals. Of all the people in Soviet society, the dissidents should stand furthest apart from regime-sponsored ideal goals. Yet such is not the case. By and large, dissidents have repeatedly shown their fascination with precisely this aspect of the Marxist-Leninist doctrines. Most dissidents, in fact, have not charged the regime with having inappropriate goals, but with using inappropriate means to accomplish highly desirable goals.

The familiar discussion of means versus ends becomes a dilemma only if one accepts the values of the ends as good in themselves. The use of bad means to attain bad ends presents no moral problem; but if one insists that bad means may not be used to achieve good ends, one is also implicitly defending the values of the ends. This is precisely the situation (or predicament) of many Soviet intellectual dissenters who attack the regime for its failure to live up to its own standards. Consider, in this respect, the anguished cry of the dissident writer, Andrei Siniavskii, who himself has been a victim of the regime's willingness to use unworthy means:

> So that prisons should vanish forever, we built new prisons. So that all frontiers should fall, we surrounded ourselves with a Chinese Wall. So that work should become a rest and a pleasure, we introduced forced labor. So that not one drop of blood be shed any more, we killed and killed and killed. In the name of the Purpose we turned to the means that our enemies used.[11]

The dissenters find a good purpose warped by the use of bad practices. They still, however, find themselves part of the social consensus on the ends—the utopian goals which are the self-professed purpose of the Soviet regime. In Siniavskii's words:

> Yes, we live in Communism. It resembles our aspirations about as much as the Middle Ages resembled Christ, modern Western man resembles the free superman, and man resembles God. But all the same, there is *some resemblance*, isn't there? This resemblance lies in the subordination of all our actions, thoughts, and longings to that sole Purpose which may have long ago become a meaningless word but still has a hypnotic effect on us and pushes us onward and onward—we don't know where.[12]

The use of the "hypnotic effect" of utopian goals by the regime to gain legitimacy is a powerful, but at the same time uncertain, technique. The more it is emphasized in regime propaganda, the more it is likely to arouse popular enthusiasm—but the enthusiasm is based on expectations that are difficult, if not impossible, to realize. Unrealized expectations can grow into disillusionment, which the regime tirelessly combats. Clearly, there are dangers in raising utopian expectations prematurely.

The goal of building communism is a paradox for the Soviet regime.

---

[11] Andrei Siniavskii [Abram Tertz], *On Socialist Realism* (New York: Vintage Books, 1965), p. 162.

[12] *Ibid.*, p. 163.

In the short run it can restore lost enthusiasm for the many immediate chores the regime sets before its people. Yet the regime pays a price: it has borrowed the people's energies, but it must repay with a finished, indeed perfect, product in the foreseeable future. If the delivery is postponed, or if the product is delivered in unfinished condition, the regime in the long run will have contributed to the demoralization of the people.

In fact, postponed delivery of communism is far more advantageous to the regime than premature delivery. The strength of utopian aspirations as a motivation for directing social energies lies in the extrapolation of ideal future goals from immediate, present efforts. Whatever satisfaction might be derived from achieving a utopian end, its utility as a source of motivation is terminated on the day when it has been achieved. Thus a utopian goal can inspire maximum effort (and even some moral laxness in the choice of means), while utopia itself, once achieved, is in desperate need of new inspirations to stoke the fires of personal motivation. This problem, as we shall see, can be met in the context of a fully developed utopia, but the premature declaration that the goal had been reached in a still imperfect Soviet society would create serious obstacles to further meliorative change.

Even the declaration that a significant attribute or element of communism had already been achieved would create problems. Depending on their degree of dissatisfaction with the existing society, individual Soviet citizens might conceivably react to this declaration with anything from outright disbelief, through disinterest, to enthusiasm. But regardless of the reaction, one element of goal orientation would be removed from the individual's set of motivations. The Soviet regime from its very inception has propagated the theme of goal orientation, of purposeful striving for specific ends set by the regime. These short-range goals have always been considered stepping stones on the way to the eventual building of communism. This has been the primary ideological technique for mass mobilization used by the Soviet regime in its rapid, and in many respect impressive, march toward modernity.

As we have implied above, along the way to communism the press of immediate goals began to obscure the ultimate purpose. This effectively weakened the justification for the self-sacrifice and striving that had pushed people toward accomplishing tasks. Thus, as already mentioned, Khrushchev had a very practical reason for refurbishing the tarnished image of communist society.

The irony of the situation, however, is that the achievement of communism is an effective inducement to mobilization when it is an aspiration, and it becomes more effective as it approaches reality. But at the magic moment when dream becomes fact, the dream no longer serves as a motivating force for social change. Thus the gradual acquisition of utopian features by a transitional Soviet society implies the gradual weakening of the regime's grip on the levers of mass mobilization. Of course, in theoretical terms this weakening is quite appropriate, since the approach to communism implies a lessened requirement for social change and, of course, a reduced need for mobilization techniques and the entire panoply of governmental activities. But in terms of political realities it is difficult to imagine the present Soviet regime yielding any significant amount of its long-practiced powers of mobilization.

Up to this point we have assumed that the goal of communism serves as a powerful stimulus to action for the Soviet people as a whole, but this assumption requires some examination. It is tempting to write of the Soviet peoples as the Soviet press does: as a unified, monolithic, "mass" of collective uniformity in political matters. The unified political system, the uniformity of the urban environments produced by centralization and planning (even when inefficient), the conformity-producing effects of the educational system, combined with the dogmatic, almost hypnotizing drone of the agitprop machine should all tend to produce more uniformity in the Soviet population than would be found in pluralistic societies, with their multiplicity of social stimuli. At least this is the common, and plausible, supposition. Without much empirical information, and with all the caution that this lack should inspire, it is still possible to raise the possibility that several different responses to Soviet utopian goals are possible for the Soviet citizen. A reasonable typology appears in the table on page 19.

Despite all notions of the monolithic unity of the Soviet masses one can imagine any of these responses ensuing from the not-always-consistent influences of Soviet life. In fact, the uniformity of Soviet life is largely an artifact of the political regime, covering a multiplicity of underlying variations—and even stark contrasts—in the Soviet environment. Above all else, the great variety of national groups (by Soviet count, forty-four major ethnic groups) assures a certain vital diversity in the population. Patterns of membership in the CPSU indicate that ethnic Great Russians are more likely to belong than members of other nationalities, and the three major Slavic nationalities are more likely to affiliate with their local branches of the CPSU than the non-Slavic groups. This variation is probably due to a complex of mutually interacting factors (such as economic level, education, relative remoteness from the power center in Moscow, varying effects of traditional culture), but it is probably a good indicator of the relative strength of Party organization and mobilization potential in the non-Russian areas. Considerations such as these lead to the supposition that negative at-

| Mode | Attitude: Communism Is | Reaction To Utopian Message |
|---|---|---|
| active belief | an important part of personal motivation, a desirable goal directly connected to daily efforts | high interest, enthusiasm |
| remote belief | a distant and desirable goal | marginal interest, rare curiosity |
| apathy | irrelevant, entirely separate from personal goals | disinterest, boredom |
| skepti-cism | an impossible dream, a fairy-tale for the naive | disbelief, irony |
| active disbelief | a misguided doctrine of the regime, a goal which is inherently bad | hostility, anger |
| cynicism | a trick of the regime to enhance its power | disdain, ridicule |

titudes toward official goals would probably be more prevalent in the non-Russian, and especially non-Slavic, areas of the Soviet Union.

There is also a striking distinction between urban and rural life—a distinction that remains despite all the efforts directed to removing it (and all the claims of success). Leaving aside the quite primitive material and cultural conditions that still characterize the Soviet countryside, there is ample evidence to support the conclusion that the peasantry is ideologically more backward than urban dwellers. In the regime's terms, the peasantry lacks sufficient "socialist consciousness" to have strong convictions about the future communist society. Once again, lower CPSU membership in the rural areas, lower educational levels (and thus less exposure to doctrine), and many impressions of outsiders (some published in the Soviet Union) lead to this supposition.[13]

[13] In addition to many newspaper articles, there is the remarkable depiction by Vladimir Soloukhin, *A Walk in Rural Russia* (London: Hodder & Stoughton, 1966), and a more lurid picture of backwardness and depravity in Andrei Amalrik's *Involuntary Journey to Siberia* (New York: Harcourt Brace Jovanovich, 1970).

The structure of the information flow also leads one to suspect less than total enthusiasm for the doctrinal goals of the regime. The Soviet educational and agitprop systems may present a largely consistent view of Soviet society, but it is a highly overoptimistic—and thus partly unreal—view. Reality always offers a sobering contrast. Reactions to this disparity may vary: those Soviet citizens with positive attitudes on the scale will probably alter their perceptions of reality to reduce "cognitive dissonance" while those with negative attitudes are more likely to doubt the descriptions flowing in from the regime. As long as this disparity exists, however, one may rightly suspect that the Soviet population will contain varying opinions on the appropriateness of the doctrine sponsored by the regime.

While it is likely that those critical of some aspects of current regime *policies* are broadly distributed in socioeconomic categories, it seems that those critical of the regime's *goals* are narrowly distributed in the population. Furthermore, they are not the primary sources of the articulate dissent much publicized in the West but are, on the contrary, distinguished by their lack of articulateness. The hypothesis is that they are *associated with a lack of political socialization efficacy,* that they are the population groups least socialized to the norms of political behavior and attitudes propagated by the regime. The critics of regime goals are distinguished by two attributes which lead to low socialization efficacy:

1) They are the least exposed to agencies of regime-directed political socialization, which include schools, factories, mass media, and youth organizations.
2) They are the most exposed to alternate sources of socialization to competing norms. These sources include diverse national cultures, religions, traditional families, and groups which have been the object of regime discrimination.

Based on these characteristics, it appears that the population groups most likely to support the regime's ends (building communism) are the relatively educated, Russian, city dwellers with skilled occupations and presumably higher social status—including many of those associated with dissident movements in the Soviet Union. Those most likely to dissent from, or be indifferent to, the regime's goals are relatively undereducated, non-Russian, peasants, possibly with religious affiliations. These latter groups are not likely to articulate their dissent; they are not the authors, nor even the readers, of *samizdat* (the underground press). Their apathy toward the regime's goals is related to their apathy toward the immediate demands of the regime. And where there is an active response from this group to such demands, it only flows from considerations of self-interest: sufficient incentives and rewards combined with effective potential sanctions for nonperformance. Much of the agitprop machine's incessant barrage is directed toward these target groups, but such is their relative psychic isolation that they are often out of range. Those within range are more likely to fall in with the existing, regime-supported consensus. We can be certain that these groups exist even if we rely only on Soviet sources of information, but there are no sources for even rough estimates of the size of these insufficiently socialized segments. Since the group is rendered effectively mute by its own characteristics and the regime's efforts, one might suspect that it is larger than appearances indicate.

The regime must not only combat the tendency toward apathy of these groups, but it must also translate the transcendental values of the utopian vision of communism into the operational values of Soviet-style socialism. The translation into operational values requires three thematic characteristics:

1) *Simplification:* the universal must be reduced to the particularistic, the abstract to the concrete, the unfamiliar to the familar
2) *Consistency:* present tasks must be clearly related to future goals, diverse immediate efforts must be related to common ends, and the goals must be shown as mutually consistent
3) *Utility:* regime goals must be related to satisfaction of personal goals; there must be a "payoff"

Each of these three thematic characteristics is found in the output of the ideology machine. Simplification is inherent in the old Bolshevik elitist notion that the people must be fed a special diet of easily digestible homilies. Thus Lenin's remarkably banal slogan, "Communism is Soviet power plus electrification of the whole country," has become a model of the unsophisticated messages that are meant to capture the presumably simple-minded enthusiasms of the people. The folk wisdom of the old Russian proverb, "Repetition is the mother of learning," has been utilized by the ideology machine in conjunction with its reduction of policy goals to slogans.

The shallowness that characterizes most of the regime's propaganda outpouring can only be understood in relation to the party elite's attitude toward the citizenry, the peasants in particular. The attitude is summed up by the word "upbringing," which is the process whereby the elite, *in loco parentis*, teaches the people how to behave and think "in a communist way." The relationship is maternalistic: proud, indulgent love for good performance is mixed with a high sensitivity to the shortcomings and failures of the people. Just as a Russian mother is likely to use "withdrawal of love" as a means of influencing the behavior of her child, so the Party is likely to use "withdrawal of reward" as a technique for imposing sanctions for the "child" people's shortcomings.[14]

Centralization of the ideology machine insures that, whether the language is Russian, Ukrainian, or Azerbaijani, the essence of the message remains the same. The supreme headquarters for generation of the ideology is the *apparat* (staff) of the CPSU Central Committee and, within that agency, the Ideological Commission of the Central Committee, generally headed by a Committee Secretary. The most authoritative reports and pronouncements, which set the tone and most of the content of ideological themes throughout the country, are issued by the top leadership on a rotating basis. The party leader, the General-Secretary, is primarily responsible for theoretical pronouncements, but other Politburo members may also act as ideological spokesmen from time to time. Traditionally, one of the roles of the political leader has been that of doctrinal innovator and developer, and the rotation of this latter aspect of leadership is one indication of the Politburo's desire to maintain a division of responsibilities and power. It is the responsibility of the Ideological Department to assure that the emphases and theme priorities of the current party "line" are consistently disseminated throughout the far-flung network of the ideology machine. This is a heavy responsibility and can only be accomplished at some loss to the integrity of the doctrinal message. In other words, simplification is in part the consequence of the need for consistency throughout the network, and reliance on banal repetition of formulas is an effective method of assuring that subtle deviations do not intrude.

Another requirement of consistency is that the official doctrine not contain internally inconsistent parts. Since the theory is supposed to be a vital explanatory device for understanding reality, reality inevitably pulls and pushes the theory in different directions as the Party attempts to cope with diverse problems simultaneously. Thus conflicting pressures are often put on the ideology, and it tends to fragment as the regime feels compelled to justify every policy with complementary doctrinal mutations.

For two basic reasons, therefore, consistency is not always achieved in practice. The conflicting demands made on theory lead to internal inconsistencies, and the vastness of the ideology-production mechanism leads to variations in the exegesis that inevitably follows the authoritative pronouncement. Realistically, however, given the great difficulties, one would have to give the Ideological Commission rather high marks for its largely successful efforts in removing inconsistencies and subtleties alike from Soviet doctrine.

[14] For an examination of Russian child-rearing practices, see Urie Bronfenbrenner, *Two Worlds of Childhood: U.S. and U.S.S.R.* (New York: Russell Sage Foundation, 1970).

The final requirement of the goal themes in the ideological output, utility, is the result of the elite's perception of the masses. Clearly they are seen as too backward ideologically to be guided solely by altruism and collective goals (i.e., the values of communism). Immediate tasks must therefore, be tied to promised rewards, although status rewards (honors, medals, banners) are also utilized heavily. Practical experience has repeatedly proven to the party leadership that material rewards (so-called material self-interest) are more effective than the cheaper "spiritual" rewards that the regime has tried to substitute. Resorting to material self-interest, however, leads to inconsistency with a primary theme of the ideological goal, for in the communist society of the future the communist man will be motivated by altruism alone and will enthusiastically support the idea of distributing "to each according to his need." Thus the requirement of utility in present agitprop goal-oriented messages is one indication of the difficulties of consistency in the doctrine as a whole. Ultimately, a question must arise at Party headquarters: if the people can be sufficiently motivated for short-run tasks by short-run material rewards, and if stirring them by longer-run utopian goals is immediately more difficult and ultimately more dangerous, would it not be easier to forget communist society as a motivating goal and stress refrigerators and washing machines instead?

But it is not easy for the leaders to forget. They too are products of intense socialization; they, perhaps more than others, have internalized the values of the ends, even while rationalizing their increasing use of inappropriate or contrary means. Their legitimate monopoly of power, their career security, their will to overcome human recalcitrance and natural obstacles—all these are bound up with the image of their purpose: the ultimate, undeniably grand purpose of building the perfectly equalitarian, fraternal, and harmonious society of communism.

## The Utopian Tradition

To any Soviet ideologist, the term "utopian" is pejorative. Following Engels, he is likely to contrast the "scientific inevitability" of communist society (as the natural outcome of socioeconomic forces) with the "idle dreams" of utopians. Utopianism is based on sentiment, not reason, says the Soviet ideologist. Some utopias can be commended for the moral correctness of human relations depicted in them, but only "scientific Marxism-Leninism" can be of practical value in planning a viable future for the Soviet Union. Within the entire range of utopian writers, it is only natural that the utopian socialists receive the highest approbation for their morally superior visions of the future. Nikita

Khrushchev himself acknowledged their contribution in his report to the Twenty-second Party Congress:

> The representatives of utopian socialism sharply criticized the system of exploitation and its vices. They painted a picture of the society of the future. But the utopians were closer to the truth when they talked about what would be absent from this society than when they talked about ways of bringing socialism into being. Nevertheless, we even now find the germs of brilliant ideas under the fantastic surface of these pictures of the ideal system. With gratitude we recall the names of the great utopian socialists Saint-Simon, Fourier, Owen, Campanella and More, and the names of our Russian revolutionary democrats Chernyshevsky, Herzen, Belinsky and Dobrolyubov, who came closer than the others to scientific socialism.[15]

Still, from a non-Soviet perspective, the Marxian communist society fits well within the ancient and voluminous literary genre of utopianism. Of course, from this perspective "utopian" is not necessarily a pejorative description. All that would be implied by including the communist society in the utopian tradition is the acceptable notion that communism is one pattern of ideal society, offered as an alternative to existing evil. The utopian literature is so vast, and it contains so many varieties of imaginary conditions, that it is very difficult to define the entire class of works properly belonging to the genre in a concise but comprehensive formulation. The critical literature—itself almost as large as the utopian literature—abounds with attempts to provide such definitions.

For our present purposes, there is no need to catalog the many and varied definitions and interpretations of utopia and even less need to enter into a comprehensive discussion of the history of the utopian tradition. The intention is merely to place the Marxian utopia, the communist society, in the context of utopianism and, in a general way, to indicate how the essential attributes of communism compare with the prevalent features of the well-known utopias of the past. To do so, it is necessary to establish some characteristics which most writings on utopia have in common.

Utopian writings are the product of literary imagination, and they generally can be considered a special category of fictional writing. They depart from most other types of fiction in that they describe imaginary situations and people in an imaginary society rather than imaginary

---

[15] Nikita Khrushchev, "On the Program of the Communist Party of the Soviet Union," *Pravda* and *Izvestiia*, October 19, 1961 (*CDSP*, vol. 13, no. 44, p. 8). To this praise Khrushchev added an almost obligatory reminder: "But only Marx, Engels, and Lenin created the theory of scientific communism and pointed out the true paths toward the establishment of a new society. . . ."

situations and people in a "real" society. Of course, all fiction filters reality through the imagination and interpretation of the author, and no fiction writer really intends or claims to provide an accurate, comprehensive description of his society. Except for science fiction, fantasy, and utopian fiction, however, writers of fiction essentially do claim that the situations they describe could plausibly occur in some past or present society. They do not consciously attempt to invent a new society, although they may inaccurately portray the past or present.

Utopian writing falls into the category of fictional writing in which the social setting is consciously invented by the author. This creates the first serious problem for utopian writers: the *paradox of plausibility*. We note that in "pure" fantasy, myth, and allegory the author makes no attempt and feels no compulsion to connect his description plausibly to past, present, or even future reality. His setting is analogous to the real world but is literally super-natural—not limited by observable natural relationships. But utopian writers generally do not feel content with this separation of the unreal from the real. They strive for a connecting link; they wish to create a *plausible extension* of reality.

The materials for the creation of utopia, these writers almost invariably tell us, already exist in society. Utopia involves the expansion of certain features to new levels and the extirpation of others. In this sense, utopian fiction is sharply distinguished from other forms of fantasy. Only in science fiction fantasy does the author also attempt a plausible extension of the real world, and this is usually accomplished through the *deus ex machina* of imaginary (but *plausible*) technological advances. Technology is not the connecting link with reality in utopian fiction, although it often plays a peripheral role. The link is generally a social process, a transformation of society mediated by the universal acceptance and consistent application of a set of principles that define social relationships and human behavior. Utopian writers affirm that these are reasonable, logical principles, and that reasonable human beings would universally adopt them, given proper conditions.

The plausible extension of reality is accomplished, therefore, through an approach which is essentially optimistic about the potential attributes of the human race, optimistic about the role of reason in organizing social change, and convinced that there is, indeed, a core of apprehensible principles which could restructure human existence and give it meaning. There is no original sin or inherent defect in the nature of man which would inevitably and enduringly turn him away from the realization of the harmony that ensues from the consistent reification of these principles in utopia.

It is precisely on this question of the nature of man that utopians and anti-utopians most differ. If there is inherent and irremediable evil in man, then attempts to construct utopia are not only futile but, more importantly, harmful. All utopias depend upon complementarity between the social relations external to man and the psychological relationships that make up his internal personality structure. Since utopias are portrayed as the reification of reasonable, logical ideas, utopian man is also described as the epitome of reason and logic in the special sense that his attributes are organized in consistent conformity with the attributes of utopian society. If utopia is to be preserved, if it is to be essentially harmonious, the reason and order of its social arrangements must be reflected in the psychology of its participants. Because the internal and external world of utopian man must be harmonized, there is no room for any inherent defects, atavistic longings for evil, or other manifestations of original sin in the basic nature of utopian man.

All of this implies a certain reduction in variety of human experience. The utopian order is a simplification of reality, a reduction of possibilities. The argument in its favor is that it is a simplification achieved by eliminating evil, or at least greatly reducing the possibility of its occurrence. Certainly each utopian writer has a list of unlovely human attributes he would like to eradicate, and thus human variety may be reduced, from the utopian's perspective, as the price one pays willingly for the elimination of evil. If this assertion can be demonstrated, any desire for greater variety is reduced to an absurd longing for a touch of evil to add zest to human experience.[16]

Since utopias simplify by eliminating existing evils, they are also radical critiques of existing society. They may not all have the biting satirical edge of a *Gulliver's Travels*, but they all start from the assumption that existing society is such a fundamental perversion of potential human virtues that a radically different alternative would be preferable. A logical but arguable extension of this is that utopian writers are basically alienated men. The point is arguable because some utopians—Sir Thomas More himself, for example—have pursued active and eminent careers in public affairs. If alienation is to include such utopians, it must have a special psychological meaning which distinguishes it from the more common anomic alienation.

This distinguishing feature is clearly the utopian conception of man's inherent nature. The utopian believes that man in a "state of nature" is inherently virtuous, and that society has warped human behavior by creating external constraints on the practice of goodness. This, of course, is the basis of the optimism mentioned earlier. In order to bring out the essential goodness of man, one need "merely" restructure soci-

---

[16] George Kateb convincingly demolishes such arguments in his *Utopia and Its Enemies* (New York: Free Press, 1963). See particularly pp. 227ff.

ety in ways that restrain evil and allow for the free expression of man's inherently good qualities.[17] Non-utopian (and anti-utopian) alienation also involves a rejection of society as it is, but it is coupled with a pessimistic view of human nature which severely limits any meliorative action and makes utopian idealism absurd. In this sense, the non-utopian sides with Hobbes, who viewed natural man as a beast with unbridled aggressive drives. Anti-utopians see existing society as the solution to man's inherent evil, and authority and repression as necessary antidotes to the anarchy that characterizes natural man. In this non-utopian alienation, existing society represents an evil, but it is a necessary evil because it prevents something even worse: the free expression of man's "natural" libidinous anarchy.

It can be argued that utopias should not be taken at face value. Is it not possible, even probable, that some utopias were not meant by their authors to be taken seriously? Certainly *Gulliver's Travels* was meant to satirize eighteenth-century England more than it was intended to display the dubious virtues of Lilliput, and even More's *Utopia* had its playful elements.[18] Aside from this possibility that some utopias were meant to be satires or clever hoaxes (at the expense of the readers), there is the more subtle distinction between those that were offered merely as devices for Platonic speculation on the ideal, and those that were seriously suggested as programs for future social action or predictions of things to come. Judith Shklar makes this distinction chronologically: the "classical" (pre-nineteenth century) utopias were Platonic while the "modern" utopias are more programmatic.[19]

---

[17] This does not mean that all utopians agree on the definition of goodness in man, or on the kind of social structure best designed to bring out this goodness in characteristic behavior patterns. The basic belief is simply that the author's definition of goodness is inherent in man, and that an appropriate social structure will (or could) make this goodness a characteristic of human behavior. An excellent example of this utopian position is given by Edward Bellamy in *Looking Backward* (New York: New American Library, Signet, 1960), p. 191: "Now that the conditions of life for the first time ceased to operate as a forcing process to develop the brutal qualities of human nature, and the premium which had heretofore encouraged selfishness was not only removed but placed upon unselfishness, it was for the first time possible to see what unperverted human nature really was like. . . . Soon was fully revealed what the divines and philosophers of the old world never would have believed—that human nature in its essential qualities is good, not bad; that men by their natural intuition and structure are generous, not selfish; pitiful, not cruel; sympathetic, not arrogant; godlike in aspiration, instinct with divinest impulses of tenderness and self-sacrifice; images of God indeed, not the travesties upon Him they had seemed."

[18] See Paul Turner's introduction to Thomas More, *Utopia* (Baltimore: Penguin Books, 1965).

[19] Judith Shklar, "The Political Theory of Utopia: From Melancholy to Nostalgia," in *Utopias and Utopian Thought*, ed. Frank E. Manuel (Boston: Houghton Mifflin, 1966), pp. 105–9.

Indeed, one can not always assume that utopias are offered as serious suggestions of things to come. In fact, Marx was one of very few theorists who affirmed that a utopian society *will be*. Most utopians seem to suggest that utopia *might be*, given certain rather improbable future developments; others, more despairing of the actual human condition, have merely described what *might have been*. In all except the first group, there is a certain tentativeness and ambiguity in the author's affirmation of utopian possibilities. But common to all is a certitude about the potentiality of human beings to live in an environment which consistently creates internal and external harmony, security, and peace. Where they do differ, the crucial factor is the author's perception of existing conditions. Those who are hopeful that utopia might be see the path to salvation strewn with surmountable obstacles. Those who see utopia as a society that might have been, as a great but lost opportunity, see no way of extricating humanity from the many traps that history has prepared for it.

Thus, while utopians may differ in their optimism about the feasibility of creating a utopia, they are all quite optimistic about the potentiality of human beings to be "utopianized." Secondly, they are all, to one extent or another, repelled by features of the society in which they live. From this it can be seen that there are really two components, or sources, of utopian writing: the author's radical critique of his own society, and the author's beliefs about the essence of natural man, i.e., man stripped of his artificial, social attributes.

To say that the serious utopian is a radical critic of society is to say that he is quite different from the meliorist critic. The meliorist perceives deficiencies which he thinks can be rectified within the context of the given institutional and social structure. He supplies a corrective to the established order. The utopian sees a pervasive, systemic evil in the established order, an evil which requires a systematic restructuring of reality. The utopian is a revolutionary, but an intellectualized revolutionary, without the personal commitment to action that characterizes true revolutionary leaders. At his most hopeful, he suggests that utopia might be, but his suggestion is clearly not a prediction. He postulates that, in an environment which encouraged good and discouraged evil, people would behave better than they now do. He does not tell us that the environment will necessarily change in this direction; he only tells us that such a development is plausible. His utopia may serve the function of a daydream: a retreat to an imaginary alternative to reality *as a substitute for taking action* to change reality. It is for him (as it may be for the entranced reader) a *passive form of wish fulfillment*.

All of this clearly distinguishes Marx (and Engels) from the archetypal utopian writer. Marx was not beset by doubts concerning the future development of mankind toward a utopian society. For Marx, the utopian society was a natural outcome of historical forces. The precise timing and particular concatenation of these forces could not be predicted in advance, because they would depend on the complex interactions of forces in each case. Marx never seemed to doubt, however, that the utopian society would eventually occur, inevitably and universally. This is a fundamental difference: far from being a passive form of wish-fulfillment, or even a mere prediction of things to come, Marx's utopia is a *call to action*.

Paradoxically, although he was one of the more assertive and optimistic utopian *thinkers* of his time, Karl Marx cannot be classified as a utopian *writer*. Marx felt that he had uncovered certain underlying forces which explained the course of human historical development. His findings were "scientific," not necessarily in the sense of precision, but in the sense—the more important sense—that his findings would ultimately be empirically verifiable. His insistence that thought is the product of perception about the material world, combined with his "scientism," led him to reject an emphasis on speculation about the future. His style was tough-minded, contemptuous of wishful thinking, and embarrassed by sentimentality. He attacked fuzzy-minded utopian thinking (which he attributed to Proudhon, among others). Thus, Marx never wrote a utopia, and in fact *could not* have written one, for to have done so would have violated the essence of his method. In all the vast output of his writing, he mentions the communist society only rarely, and then in passing.

Although Marx disqualified himself as a utopian writer, we must still drag him—against his will, no doubt—into the camp of utopian thinkers. He shares with the others an optimism about the potentiality of human beings for essential perfectability. He shares with them a profound sense of alienation from his own society, and is a radical critic of its institutions; like other utopians, he recognizes basic flaws in the existing system which can only be removed by a total re-formation of society, not merely by its reform. The crucial difference is Marx's commitment to action. His own life was filled with vigorous political efforts, mainly to organize an effective working-class movement. But, more importantly, he was a philosophical activist.

There is no contradiction in Marx between purposive human action and historical determinism. History will follow a predictable pattern in a specific sense: the sequence of historical stages is inviolable. But the pace and circumstances of this development are not fixed and are subject to human intervention. Marx's determinism does not and could not lead to quietism. In fact, Marx's analysis indicates not only that human action is necessary for historical development, but also that progressive human action is just as predictable (i.e., just as dependent on socioeconomic forces) as the sequence of historical stages.

This clearly separates Marx from the mainstream of the utopian tradition. While there is a small subgroup of utopians who predicted utopia with certainty, by far the largest group was only certain that utopia would necessarily develop under particular preconditions that were both plausible and problematic. They suggested that the preconditions for utopia are a matter of human choice, and that rational men would choose those preconditions. They did not predict that this choice would be made. But Marx saw a logic not just in man; he saw it in the historical development of man. In this, he follows the Hegelian pattern of seeing "reason in history"—but not in a Hegelian history which evolves independently of man's conscious action. The utopian describes what would happen *if* man became operationally, and not just potentially, rational, and structured his environment to bring out his best qualities. Marx, on the other hand, was certain of man's eventual rationality because *historical* rationality would create the preconditions for man's consciousness.

Thus Marx was a utopian without a utopia. He does not fit within the literary genre, but he sits quite comfortably within the philosophical tradition, sharing with it a rejection of existing society and a belief in the essential goodness of natural man. His communist society is utopian in general outline, but its lack of detailed exposition makes it a non-literary utopia.

Marx also shares with the mainstream of the utopian tradition a number of assumptions about the nature of utopia. Foremost among these is the assumption that man is the product of his environment, that he is molded by social patterns and can, therefore, be designed to specifications with fair accuracy simply by creating appropriate social conditions. According to this conception, man is not a tabula rasa upon which society can write its behavioral formulas without limit. Man is, instead, a composite of a very wide range of potential behaviors. Social conditions—essentially the structure of sanctions and rewards—either encourage or discourage the actual display of particular behaviors from the large potential behavioral repertoire. Marx and the utopians agree that existing society is culpable in containing advantages for vile and reprehensible behavior while discouraging the display of man's potential for goodness. For them, man is no more to blame for his observable vileness than is a dog trained to kill. From this reasoning comes the utopian interest in specifying a consistent pattern for society that will encourage the equally consistent display of good behaviors by its members. Deviations from goodness might still occur in most utopian societies, but they would be contingent, not essential, behaviors.

Because of this emphasis on the malleability of man, most utopias stress the importance of socialization, or the training and education of young people. This emphasis is most clearly presented in B. F. Skinner's *Walden Two*, with its "modern" social science hubris concerning the manipulation of human behavior by conditioning. But Skinner has only brought into clearer focus the implications of earlier utopias. If utopian values are not alone inherent in man, they alone must be developed by utopia out of man's large inventory of potentialities. Marx, however, did not stress socialization, because he believed that the material conditions of life molded man's consciousness. Utopian conditions would, presumably, mold a utopian consciousness. It is interesting to note that the only extant Marxian literary utopia, William Morris's *News from Nowhere*, deemphasizes socialization and denies the need for, or desirability of, formal education altogether.

A universal assumption of utopians is that the utopia must be self-contained and isolated from outside contamination. Thus utopias are usually situated far from existing civilization, on an island, or even another planet. In an earlier day, this solution might have seemed plausible, but, as George Kateb ruefully remarks: "There is no longer the possibility of utopia abiding in solitary innocence: the rest of the world stands ready to impinge, and if utopia can be utopia only without threats to its life, and without a military establishment meant to meet those threats, the whole world must be utopia for any part of it to be."[20] Marx, of course, chose the second alternative: the whole world would eventually be his utopia. However, Marx indicated that the whole world would not enter communism simultaneously, and the transitional problems of a world partly communist, partly proto-communist, and partly anti-communist remain a difficulty for Marxian philosophy.

The two sources of utopia—alienation from the author's society and belief about the essence of natural man—also form the two dimensions of variance in the characteristics of literary utopias. It is certainly not surprising that utopias are essentially simplified extensions of the author's society, or that the author's imagination of "what might be" is limited ultimately by his knowledge of "what is" and "what has been." The author removes features of existing society that he perceives as

[20] Kateb, *Utopia and Its Enemies*, p. 21. This is the central theme of Aldous Huxley's *Island*, where the island utopia of Pala is destroyed by the depravations of an insatiably greedy outside world. Outside contamination has also been a major problem for experimental utopian communities, such as those attempted in nineteenth-century America. Similarly, the Israeli *kibbutzim* have only been able to survive by isolating their members as far as possible from the contamination of the larger Israeli society. Thus, if one gives it credit for utopian aspirations, there is some logic in the attempts of the Soviet regime to isolate the country from foreign, corrupting influences.

harmful to the development of good human attributes; he enlarges other incipient features of existence which further that development; and he reverses some existing social relationships to achieve the same end. In all of this, however, he is bound by his knowledge of, and reaction to, the human condition as he knows it. Thus it seems quite natural that the utopian literature of the nineteenth century was virtually unanimous in adopting some form of socialism as the alternative to the existing evils of unrestrained capitalism. This relationship is even more obvious in the case of Marx, who concentrated his energies on a sustained critique of the capitalist system as a foundation for his utopian aspirations.

Differing beliefs in the essence of natural man also account for many variations in the specific organization of utopian society. While all utopians grant natural man the *potentiality* for goodness, they do not all agree that he has a natural *propensity* for it. Thus some utopians (William Morris, for example) view utopia as the removal of existing barriers to goodness and emphasize in their societies the freedom through which man will be able to achieve his natural inclination. Others (like Edward Bellamy) suspect that man's potentiality for evil might inadvertently be reinforced by utopian freedom, and they strive to structure utopia through hierarchical authority in order to avoid such accidental evil. The authoritarian utopias (such as More's) also necessarily deny the principle of equality in governance, while egalitarian utopias (such as Morris's) necessarily deny the importance of authority in governance.

All utopias make some provision for the natural variations in human attributes, even in the highly structured conditions of utopia. A hierarchy of natural human variations conforming to principles of justice is the basis of Plato's *Republic*; and, from a diametrically opposed viewpoint, it is caricatured (and made unnatural) in Aldous Huxley's dystopian *Brave New World*. Marx took the view that man has a propensity for goodness and a potentiality for far greater and more diverse accomplishments than has ever been realized. Marx foresaw a utopian man who would require no social restraints and who would develop fully, in accordance with his many potentialities.

What is the goal of utopia? The specific aim of each model is integrally connected with the author's critique of existing society. One of the distortions produced by existing society, the utopian tells us, is that men are given false goals and are thus turned away from realizing the best that resides in them. Utopia substitutes goals that are congruent with man's *self-realization of goodness*. The consequence of this, in all utopias, is *subjective happiness*. Whatever the social conditions—democratic or dictatorial, affluent or ascetic, technologically primitive or futuristically advanced—the inhabitants of utopia feel they are happy. They are at peace with the world because the world is at peace with them, because it offers no contrast to their conceptions of what ought to be. Such conflict as might remain—and not much does—is entirely incidental and is reduced to the level of triviality. If subjective happiness is to be the end result, socialization becomes the key to utopia, for it is doubtful that men would have the "right attitude" toward conditions in utopia without instruction (formal or informal) in apprehending what the right attitudes are. At the very least, social conformity through pressure of elders and peers would be needed to assure continuity in utopian generations.

If subjective happiness is the consequence of self-realization in utopia, it is usually a manipulated self-realization. There is not a vast difference *in this dimension* between *Walden Two*, for example, and *Brave New World*. In both, the inhabitants have achieved a variety of contentment through a manipulated congruence between the self and the external world. The most fundamental and indeed obvious difference between these two societies is the authors' attitude toward them. Skinner argues for his utopia. Huxley artfully makes us feel revulsion at the kind of peace—bought with the occasional help of "soma" pills—which can be found in his dystopia. Despite this, one might, if forced to make a choice, find some aspects of Huxley's model preferable to Skinner's. And if the society depicted in *1984* fills the reader with horror, does it not also retain *the possibility* of subjective happiness for its inhabitants? Has anyone forgotten what Orwell knew quite well: there were, and still are, ardent defenders of Stalinism in the Soviet Union?

In spite of the diversity of forms which utopia takes in the literature, there is a single ethical core which is common to a surprisingly large majority and is embodied in the social institutions of communism. Close integration of the individual into the community is a sine qua non, along with some degree of sharing of social resources. Associated with this is cooperative rather than competitive labor, purposeful achievement for societal ends rather than self-indulgence or private hedonism, and an ethic of social responsibility for each member rather than of struggle for survival of the fittest. Those who argue for individual exertions instead of communal effort, for competition among men in an arena that is free of unnatural handicaps for the strong, these people attack utopias; they don't write them.[21]

The communistic elements of the well-known utopias vary, but they

---

[21] A good example of this is Ayn Rand's novel *Atlas Shrugged*, which contains a forceful argument against typical utopian values. It is, however, possible to speak of an asocial utopia in the sense of individual self-realization outside the social environment. Henry Thoreau seemed to be seeking such a personal utopia in his *Walden*, and there are some elements of this in anarchist and Buddhist thought.

are generally quite prominent. Plato's *Republic*, for all of its semimilitary hierarchy, includes women among its communal goods. More's ascetic communism seems to be an ideal reflection of the Christian monastic code, a code which attracted him throughout his life. Other premodern Christian writers, like Campanella and Saint Augustine, drew their inspiration from the ethical communism of early Christianity —a sharp contrast with later Church doctrine and with medieval European society. The modern utopias are, in the main, inspired by alienation from capitalist society and offer socialism as a cure for the ethical deficiencies of that system. Yet, whatever the specific historical influence, the remarkable fact is that the vast majority of literary utopias, and *all* known experimental utopian communities (both religious and secular), have been based on communist principles of organization.

In this context, Marx can be seen as a not very explicit (and therefore, not very significant) contributor to the overwhelming consensus. As we shall see in the next section, his major contribution to the utopian tradition was in his theory of transition to communism (precisely the area where the tradition is weak), and not in the depiction of the developed communist society (where the tradition is relatively strong). Even with Marx's contribution, however, the theory of transition remains the crucial weak point in utopianism. The plausible link to "nowhere" can be more easily built in an imaginative literary work than it can in reality.

This is the quintessential core of the problem, for Marx's utopia, however vague and derivative it may be, is the only utopia which has ever become the guiding principle for directed, planned social change in a modern mass society. For the creators of the utopian literary tradition, a plausible link to utopia could suffice, but for the Soviet builders of communism, a solid bridge had to be constructed, sturdy enough to withstand the accumulated weight of history. And for guidance in building this edifice, they turned to the collected works of Marx, Engels, and Lenin.

## The Marxist Tradition

Marx and Engels left a rich and voluminous literary heritage. This large body of work has, in turn, been amplified by numerous Marxist, un-Marxist, and anti-Marxist commentaries. Fortunately, it is not necessary to summarize this vast and complex literature for the purposes of this study. Our concern is to outline the main sources of influence on contemporary Soviet thinking about communist society. It is thus quite proper to consider only those parts of the Marx-Engels legacy that have been used by present-day Soviet writers in thinking about the Soviet future. Furthermore, our aim is to present a rough approximation of Soviet interpretations of the selections from Marx, Engels, and Lenin that they have used. Because these Soviet interpretations have often been ahistorical simplifications of Marx's thought, there has been an unfortunate tendency in the Soviet Union to reduce Marx to the rather banal, dogmatic level of "Marxism-Leninism." While Marx has been poorly served by his Soviet adherents, it is more important for our purposes to follow their interpretations than to attempt the more difficult task of rendering an accurate synthesis of Marx's work.

As already indicated, Marx never wrote a systematic description of communist society, although glimpses of that society appear from time to time in his writings. Communism, in Marx's thinking, appears most often as a dialectical outcome of transformations in previous social relations. Quantitative changes accumulate incrementally until a new qualitatively different stage is reached. A transformation occurs through the agency of revolution, revolution which restores a lost balance between productive forces (or modes of production) and social relations (or relations of production). That is, the relationships among people (and particularly property relations) are brought into harmony with the way in which they produce goods for society. The socialist revolution restores this balance in such a way that no further revolutions are necessary, since it produces conditions for the widest possible blending of personal and social interests. Man no longer stands against society; he is at one with society, because society is no longer an instrument for furthering the interests of a particular class of members.

This sort of Marxist reasoning is, of course, well-known, but it is important to restate it as an introduction to Marx's treatment of communism.[22] For Marx, communism is the dialectical synthesis of man's need to be an integral part of society as opposed to—but combined with—man's ultimate need to be free of the constraints which precommunist society always imposed on him. Freedom of the self in harmony with the interests of the societal community is the goal and special characteristic of communist society.

Freedom as Marx uses it has definite Hegelian overtones. It is not a license to do anything whatever, but the opportunity to do what a conscious, rational person would do to further his interests. In precommunist societies, freedom is always illusory, for there man is inherently

[22] For the purposes of this discussion, no distinction is made between the thought of Karl Marx and that of Frederick Engels. Such a distinction serves no useful purpose in a discussion of influences on Soviet thinking since the prevailing Soviet view is that the two were always in total agreement. In general, those non-Soviet writers more favorably disposed toward Marxism adopt this view, while those more inclined to a critical appraisal tend to emphasize differences in the writings of Marx and Engels.

separated (or alienated) from the results of his own activities. In fact, his activities often further the interests of his enemies. But in communist society, the absence of the property relations that differentiate men into intrinsically hostile classes permits an essential correspondence between self-interest and societal interest within any conscious act. Precommunist society gives man only the freedom to act against his inherent interests and prevents him from acting to further those interests; communist society, on the other hand, uniquely grants man the freedom to act in his self-interest, because his interest is society's. Man's "communist essence" is fully revealed in this society and leads to (or is a component of) *consciousness*, a cognition of the true content and meaning of consequential acts. Communism permits man to design his activities so that they will produce the intended consequences. According to Engels, only after the socialist revolution "will the social causes set in movement by [man] have, in the main and in a constantly growing measure, the results intended by him."[23] The rational ordering of society, and indeed the whole rationale of economic planning, is based on this perception of the unique communist property of enhancing predictability through the elimination of fundamental internal contradictions.

The primary internal contradiction that is eliminated, class struggle, permits the state to disappear, with the result that communist society is not "civil society," Marx's term for political communities. In civil societies, conflict over the unequal distribution of property necessitates a special mechanism—the state—for maintaining the dominance of the property-holding class. Communist society strips away the property barrier to the essential communal unity of natural man in his struggle to comprehend existence. It is a noble and thoroughly attractive vision, and a supremely confident, optimistic view of man's future.

The essence of this vision—in fact, probably its inspiration—is the end of man's alienation. Alienation is viewed by Marx as the result of the division of labor in society that is connected to unequal property relations. In *The German Ideology* (an early, long unpublished work), Marx wrote that the division of labor and private property are "identical expressions," the first referring to activity and the second to the product of the activity. The division of labor (under capitalist conditions) thus becomes a central obstacle to community and a cause of alienation:

> The division of labor implies the contradiction between the interest of the
> separate individual or the individual family and the communal interest of

[23] Frederick Engels, *Anti-Dühring* (Moscow: Foreign Languages Publishing House, 1959), p. 391.

all individuals who have intercourse with one another. . . . The division of labor offers us the first example of how, as long as man remains in natural society, that is, as long as a cleavage exists between the particular and the common interest, as long, therefore, as activity is not voluntarily, but naturally, divided, *man's own deed becomes an alien power opposed to him*, which enslaves him instead of being controlled by him.[24]

It is not the division of labor *per se*, but the "natural" (rather than the "voluntary") division that results in man's alienation from the consequences of his acts. What is this "natural" division of labor? Essentially, it is that division which occurs under the "natural" haphazard irrationality of capitalism, where men are forced by circumstances of birth and accident to work at whatever is available to them rather than choose work that suits their personalities and talents. Again, communism is seen as the society which permits the free expression of man's innate capabilities. Under capitalism, Marx writes, "each man has a particular, exclusive sphere of activity, which is forced upon him and from which he cannot escape. He is a hunter, a fisherman, a shepherd, or a critical critic, and must remain so if he does not want to lose his livelihood."[25] In a widely quoted phrase (from *The German Ideology*) Marx contrasts this situation with that in communist society "where nobody has one exclusive sphere of activity but each can become accomplished in any branch he wishes, [where] society regulates the general production and thus makes it possible for me to do one thing today and another tomorrow, to hunt in the morning, fish in the afternoon, rear cattle in the evening, criticize after dinner, just as I have a mind, without ever becoming hunter, fisherman, shepherd or critic."[26]

Of course, one must not take this view of communism too literally; it is clear from other writings that Marx had no such bucolic image of it and was merely highlighting the basic distinction between communism and all previous societies: that for the first time there would not be any "fixation of social [productive] activity," or "consolidation of what we ourselves produce into an objective power above us, growing out of our control, thwarting our expectations, bringing to naught our calculations."[27] Communism would not "type" or define people by their productive activities—activities which, in noncommunist society, were not voluntarily entered into, and which thereafter form barriers to various

[24] Karl Marx and Frederick Engels, *The German Ideology* (New York: International Publishers, 1947), p. 22. Emphasis added.
[25] *Ibid.*
[26] *Ibid.*
[27] *Ibid.* That this approach is derived from Marx's early use of Feuerbach's "transformative method" is suggested by Shlomo Avineri's *The Social and Political Thought of Karl Marx* (Cambridge: At the University Press, 1971), pp. 12–27.

avenues of self-realization. This again is a unique feature of communist freedom.

It must be admitted, however, that the process by which man will realize this freedom is not made clear by Marx. From the above-quoted phrase we learn that "[communist] society regulates the general production and thus makes it possible" for the individual to exercise his various productive inclinations. But regulation of the general production would seem to require the regulation of human labor resources, and in any case it is difficult to imagine a productive industrial society in which individual whims could be so readily served. Fortunately, there is another oft-quoted sentence in Marx's later *Critique of the Gotha Program* which refines his meaning considerably:

> In a higher phase of Communist society, after the enslaving subordination of the individual to the division of labor shall have disappeared, and with it the antagonism between intellectual and manual labor, after labor has become not only a means of life but also the primary necessity of life; when, with the development of the individual in every sense, the productive forces also increase and all the springs of collective wealth flow with abundance—only then can the limited horizon of bourgeois right be left behind entirely and society inscribe upon its banner: "From each according to his abilities, to each according to his needs."[28]

Marx's picture of communist man is not, then, one of an individual who lightheartedly dabbles in pleasurable pursuits, and we can dismiss the flippant, ironic rusticity of the picture given in *The German Ideology*. (Engels later expressed relief, in fact, that altered circumstances prevented the publication of *The German Ideology*.) For communist man, labor becomes "the primary necessity of life," and the "antagonism" between mental and physical labor disappears. He will have internalized a need to labor for a society which has, in turn, a primary purpose of satisfying his aspirations for the fullest self-development. Under such conditions, it does not seem too severe a restriction on "absolute" freedom that communist man would define his personal goals in terms consonant with social approval. As in any other society, utopian or not, subjective happiness would be the ultimate result, and there would be no consciousness of social constraint.

Here we see a further refinement of what was said earlier about Marx in relation to the utopian literary tradition. Like the utopians, Marx postulated that the innate, latent goodness of man could be developed by appropriate social conditions, but in his formulation this goodness is not an abstract moral term. Rather, it is an expression of rationality, a

---

[28] Karl Marx, *Capital, The Communist Manifesto and Other Writings*, ed. Max Eastman (New York: Modern Library, 1932), p. 5.

logical human response to conditions in which self-interest has been radically redefined. The ethic of communism is a result of new social conditions, and these communist social conditions naturally (and dialectically) arise from the contradictions of the previous social order. Engels remarks in *Anti-Dühring* (endorsed by Marx) that "all moral theories have been hitherto the product, in the last analysis, of the economic conditions of society obtaining at the time."[29] Thus, continues Engels, "a really human morality which stands above class antagonisms and above any recollection of them becomes possible only at a stage of society which has not only overcome class antagonisms but has even forgotten them in practical life."[30] Engels's point is that a moral preference for one form of society over another counts for naught, that social processes are governed by causal factors in the tangible human relationships of a given society. Ideas are a reflection (not necessarily accurate) of a given social reality, and ethics too are dependent on the circumstances of human interaction. Thus, only at the highest stage of human development, communism, when class antagonisms have not only been abolished, but even "forgotten . . . in practical life" can a new "really human" morality be derived from a new "really human" society.

In *Anti-Dühring*, Engels gives us some further clues concerning the outward shape of communist society. The state has always been the instrument with which the dominant class has subjugated the rest, but under communism

> as soon as there is no longer any social class to be held in subjection; as soon as class rule, and the individual struggle for existence based upon our present anarchy in production . . . are removed, nothing more remains to be repressed, and a special repressive force, a state, is no longer necessary.[31]

He continues: "State interference in social relations becomes . . . superfluous" and "withers away of itself." The state is unnecessary, not because its *supposed* role as mediator of now nonexistent class antagonisms is obsolete, but because its *actual* role as the weapon of the ruling class has been obviated by the elimination of class rule. Marx makes it clear (in *The Poverty of Philosophy*) that in a classless society "there will no longer be political power, properly speaking, since political power is simply the official form of [class] antagonism in civil society."[32] Given this definition of politics, Engels's conclusions about

---

[29] *Anti-Dühring*, p. 131.
[30] *Ibid.*, p. 132.
[31] *Ibid.*, p. 387.
[32] Karl Marx, *The Poverty of Philosophy* (Chicago: Charles H. Kerr, n.d.), p. 190.

the sphere of regulation under communism seem logically appropriate: "The government of persons is replaced by the administration of things, and by the conduct of processes of production."[33]

The "administration of things" is presumably a technical, rational operation, free of the ethical judgments which might cause men to differ even when self-interest and social interest are harmoniously combined. Here again, if values flow from a common interest in a harmonious society, rational men cannot be expected to disagree about them. The prospect that is opened up to man is a lasting solution to the problem of social organization and a diversion of his energies into the everlasting struggle to conquer the natural world.

The bright prospect of man's future is predicated on a great increase in the productive forces of society. Both Marx and Engels make it clear that man cannot be truly free unless he is unshackled from the grim necessity of producing for survival. According to Marx, "the realm of freedom actually begins only where labor which is determined by necessity and mundane considerations ceases; thus in the very nature of things it lies beyond the sphere of actual material production. . . . Freedom in this field can only consist in socialized man, the associated producers, rationally regulating their interchange with Nature, bringing it under their common control, instead of being ruled by it as by the blind forces of Nature, and achieving this with the least expenditure of energy and under conditions most favorable to, and worthy of, their human nature."[34] Even under communism, some time will have to be given to production in the "realm of necessity," but Marx envisions the shortening of the working day, and increased time given to "that development of human energy which is an end in itself" (as he put it in the third volume of *Capital*), i.e., to those pursuits which have as their sole purpose the self-realization which is the ultimate purpose of communism.

These pursuits would be many and varied. Marx and Engels emphasized that the artificial "antagonism" between mental and physical labor under capitalism, and the resulting status differential, would naturally disappear under communism. Indeed, their bucolic and probably not quite serious example of diverse occupations in *The German Ideology* is a neat blending of intellectual and simple physical labor. The point is a commendably sensible one: hardly anyone would deny either the advantages of combining physical and mental exercise for healthy human development or Marx's point that the existing society creates obstacles to the free combination of these activities in the characteristic lifestyle

[33] *Anti-Dühring*, p. 131.
[34] Karl Marx, *Capital*, 3 vols. (New York: International Publishers, 1967), 3: 820.

of contemporary man—the more so as the society becomes increasingly developed economically. Although Marx did not express it this way, the sameness of routinized existence leads to boredom, and he prescribed a stimulating variety in daily life which might very well be an antidote.

While Marxian variety in lifestyle is highly attractive, several questions inevitably arise concerning its implementation. Even given universally perfected consciousness, highly adaptable and talented people, and the greatest willingness to cooperate in the general welfare, is it possible to imagine (as does Engels in *Anti-Dühring*) a society in which "socialized production upon a predetermined plan" is combined with a directing structure in which "the government of men is replaced by the administration of things"? Would not planning itself tend to reduce the stimulating spontaneity of the communist lifestyle envisioned by Marx? In fact, is not variety, if planned and predetermined, still a routine which can eventually lead to enervation rather than stimulation? One need not conclude that quarrels over work assignments would inevitably ensue in communist society to question whether planned work assignments, even when willingly accepted, really are compatible with Engels's description of communism as "the ascent of man from the kingdom of necessity to the kingdom of freedom."[35]

Marx and Engels suggest a tentative way out of this paradox: man's productivity and social wealth will be immensely multiplied to the point where society's "necessary labor" for material needs will consume only a small portion of his time and energy. Consequently, man's energies will be devoted to creative, personal self-fulfillment, to "that development of human energy which is an end in itself." This pursuit, however, accentuates an individualism which would have to be reconciled with the prior claims of communal responsibility. While this hardly amounts to an inherent contradiction in communist society, it does amount to a problem with which, as we shall see, contemporary Soviet ideologists must wrestle. If unimaginable abundance under communism leads to a reduction of the sphere where necessary, planned work will occupy man, this certainly cannot be the solution to the planning versus freedom dilemma for the foreseeable future in the Soviet Union (or any other country, for that matter).

The other features of the Marx-Engels communist society do not seem to differ markedly from the generic attributes of utopian communism since the time of Plato. The freer association of the sexes envisioned by Plato for his "guardian" class will be the norm for the entire society of Marxian communism. In the latter, however, it develops, dialectically, from the flaws of the bourgeois family, which is seen as a

---

[35] *Anti-Dühring*, p. 391.

distorted relationship in which capitalist property relations are extended to wife and children. Thus Marx and Engels assert that "the bourgeois sees in his wife a mere instrument of production."[36] Since, in their view, the institution of bourgeois monogamy had already broken down, and become a mere hypocritical facade covering widespread adultery and prostitution, communism will merely "introduce, in substitution for a hypocritically concealed, an openly legalized community of women."[37] But Engels made it clear that communism would not entail the kind of "group marriage" that made the Oneida Community in the United States so notorious. Sexual love will determine the pairing of the sexes under communism, and since "sexual love is by its nature exclusive . . . the marriage based on sexual love is by its nature individual marriage."[38] Thus "the equality of women . . . achieved [under communism] will tend infinitely more to make men really monogamous than to make women polyandrous."[39] To this Engels adds that communist monogamous marriage will exclude two features of bourgeois marriage: male supremacy, and indissolubility of the relation even "if affection definitely comes to an end or is supplanted by a new passionate love." As to the communist family as a unit of society, Engels gives the following interesting, albeit brief, description:

> With the transfer of the means of production into common ownership, the single family ceases to be the economic unit of society. Private housekeeping is transformed into a social industry. The care and education of the children becomes a public affair; society looks after all children alike, whether they are legitimate or not.[40]

This passage seems to imply a society in which the kitchen, the vacuum cleaner, and the nursery are all separated from the marriage relationship, and it has provided much fuel for Soviet debate over the relative viability of parents versus boarding schools as the agents of future upbringing.

Other questions about communist sexual relations Engels dismissed with a characteristic warning that only future conditions could determine the form of future social relationships.

> But what will there be new? That will be answered when a new generation has grown up . . . When these people are in the world, they will care precious little what anybody today thinks they ought to do; they will

---

[36] Karl Marx and Frederick Engels, "The Communist Manifesto," in *Selected Works*, 2 vols. (Moscow: Foreign Languages Publishing House, 1958), 1:50.

[37] *Ibid.*, p. 51.

[38] Frederick Engels, *The Origin of the Family, Private Property, and the State* (New York: International Publishers, 1942), p. 72.

[39] *Ibid.*, p. 73.

[40] *Ibid.*, p. 67.

make their own practice and their corresponding public opinion about the practice of each individual—and that will be the end of it.[41]

As previously mentioned, their scientific "materialist" approach to questions of past, present, and future social forms drastically limited speculations by Marx and Engels about the details of communist society. The picture they left was only a sketch. They were confident that future generations, given a vastly different material world, would know how to complete the picture.

Marx and Engels did, however, provide more details on the process of transition to communism—the plausible link from the present to utopia that is often so weakly developed in the utopian literature. They repeatedly insisted that a socialist revolution would be required in order to set the stage for the development of communism. There could be no success in reforming a basically exploitative system; only the totality of revolution could wrench history forward from capitalism to socialism. The postrevolutionary period was defined by Marx as "a political transition period during which the state can be nothing else than the *revolutionary dictatorship of the proletariat.*"[42] Although capitalist society had already prepared the groundwork for socialism, a period after the revolution would be required to solidify the new social relationships implied by the victory of the proletariat. Since the proletariat would include the vast majority of the people, its temporary dictatorship would be a profoundly democratic one, and it would enact policies for the benefit of the vast majority while suppressing the unregenerate former exploiters. The overall task of this period was defined in *The Communist Manifesto*: "The proletariat will use its political supremacy to wrest, by degrees, all capital from the bourgeoisie, to centralize all instruments of production in the hands of the State, i.e., of the proletariat organized as the ruling class; and to increase the total of productive forces as rapidly as possible."[43] This would have to be done "by means of despotic inroads on the rights of property" such as "a heavy progressive or graduated income tax, abolition of all right of inheritance, confiscation of the property of all emigrants and rebels," etc.[44] The granting of credit, and the means of transportation and communication would all be centralized "in the hands of the State." In addition, the state would establish the "equal liability of all to labor [through] the establishment of industrial armies, especially for agriculture," would bring about "the gradual abolition of the distinction between town and country, by a

[41] *Ibid.*, p. 73.
[42] Karl Marx, *Critique of the Gotha Programme* (New York: International Publishers, 1933), pp. 44–45.
[43] Marx and Engels, *Selected Works*, 1:53.
[44] *Ibid.*

more equable distribution of the population over the country," and would inaugurate "free education for all children in public schools [including] the combination of education with industrial production."[45] Judging from Marx's approving comments on the policies of the Paris Commune of 1871, one could also surmise that all those in public service during the dictatorship of the proletariat would receive workmen's wages, and that the members of the directing body would be elected by universal suffrage, combine legislative and executive functions, and be primarily workingmen or their "acknowledged representatives."[46] In addition, the police force would be "stripped of its political attributes" and made a responsible agent of the proletariat, churches would be disestablished and disendowed, magistrates and judges would be made "elective, responsible, and revocable" as would be members of the administration. Marx also approved of the idea that the Paris Commune was "to serve as a model to all the great industrial centers of France" and that "the Commune was to be the political form of even the smallest country hamlet," with each district sending delegates (bound by formal instructions) to a so-called National Delegation in Paris. Representative democracy as a political form during the phase of the proletarian dictatorship was thus specifically endorsed by Marx in this particular case. In a sense, the historical process had validated these proletarian institutions, which Marx recognized as appropriate for the conditions under which they were born (or planned). It is not certain, however, that Marx saw these institutions arising in future, presumably different, circumstances. In any case, he never set down a theoretical analysis of the form of the dictatorship of the proletariat *in extenso*.

Both the dictatorship of the proletariat and socialism itself were to be built upon the completed foundation of capitalism. The capitalist system had created the necessary preconditions, i.e., highly developed forces of production, for a relatively rapid transition to socialism. Marx explained this aspect of what became known as "historical materialism" in the following way:

No social order ever perishes before all the productive forces for which there is room in it have developed; and new, higher relations of production never appear before the material conditions of their existence have matured in the womb of the old society itself. Therefore mankind always sets itself only such tasks as it can solve; since, looking at the matter more closely, it will always be found that the task itself arises only when the

---

[45] *Ibid.*
[46] Karl Marx, "The Civil War in France," in *Selected Works*, 1:519.

material conditions for its solution already exist or are at least in the process of formation.[47]

Thus the bourgeois society creates the material preconditions for socialism, and the socialist revolution transforms the relations of production (i.e., the relations among people in the productive process) into harmonious balance with the productive process. Capitalist relations of production, while appropriate for progressive development during the early period of capitalism, eventually become an anachronism: "From forms of development of the productive forces these relations turn into their fetters," writes Marx, and at that point "begins an epoch of social revolution."[48]

Under the socialist system, people would labor according to their ability and receive goods in proportion to the value of the labor performed. According to Marx, the socialist worker "receives from society a voucher that he has contributed such and such a quantity of work and draws through this voucher on the social storehouse as much of the means of consumption as the same quantity of work costs. The same amount of work which he has given to society in one form, he receives back in another."[49] This system, while just according to bourgeois standards, is unjust by communist standards because "it tacitly recognizes unequal individual endowment and thus capacities for production, as natural privileges. *It is therefore a right of inequality in its content as in general is every right.*"[50]

This inequality would be eliminated in the second phase of postrevolutionary society, the full communist society. Since, for the first time in human history, there would be no antagonism between the forces of production and the producers, the development of communism would proceed smoothly and gradually. Communist consciousness would make labor a "primary necessity of life" and would fully support the distribution of goods according to the needs of the individual, without regard to the value of his labor.

The communist society which Marx bequeathed to his successors contains many unresolved problems. In contrast to other utopians, Marx deinstitutionalized his utopia, depending instead on the internal control mechanism of communist consciousness to establish the essential harmony of society that is always a primary utopian goal. In so doing, he did not express merely a fundamental faith in the qualities of mankind, but rather a belief in the primacy of man's social identity in

[47] Karl Marx, "Preface to a Contribution to the Critique of Political Economy," in *Selected Works,* 1:363.
[48] *Ibid.*
[49] *Critique of the Gotha Programme,* p. 29.
[50] *Ibid.,* p. 30.

structuring his thought and behavior: "It is not the consciousness of men that determines their being, but, on the contrary, their social being that determines their consciousness."[51] That common ownership of the means of production and the end of structural property inequality could lead to fraternity, altruism, and maximum cooperation between men seems at least possible. But it is more difficult to accept some of the other assumptions behind the Marx-Engels version of communism. The insistence on absolute equality seems a value preference not necessarily connected to the material conditions of communist society. While it is perhaps a laudable preference, it does raise many vexing problems for those who later take on the obligation to carry through the plan. Since the genetic endowments of men will still be unequal under communism —despite a far greater fulfillment of potentialities—communist society is saved from the baneful effects of hierarchy and inequality by the advent of poly-functional man, the man of many skills and talents who moves easily from the workmen's bench to the director's chair and back again, without complaint. The Marxist method of analysis renders invalid any objections to this vision based on our knowledge of present society and its endemic specialization. After all, the conditions of life will be different under communism, and communist man cannot be measured by the inadequate yardstick of contemporary man, warped and dwarfed by the conditions of capitalism. Still, the poly-functional communist man is easier to imagine in a society where "hunters, fishermen, and critical critics" predominate than in a highly productive, industrialized society with (as we now know) widespread applications of highly complicated technology in daily life. This problem, and other similar problems of balancing freedom and equality on the one hand with the necessity for close coordination and rational planning on the other, has remained to bedevil the Soviet planners of the new society based on Marx's vision of the future.

If, as Marx postulated, socialism could only be built upon the base of revolutionized capitalism, it could not be an immediate prospect for

---

[51] "Preface to a Contribution," in *Selected Works*, 1:363. Shlomo Avineri argues that Marx was not a materialist reductionist, and did not intend to suggest that man's thought is merely a reflection of the existing material world. Avineri dissociates Marx from the reductionist position of Engels (in *Dialectics of Nature*) and Lenin (in *Materialism and Empirio-Criticism*). While the point is valid, it is not emphasized here for two reasons: Marx unfortunately left himself vulnerable to this misinterpretation in several of his more summary formulations; and Soviet philosophers have consistently followed this misinterpretation because of Lenin's appropriation of it. Thus, what Marx actually thought, and the contrast between his thinking and that of Engels and Lenin, is less important for our purposes than the accepted Soviet misinterpretation of Marx and the Soviet insistence that the three were always in agreement. See Avineri, *The Social and Political Thought of Karl Marx*, chapter 3.

most of the world, where capitalism had not yet appeared. The prospect for Russia was thus dim. Both Marx and Engels became interested in Russian conditions and both acquired a reading knowledge of Russian in order to study those conditions more fully. Their influence among Russian radicals grew immensely in the last two decades of the nineteenth century and as a consequence they were repeatedly asked for advice about the prospects for revolution in Russia. Many Russian revolutionaries had looked to the communal property arrangements of the Russian peasant village as an embryo from which socialism could grow directly, without the necessity of first building an industrialized capitalism. Engels, however, insisted that this could be done only if a successful socialist transformation took place in Western Europe. In 1874, Engels asserted that "if anything can still save Russian communal ownership and give it a chance of growing into a new, really viable form, it is a proletarian revolution in Western Europe."[52] Almost twenty years later, he reaffirmed that position in a general, theoretical context:

> No more in Russia than anywhere else would it have been possible to develop a higher social form out of primitive agrarian communism unless —that higher form was *already in existence* in another country, so as to serve as a model. That higher form being, wherever it is historically possible, the necessary consequence of the capitalistic form of production and of the social dualistic antagonism created by it, it could not be developed directly out of the agrarian commune, unless in imitation of an example already in existence, somewhere else.[53]

For most of his life, V. I. Lenin wrestled with the same problem: what is to be done in a precapitalist society to bring about the socialist revolution? Lenin took the first step by attempting to show (in *The Development of Capitalism in Russia* [1898]) that capitalism had actually progressed much farther than had been imagined. If this were true, a socialist revolution could take place within Lenin's lifetime. If it were not true, however, he and other Marxists of his generation would have the limited role of pushing forward the more progressive bourgeoisie to the fullest development and eventual breakdown of capitalism. The full story of Lenin's theoretical development has been told elsewhere and need not be outlined here.[54] That Lenin was able to

---

[52] Frederick Engels, "On Social Relations in Russia," in *Selected Works*, 2:58.

[53] Engels to Danielson, October 17, 1893, in Karl Marx and Frederick Engels, *Selected Correspondence, 1846–1895*, trans. Dona Torr (New York: International Publishers, 1942), p. 515.

[54] See *inter alia* Leopold Haimson, *The Russian Marxists and the Origins of Bolshevism* (Boston: Beacon Press, 1955); John Plamenatz, *German Marxism and Russian Communism* (New York: Harper & Row, 1965); Adam B. Ulam, *The Bolsheviks* (New York: Macmillan, 1965).

overcome his Marxist scruples concerning premature revolution is obvious, and Marx, in his enthusiasm for the Paris Commune of 1871, could be held guilty of the same flexibility when practical opportunities arose.

Lenin was a tough-minded Marxist, and a tactical genius *nonpareil*. He was not given to utopian speculation and wrote little about his expectations of future social development. For Marx and Engels, reticence about the details of communism was based on their insistence on a scientific approach to a history bounded by developments in the material world. For Lenin, the reticence came from a disdain for sentimentality and for the weakness he saw issuing from utopian speculation. His tremendous energies were always captured by immediate problems, even more so after seizing power than during his long years in exile. The fifty-five volumes of his *Complete Collected Works* are filled with polemics, articles, and letters directed toward specific and often urgent tasks. The one text usually cited by Soviet theoreticians for Lenin's views on communist society is *State and Revolution,* a work that is quite atypical of Lenin's usual immediate perspective. Written during 1917, just before the November Revolution, it contains a mixture of long-term speculation about future developments and cautionary reminders about the dangers of expecting such developments to occur rapidly after the revolution.

Lenin's implicit solution to the dilemma of Marxist revolution in precapitalist society was to start a revolution in the name of the proletariat, *then* use political power to create the material conditions which should have preceded the revolution. This solution was necessary in order to accommodate his theory of revolution to the special circumstances of 1917 Russia. It involved, above all else, a new interpretation of the roles of the proletariat and the communist vanguard in the revolutionary process. Of all the things that distinguish Lenin from Marx, nothing is more important than their quite different attitudes toward the proletariat and its capabilities for carrying through a revolution and establishing socialism. Marx saw the proletariat as a creature of history —warped and deformed by capitalism, but capable of regeneration given the dialectically reversed position it would occupy in socialist society. Lenin had to deal with the contemporary Russian masses, more a backward peasantry than a proletariat. To fashion a revolution out of this flesh required a different approach, one in which the role of leadership necessarily had to be magnified. And if Marx could rely on increased consciousness at the time of the socialist revolution—for after all, material conditions would have developed such consciousness by that time—Lenin could not expect such an improvement if his revolution were to occur within his lifetime.

Lenin's opinion of the Russian peasant-proletariat was both realistic and uncomplimentary. They were not capable of class consciousness, he argued but only of "trade union consciousness," the desire to ameliorate their living conditions without grasping either the basic cause or remedy of their suffering. Lenin's attitude is clearly revealed by his remarks at a decisive secret meeting of the Bolshevik Central Committee, just prior to the revolution, when he was urging his plan for immediate insurrection on his colleagues. His position was that "the Party could not be guided by the temper of the masses because it was changeable and incalculable; the Party must be guided by an objective analysis and an appraisal of the revolution."[55] Even in his most "utopian" work, *State and Revolution*, Lenin made it clear that the Russian masses would need much guidance from the Bolshevik vanguard to establish a dictatorship of the proletariat. Lenin's picture of this stage was based on two assumptions. The first was that "capitalism simplifies the functions of 'state' administration . . . functions which are already fully within the ability of the average town dweller and can well be performed for 'workmen's wages.' "[56] Thus it would be possible "to *smash* the old bureaucratic machine at once and to begin immediately to construct a new one that will make possible the gradual abolition of all bureaucracy."[57] But the new "proletarian bureaucracy," while acting in the name of the proletariat, would still have many of the characteristics of the old. It could not be otherwise, Lenin argued, because of his second assumption: that the people were not yet ready (and would not be for some time to come) to assume the responsibilities of socialism. And here, Lenin squarely confronts the problem of premature revolution:

> We are not utopians, we do not "dream" of dispensing *at once* with all administration, with all subordination. These anarchist dreams, based upon incomprehension of the tasks of the proletarian dictatorship, are totally alien to Marxism, and, as a matter of fact, serve only to postpone the socialist revolution until people are different. No, we want the socialist revolution with people as they are now, with people who cannot dispense with subordination, control and "foremen and accountants."[58]

After a "protracted" period of gradual evolution, an order would be created where "the functions of control and accounting, becoming more and more simple, will be performed by each in turn, will then become a

---

[55] "Minutes of the Meeting of the Central Committee of the R.S.D.L.P. (B), October 29, 1917," in V. I. Lenin, *Selected Works*, 3 vols. (New York: International Publishers, 1967), 2:437.

[56] Lenin, "State and Revolution," in *Selected Works*, 2:303.

[57] *Ibid.* Emphasis here and in following quotations from "State and Revolution" appeared in the original text.

[58] *Ibid.*

habit and will finally die out as the *special* functions of a special section of the population."[59]

As can be seen, Lenin attached great importance to "accounting and control" in the development toward communism, as though the whole transition amounted to the perfection of a bookkeeping procedure. But for Lenin these words became a metaphor for describing the fully conscious, rational man who has the tools to control his environment—essentially the kind of man envisioned by Marx and Engels. Lenin wrote that "accounting and control . . . is *mainly* what is needed for the 'smooth working,' for the proper functioning" of socialism, and that the "door will be thrown wide open for the transition from the first phase of communist society [i.e., socialism] to its higher phase [only] when *all* have learned to administer and actually do independently administer social production, independently keep accounts and exercise control over the parasites."[60] Until, and as long as, men are unable to raise themselves to this level, "the socialists demand the *strictest* control by society *and by the state* over the measure of labor and the measure of consumption."[61] The institutions which Lenin created after the Revolution and which have survived to this day are based on this compromise with reality, on the contrast between Soviet men and communist man.

The distinction that Lenin made between actual Soviet men and the new communist man has had a great influence on contemporary Soviet theorists. According to Lenin, the process by which the former grows into the latter is one of habituation to obvious social rules under conditions which make that habituation "natural." The state will wither away, he explained, only when men "freed from capitalist slavery, from the untold horrors, savagery, absurdities and infamies of capitalist exploitation . . . gradually *become accustomed* to observing the elementary rules of social intercourse that have been known for centuries and repeated for thousands of years in all copy-book maxims. They will become accustomed to observing them without force, without coercion, without subordination, *without the special apparatus* for coercion called the state."[62]

It cannot be denied that there is here a subtle shift of emphasis away from the Marx-Engels explanation for the gradual disappearance of the state. The Marx-Engels state is an instrument of class struggle and disappears because it is obviously superfluous in a classless society. Lenin's notion of the state combines this function with that of enforcer of social

[59] *Ibid.*
[60] *Ibid.*, p. 345.
[61] *Ibid.*, p. 341.
[62] *Ibid.*, p. 335.

behavior norms, a kind of parental coercive authority for assuring good conduct. Thus he writes:

> The expression "the state *withers away*" is very well chosen, for it indicates both the gradual and the spontaneous nature of the process. Only habit can, and undoubtedly will, have such an effect; for we see around us on millions of occasions how readily people become accustomed to observing the necessary rules of social intercourse when there is no exploitation, when there is nothing that arouses indignation, evokes protest and revolts, and creates the need for *suppression.*[63]

But Lenin also sadly noted that the people of his generation could not by any flight of imagination be likened to such morally inner-directed specimens. The prediction that communism will arrive "presupposes not the present productivity of labor and *not the present* ordinary run of people, who . . . are capable of damaging the stocks of public wealth 'just for fun,' and of demanding the impossible."[64] This, as we shall see, has been the melancholy lament of Lenin's successors as well. The task of converting "the present ordinary run of people" into models of deportment fit to live in full communism has become a perennial, major goal of the Soviet government, a goal which has so far been utterly frustrated.

Even under communism, there would be rare violations of social norms, Lenin acknowledged. He recognized both "the possibility and inevitability of excesses on the part of *individual persons*" and "the need to stop *such* excesses." This enforcement of social norms would be accomplished, however, not by a "special apparatus of suppression" but by "the armed people themselves, as simply and as readily as any crowd of civilized people, even in modern society, interferes to put a stop to a scuffle or to prevent a woman from being assaulted."[65] Here again, the Leninist emphasis is on habitual behavior, departures from which—under communism—can be viewed as individual aberrations.

Lenin's decision to make a "premature" revolution resulted in the emphasis in his later thought on creating the material conditions of mature capitalism as a prelude to socialism and eventual full communism. Individual behavior, productive forces, social relations—all would be deliberately created by a regime which had taken political power in the name of a proletariat still in its infancy. Due to the backwardness of Russia, Lenin wrote (in May 1918), the road to socialism would have to pass through the intermediary stage of "state

[63] *Ibid.*
[64] *Ibid.*, p. 341.
[65] *Ibid.*, p. 336.

capitalism" under the control of the proletarian state.[66] The logic of his position was dictated by the circumstances that he had created by taking power before the maturation of capitalism. The "left-wing communists" had looked forward to a relatively rapid implementation of socialist principles, but Lenin said again and again that such visions would have to be postponed:

> At present, pretty-bourgeois capitalism prevails in Russia, and it is *one and the same road* that leads from it to *both* large-scale state capitalism and to socialism, *through one and the same* intermediary station called "national accounting and control of production and distribution." . . . Is it not clear that from the *material*, economic and productive point of view, we are not yet on "the threshold" of socialism? Is it not clear that we cannot pass through the door of socialism without crossing "the threshold" we have not yet reached?[67]

Soviet history since Lenin's time has certainly followed the course predicted by him—at least in this respect. Communist utopianism, a visible phenomenon in the left wing of the Bolshevik party at the time of the November Revolution, was rapidly suppressed and discredited after it became associated with oppositionist activities. Under Stalin this trend was accentuated, and the goal of a fully communist society was obscured by the awful consequences of his social policies. That it resurfaced under Khrushchev is a testimony to the durability of the idea and to the central place it occupies in the regime's legitimacy.

### The Troubles of Transition

Whether one views the Soviet theory of communist society from a Marxian or a utopian perspective, the most troubling single problem is precisely the problem that confronts the present regime: transition to the future society. In a sense, this regime has an appropriate heritage for a "forced march" through transition to communism. As we have suggested, Lenin's premature revolution necessitated paternalistic efforts by the regime to establish a radically different model of society and man. The regime adapted itself to this task, which is still the ostensible ultimate purpose of its policies.

But the regime seems to have lost its energy and determination to drive forward to utopia. Utopias, including the Marxist version, are the product of alienated thought, and they hold their greatest attraction for alienated people. Satisfaction with the imperfect state of things is cer-

[66] Lenin, " 'Left-Wing' Childishness and the Petty-Bourgeois Mentality," in *Selected Works*, 2:696–97.
[67] *Ibid.*, pp. 698–99.

tain to reduce one's enthusiasm for utopian visions—the more so as these visions might threaten to impinge on the relative comforts of life already achieved. Revolutionary times are alienated times and, consequently, times for utopian thinking. Rapidly changing societies are disorienting societies, and they stimulate utopian, wish-fulfilling alternatives. Russia in 1917 was both of these, and the population was receptive to utopian themes presented by the more radical groups, among them the Bolsheviks. When the Bolsheviks, under Lenin's firm and realistic guidance, retreated from utopianism, they met much opposition from some of their former supporters.

Having taken a forced march through industrialization, collectivization, and state socialism, Soviet society today seems less receptive to utopian visions than it did on the morrow of the November Revolution. The forced march tended to dehumanize its goals and brutalize its leaders. When the march ended, the society paused with evident relief, and it has shown signs of relative stagnation in recent years. There is more to be satisfied with in the Soviet Union today, and more privilege to be protected from the radically egalitarian designs of full communism. The vestigial utopianism that remains in the Soviet Union is not the product of general alienation *from* society but the product of inculcation *by* society, through the educational and propaganda agencies of the Soviet regime. The regime's sponsorship of utopia has thus tamed its potentially disruptive potential in the short run. Communism is not an alternative to the present society, the regime says, it is immanent in the present society. Idealism has thus been co-opted, incorporated into the legitimizing doctrine of the present establishment.

Still, utopianism presents a fundamental and, it would seem, insoluble dilemma to the Soviet party-state. By incorporating utopian goals into its legitimizing doctrine, it has accepted a standard of perfection against which its present performance can be judged. Despite its ability, through monopolization of the media, to structure this judgment in its own favor, it has inevitably armed its potential critics with a powerful weapon. Although Khrushchev's theme of the immediacy of full communism has been cast aside by the present leadership, it is still said that the Soviet Union is in a transitional stage leading to communism. Even the relatively conservative formulations of recent years do not deny the transitional nature of contemporary society, no matter how "prolonged" the transition may be:

> It is incorrect to assume that the socialist state of the entire people is on the point of withering away and of handing over all its functions to public organizations. It is incorrect to think this, because mature socialism is not a way station on the road of social development but a prolonged period in

society's forward movement. "Communism," Lenin said, "can develop only when socialism has become fully consolidated."[68]

The regime explicitly accepts, and indeed inculcates, the belief that the future will justify the present. In this way, present deprivations can be justified by future compensations, present shortages by future surpluses, present sacrifices by future rewards.

But for how long? The limit is indeterminate, but it is finite. The clock is forever ticking, and it is only a matter of time before the regime will be forced to confront the inevitable consequences of its promises. What are these consequences likely to be? Least likely is a revolutionary threat to the regime's power. The regime has institutionally and ideologically permeated Soviet life, and there would be no vehicle for such an outside threat. Much more likely is the threat from within: the fractionation and diffusion of power to the many specialized components of the socioeconomic structure—a process that has apparently already begun. Despite Lenin's practicality, the dictum of absolute unity of command in Leninism was always ultimately justified by utopian premises. Within the corpus of Leninist theory, only the building of communist society could legitimize the monopoly of power accorded the Communist party and the insistence that all particularized interests be pressed into the mold of the Party's policy goals. Thus the basic threat in the loss of utopian legitimacy is the threat to the Party's *legitimate* monopoly of power. In the absence of this legitimacy, the professional claims of expert groups, and all the other conflicting forces of a modern, differentiated society would tend to fractionate the Party and make competitive politics increasingly public.

Of course, it is possible that this development would not be perceived as a threat by the Party. It could adapt, as in fact it has already, to the changing social environment and accommodate competitive politics within a more diversified party structure. If it did so, the realm of freedom for expression of individual opinion would necessarily grow and the whole tenor of Soviet politics would markedly change. Ironically, the loss of utopian idealism could eventually lead to a liberalization of Soviet society.

The other alternative open to the regime at some future date would be to declare that communism had been achieved. As suggested earlier, this option contains inherent dangers if future Soviet society has not achieved subjective happiness for virtually all its members. However, it could be argued that a more affluent—even if not more egalitarian—society and a more effective indoctrination program could approximate

---

[68] A. Yegorov, "Partiia nauchnovo kommunizma," *Kommunist*, 1973, no. 2, p. 53 (*CDSP*, vol. 25, no. 13, p. 11).

the affirmation of society that virtually all utopias achieve. To inspire further efforts from the population, the regime could still define a post-communist stage with even more spectacular attributes. It would seem that such a declaration would eventually be a necessity if the regime is to retain its goal-oriented legitimacy. It might not escape the diffusion of its present power to specialized interests, but it could at least retain its old function of setting social goals; and it could keep possession of the "commanding heights" in directing and coordinating society's more leisurely march toward those goals.

## Questions of Scope and Method

The next three chapters represent an attempt to create a synthesis of Soviet thinking about communism during the Khrushchev years—the years when such thinking was encouraged by the highest authorities. In order to create such a composite picture, several compromises were required. Chronological order was sacrificed, because it was found that there was little, if any, sense of development and progression of ideas with the passage of time. The Soviet picture of communism has thus been arranged topically, rather than chronologically. Since an attempt has been made to fit the pieces of the mosaic together into a reasonably complete and consistent whole, the impression could be created that the result is an authoritative, comprehensive doctrine of the regime, a blueprint for the future. Such is not the case. As will be seen, there are several areas of speculation where Soviet theorists differ, and these differences have been outlined where appropriate. In addition, not all forecasts of future developments are equally authoritative. As a general rule, it was found that the more detailed the description, the less authoritative the source (i.e., the lower the institutional affiliation of the author in the hierarchy of political authority). As might be expected, the more detailed descriptions were usually offered with greater diffidence and with all the natural disclaimers of finality and exactitude, while the more general and formalistic predictions were asserted with more assurance and even a certain dogmatic finality.

Much of the literature surveyed was extremely cautious and reticent about details. For reasons already described, not many Soviet theoreticians display valor much beyond the practical limits of discretion. Despite the resultant vagueness, there seems to be a remarkable degree of cohesion in the composite image of the future. Most of the inconsistencies seem to arise not so much from differences between theoreticians as from basic incompatibilities in the thoughts of individual theoreticians.

Combined with this synthesis of Soviet thought on communism, making it as far as possible a coherent whole, there is a critique of the doctrine based solely on *Soviet* premises. Although it would be possible to analyze Soviet theory on social development in an industrial society from a Western point of view, comparing it with the considerable Western literature on the subject, I have confined the critique in most instances to the internal inconsistencies of the doctrine itself, or to brief mention of some well-recognized present trend which would seem to cast doubt on some aspect of the Soviet theory. Giving Soviet theorists every benefit of the doubt in this way helps to focus attention on the internal weaknesses of the doctrine which would have to be removed even if its basic assumptions turned out to be correct. Although this might be considered the least rigorous standard of evaluation possible, it does have one special advantage: it avoids (as much as feasible) the counter-argument, so often used by Soviet theorists, that "bourgeois" studies of the Soviet Union are based upon, and motivated by, a fundamentally hostile bourgeois world-view, and are thus inherently invalid.

Most of the materials used in this study were surveyed over a two-year period, half of which was spent in Moscow. In addition to the vast output of books and articles on the subject, dissertations and interviews were also used. Because of the huge output of commentary, it was impossible to read absolutely everything that purported to deal with the future communist society, but an effort was made to examine all the most important likely sources of commentary. It must be said, in all candor, that most of the materials read in preparing this study were not terribly enlightening. Formalistic, stereotyped discussions predominated; fresh, imaginative views were distinctly in the minority—and their merit was no doubt magnified by comparison with the rest. For this reason, only a small percentage of the works read were included in the text.

The plan of the next three chapters is based on the tripartite division of the subject usually found in Soviet sources. Chapter II synthesizes the Soviet discussion of the all-important transitional stage from socialism to communism, the stage through which the Soviet Union is now passing, according to the theory. The discussion thus centers around the various transformations that the USSR is expected to undergo in the near and "almost near" future. Of course, these transformations should have the most immediate relevancy to Soviet policy formation in the next few decades, unless policy and theory become totally unlatched.

Chapter III is an attempt to construct a picture of the future communist society as envisioned by Soviet writers. The picture has been put together from bits and pieces, and a special effort has been made to fit the pieces into a reasonably consistent whole. Where this has been impossible, the discussion focuses on the apparent incompatibilities of the component parts. Occasionally, suggestions are offered for resolving these inconsistencies in a spirit of helpfulness that will undoubtedly go unrecognized by Soviet readers. This chapter also includes a brief review of Soviet writings on the future of communism throughout the world, and the prospects for development beyond the communist stage.

A comprehensive composite picture of the "new communist man," the inhabitant of communist society, is given in chapter IV. His psychological and behavioral characteristics are considered in the context of his environment, and the two are linked together, following the usual Soviet procedure.

Chapter V, the final chapter, is a review of developments in the Soviet theory of communism since the Khrushchev period. Both the decline of references to communist society and the increasingly conservative description of that society (in the sense of being closer to present reality) are considered in connection with the political concerns of the post-Khrushchev regime.

Of course, the truly "final" chapter cannot yet be written. While the fate of the Soviet vision of utopia is not yet a pressing problem for the regime, it will continue to be both a "cherished dream of the men and women of labor" and a disturbing challenge to the Soviet leadership as long as it remains in the future. And as long as it is used to legitimize the present political system and to prod new generations into greater efforts and sacrifices, it cannot be forgotten. Marx has indeed left a troublesome legacy.

# CHAPTER II  THE TRANSITION FROM SOCIALISM TO COMMUNISM

The original assumption by Marx and Engels that the socialist revolution would occur in the countries most highly developed economically has had an important effect on the further development of Marxist doctrine in the Soviet Union. Marx could foresee a rapid transition to socialism because the attributes of a highly developed capitalist society were precisely the physical preconditions for the establishment of a socialist society. The Bolsheviks, however, inherited a country with an underdeveloped, partially capitalist economy and a population consisting mainly of uneducated, backward peasants. The entire progression to communism, therefore, has been necessarily prolonged, and the Soviet leaders have had to *build* communist society, creating by design what should have been a natural consequence of historical development.

Because of the artificiality of this building of socialism and communism, Soviet theorists have been faced with the problem of theoretically defining their progress in terms of stages and substages unknown to Marx and Engels. This task is so crucial in doctrinal terms that it has generally been left to the Party leadership. It was Stalin who proclaimed the consolidation of socialism in 1936, Khrushchev who announced the commencement of the period of "full-scale construction of communism" at the Twenty-first Party Congress in 1959, and more recently Brezhnev who defined yet another stage of "developed socialist society" at the Twenty-fourth Party Congress in 1971. The task of exegesis, however, has traditionally been left to less important party officials, academics, and propagandists. Their writings reveal that, within certain narrowly defined limits, there is room today in the Soviet ideological world for differences of opinion and public debate.

The process of transition from socialism to communism is intimately connected with the subject of the future communist society itself, especially since Marxism is a philosophy which conditions its adherents to viewing life as process and flow, rather than as a collection of static categories. Furthermore, it is possible to deduce certain unmentioned features of the Soviet-style communist society from statements concerning the transition, on the assumption that basic social policy of the transitional period is bound to have, and is meant to have, desired consequences under full communism.

## The Process of Transition

Soviet theory starts from the assumption that the "realm of consciousness" to which Marx and Engels looked forward has already arrived in the Soviet Union. The logic behind this assertion is not particularly obscure. The socialist revolution has already taken place; private ownership of the means of production has been eliminated; and a party, "armed" with the scientific theories of Marxism-Leninism, has been formed to guide[1] the working masses forward. Certain economic and educational tasks remain before society can enter the higher stage of full communism, but this progress is assured due to the conscious use of historical laws by the Communist party. Small errors are still possible, but the main points of policy are the product of the conscious application of Marxism-Leninism and cannot, therefore, have unintended consequences.

The special position of the Party and the entire swing toward voluntarism evident in contemporary Soviet doctrine are necessitated by the essentially artificial nature of the Soviet position in terms of Marxist orthodoxy. As already mentioned, the Soviets must with a conscious effort build those material conditions which capitalism was supposed to deliver upon its demise, and this effort naturally involves the conscious desires of the builders. The attempt to stay as close as possible to the Marxist tradition, however, creates a certain ambivalence in Soviet doctrine on the question of historical inevitability. On the one hand, Soviet writers declare that the transition to communism involves objective laws "acting outside of and independent of people's consciousness,"[2] while on the other, they must state as a practical necessity that "the Soviet people cannot wait until the happy future descends on them from the heavens, but must create it with their own hands, their ardent efforts."[3] This sort of dualistic formulation naturally gives rise to some doubt as

[1] The Russian word, *rukovodit'*, invariably used to describe this guidance, literally means "to lead by the hand" and is quite expressive of the relationship between party and people openly fostered in Soviet publications.

[2] P. I. Nikitin, *Chto takoe kommunizm* (Moscow: Izdatel'stvo Moskovskovo Universiteta, 1961), p. 87.

[3] L. Il'ichev, "Moshchnyi faktor stroitel'stva kommunizma," *Kommunist*, 1962, no. 1, p. 17.

to the efficacy of human will in the process of creating something that is
ultimately "independent of people's consciousness." The problem here
is inherent in any system of thought that maps out a definite and inevitable course for the future: those who accept the course are likely to react
with some sort of passive, fatalistic expectation of an irrevocable destiny. Passivity, of course, is as foreign to Soviet doctrine as it was to
Marx. The Soviet theoreticians, therefore, have had to steer a very
careful course between this danger and the alternate danger of losing
the confidence that comes from the idea that the Party's goals are
historically inevitable. The generally accepted formula has been put as
follows:

> Marxist-Leninist philosophy states that society develops according to laws
> which are not only independent of the consciousness and will of people
> but which themselves determine the will, consciousness and actions of the
> people. However, Marxism-Leninism has always been alien to a fatalistic
> view of the historical process. The people, setting one or another goal
> before themselves in their activities, can themselves hasten or retard the
> development of society.[4]

It can hardly be denied that there still exists a logical contradiction in
this statement, for if society develops according to certain laws which
are not only independent of but which actually determine "the will,
consciousness and actions" of people, then people, the dependent variable, can hardly be expected to affect the laws, which are the independent variable. Perhaps we can surmise that these independent laws
determine only the *direction* of social movement, not the *pace*, in which
case the people can either "hasten" or "retard" the inevitable outcome.
This is no doubt the most efficacious solution for the Soviets, and the
one which they generally arrive at by implication. In actual practice,
however, the emphasis is usually put on the motive power of deliberate
activity.

According to doctrine, a transitional stage is the normal condition for
all of mankind, simply because the historical process is viewed as one of
continual motion. One of the central tasks of Soviet doctrine, therefore,
is defining from what stage to what stage the transitional phase is moving. Its other important job is defining the predominant characteristics
of the transitional process itself. It is in the nature of things that the
question "From what?" can be answered definitively only in retrospect.
The "scientific" presumptions of Soviet doctrine, however, demand a
definitive answer to the question "To what?" as well. This is always a
crucial question, for the characteristics of the transitional phase (which

[4] K. V. Moroz, *Dialekticheskii materializm—ideinoe oruzhie bor'by za kommunizm* (Moscow: Izdatel'stvo VPSh i AON pri TsK KPSS, 1960), p. 68.

in nondoctrinal terms amount to the policy of the regime) must match the predicted features of the next historical stage if theory and practice are to coincide. Although necessity is often the mother of doctrinal invention in this regard, the future is usually open to a choice between several courses of action, and this choice must always be couched in doctrinal terms in order to maintain its legitimacy. The question of whether the doctrine determines present policy or is merely adapted to fit the requirements of present policy is a complex one and is beyond the scope of this study. It is important to emphasize, however, that at all points doctrine and policy, theory and practice, must necessarily be made to coalesce.

Because of the great stress which the Soviet theorists place on historical movement, their theoretical descriptions of transitional periods tend to concentrate on processes rather than on static categories. Thus, certain features of the next stage "are constantly appearing" in daily life, while various institutions are "being strengthened" and others "are gradually being combined" into some sort of supposedly superior organizational arrangement. In fact, this characteristic emphasis on the near future of institutions is often combined with an equally characteristic neglect in clearly defining the functions of each present-day institution.[5]

As previously mentioned, Khrushchev defined the transitional stage of his leadership at the Twenty-first Party Congress as the period of "full-scale construction of communism" (*razvërnutoe stroitel'stvo kommunizma*), as distinguished from the previous "gradual transition to communism" (*postepennyi perekhod kommunizmu*).[6] As was characteristic of the entire Khrushchev period, this new terminology was filled with a new sense of optimism (perhaps overoptimism) concerning the possibilities for future economic development. The phrase quickly became standard terminology and has since been used in all Soviet documents—although with decreasing frequency since Khrushchev's fall. Its major function was to change the concept of communist society from a distant goal of the unspecified future to an immediate goal directly connected with present-day life. The nearness of the goal to contemporary life was emphasized by Khrushchev from the beginning, when he said: "In our society there are many tangible and visible features of communism which will be [further] developed and per-

---

[5] An excellent, although no doubt unintentional, example of the tremendous proliferation of overlapping organizations is provided in N. G. Aleksandrov, ed., *Sovetskoe gosudarstvo i obshchestvennost' v usloviiakh razvernutovo stroitel'stva kommunizma* (Moscow: Izdatel'stvo Moskovskovo Universiteta, 1962). See especially the articles by Ia. L. Kisilev and A. A. Abramova.

[6] See P. I. Epischchev, L. M. Glazov, *O vozrastaiushchei roli KPSS v stroitel'stve kommunizma* (Leningrad: Obshchestvo po rasprostraneniiu politicheskikh i nauchnykh znanii RSFSR, 1959), pp. 16–37.

fected."[7] This remark can only mean that the present stage is already partially communistic, and it gave rise to some statements by lesser theoreticians that "we already live under communism" although "this communism is not yet mature or complete."[8] The overzealous application of Khrushchev's thesis apparently became quite troublesome, for at the Twenty-second Party Congress, in 1961, he specifically rebuffed "some comrades [who] propose going considerably farther than the planned targets" and want to introduce "equal pay for all, irrespective of qualifications or the nature of the work performed."[9] Of course, this was not the original intention of Khrushchev's thesis. It was closely connected with an analysis of the transitional process, as Khrushchev explicitly stated in his Twenty-first Party Congress address. The point that he wished to make was that, despite all the differences between communism and socialism, "there does not exist some sort of wall between them, dividing these phases of social development. Communism grows out of socialism, and is its direct continuation."[10] The idea of direct continuation is important, because the Soviet theorists want to make clear that there it no need for any kind of "social revolution" or even a "great leap" during the transition to communism. Peaceful, harmonious, and gradual development at an ever-increasing tempo is the model for the transitional period.

According to Khrushchev's analysis, the period of full-scale construction of communism corresponded to a new phase in the history of the Soviet state. The "dictatorship of the proletariat," a phrase that goes back to Marx and Engels, has been defined as the social system belonging to the transition from capitalism to socialism. Therefore, with the consolidation of socialism and the emergence of only two fraternal laboring classes, the workers and peasants, the need for a dictatorship of one class over another ceases to exist. The new form of the Soviet state is given the appellation "all-people's socialist state." It is considered "the indispensable form of organization of society between the dictatorship of the proletariat and communist social self-management"[11] (*obshchestvennoe kommunisticheskoe samoupravlenie*), the

[7] N. S. Khrushchev, "Kontrol'nye tsifry razvitiia narodnovo khoziaistva SSSR na 1959–1965 gody," in *Vneocherednoi XXI S'ezd Kommunisticheskoi partii sovetskovo soiuza: Stenograficheskii otchët*, 2 vols. (Moscow: Gosudardstvennoe izdatel'stvo politicheskoi literatury, 1959), 1:94.

[8] Nikitin, *Chto takoe kommunizm*, p. 82.

[9] N. S. Khrushchev, "On the Program of the Communist Party of the Soviet Union," in *The Road to Communism: Documents of the 22nd Congress of the Communist Party of the Soviet Union* (Moscow: Foreign Languages Publishing House, n.d.), p. 294.

[10] Khrushchev, "Kontrol'nye tsifry," p. 94.

[11] Aleksandrov, *Sovetskoe gosudarstvo i obshchestvennost' v usloviiakh razvernutovo stroitel'stva kommunizma*, p. 82.

last-named form being one aspect of full communism. Although the obvious intent of this new definition is to indicate that the Soviet state, in some sense or other, belongs to the entire people, the concept has been given further meaning by Soviet analyses of the role of the state and its various organs during the transition.

The state, as already mentioned in chapter I, was supposed to wither away after the socialist revolution, according to the original concept of Marx and Engels. The Soviet theorists, faced with a situation different from the one Marx foresaw, have had to preserve the state and, indeed, have made more of it than ever before. They are still, however, under a doctrinal obligation to permit it to "wither away" at some future time, and this issue has come to the forefront as a result of the Khrushchevian assertion that full communism was fast approaching.

This doctrinal necessity creates a paradox for Soviet theory, since a logical preparation for the withering away of the state would be the elimination of some functions and the transferral of others during the present period—in other words, a weakening of the present state. However, weakening of the state apparatus is quite definitely not the intention of the Soviet leadership, and the leaders must, therefore, seek a "dialectical" method of resolving the difficulty. They accomplish this feat by claiming that the state is actually *strengthened* in the process of withering away.[12] This strengthening of the state is accomplished by drawing countless citizens into the daily work of state organs, and by the general "democratization" of the state structure. A second strengthening device is the transferral of certain functions from state organs to "public organizations." Now, the introduction of more democratic procedures into the state administration can be viewed as a means of strengthening the state, but the removal of various functions from state control would hardly seem a method of strengthening it. Nevertheless, the following statement from the Soviet law journal, *Sovetskoe gosudarstvo i pravo,* is far from unusual:

> From the fact that certain functions of state agencies have been turned over to public organizations . . . the conclusion must not be drawn that the socialist state has been weakened. On the contrary, the shifting of particular functions from state agencies to public organizations inevitably leads to the strengthening of the socialist state and in no way lessens its active role in the building of communism.[13]

---

[12] See V. Platkovskii, *Politicheskaia organizatsiia obshchestva pri perekhode k kommunizmu* (Moscow: Gospolitizdat, 1962), p. 45.

[13] A. I. Denisov, "O sootnoshenii gosudarstva i obshchestva v perekhodnyi ot kapitalizma k kommunizmu period," *Sovetskoe gosudarstvo i pravo,* 1960, no. 4, p. 30.

Since no really satisfactory explanation is offered for this phenomenon, one can only assume that in relinquishing certain unnecessary functions to public organizations the state is able to carry out its essential tasks more efficiently. Although a great deal has been made of the democratization of the state, the most authoritative document on the subject, the Party Program of 1961, takes a more cautious position. It calls for the "extension and perfection of socialist democracy" and the "active participation of all citizens in the administration of the state," but at the same time advances the goal of promoting "the Leninist principle of democratic centralism," which in the past has always meant far more centralism than democracy. The program goes on to make this meaning more specific: "It is essential to strengthen discipline, constantly control the activities of all the sections of the administrative apparatus, check the execution of the decisions and laws of the Soviet state and heighten the responsibility of every official for the strict and timely implementation of these laws.[14] Since the officials will still be responsible for the implementation of laws, there is little doubt that what the Soviet theorists have in mind is not more democracy as we define it but more *participation* of average citizens in the day-to-day operations of the all-encompassing state. On the other hand, the mere existence of this participation might possibly lead to greater democracy, not only in the sense of increased public involvement in busywork, but also public participation in local, minor decisions. Indeed, the thought that this sort of activity could be the entering wedge for the future evolution of a more democratic system should not be dismissed out of hand.

At any rate, the soviets, as the basic building blocks of the state structure, are to be reinforced during the transition.[15] This point is made quite clear by the Party Program, which states that "the role of the soviets, which are an all-inclusive organization of the people embodying their unity, will grow as communist construction progresses.[16] The program goes on to declare that the soviets "combine the features of a government body and a mass organization of the people"—a combination which assures the soviets a special place in the theory of transition.[17] The point is that the state is transferring some of its functions to public organizations; the soviets are officially state organs, but they also

[14] *The Road to Communism*, p. 548.

[15] Solomon M. Schwarz has advanced the interesting idea that Khrushchev himself did not support an increased role for the soviets, but instead favored the public organizations. See his article, "Is the State Withering Away in the USSR?" in *The U.S.S.R. and the Future: An Analysis of the New Program of the CPSU*, ed. Leonard Shapiro (New York: Frederick A. Praeger, 1963), pp. 161–70.

[16] *The Road to Communism*, p. 548.

[17] *Ibid.*

resemble public organizations (trade unions, for example) in that they are the point of contact between the state apparatus and the masses. Therefore, the soviets will transform themselves, according to the program, and "operate more and more like social organizations, with the masses participating extensively and directly in their work."[18] Thus, the program states quite clearly that the process of democratization is also to apply specifically to the soviets. If the present trend toward greater responsibilities for local soviets continues, the net effect of these changes would presumably be a greater involvement of the "little people" of Soviet society in local affairs. At the very least, the emphasis on public participation in current doctrine raises this as a strong possibility.

The increasing importance of the soviets has been repeatedly stressed since Khrushchev's time. The role of the standing committees of soviets at all levels, from national to local, was significantly enlarged in the period from 1966 to 1970. These committees apparently involve the elected deputies in auxiliary and supervisory functions on a more continuous basis than ever before. Since there were in 1972 approximately 300,000 such committees with a membership of 1.7 million deputies nationwide,[19] their increased participation is potentially significant. The status of soviet deputies was further heightened by the law of September 20, 1972, which expanded and gave a legal basis to the rights and privileges of deputies. While it would still be unrealistic to interpret these changes as a quantum leap in the attribution of new power to soviet deputies, the potential for such future development has certainly been enhanced by these trends.

Although much has been made of the new, more democratic role of the soviets in the building of communism, Soviet theory has neglected one important aspect of it. This is the relationship between the soviets and the rest of the government apparatus itself. In theory, the increasing resemblance of the soviet to a public organization is dependent on its attracting more citizens to its daily work, thus making it a sort of locally-based mass organization. From a juridical point of view, however, the chief distinction of a public organization is its "non-state" (*vneshtatnyi*) character, which theoretically implies a certain independence in its relations with the state. The soviets, on the other hand, are presently a juridical component of the state, and this might prove awkward in the future when the state withers away and the soviets remain as a thriving

---

[18] *Ibid.*
[19] Figures given by I. V. Kapitonov, *Pravda*, September 21, 1972. (For a translation of this speech, see *Current Digest of the Soviet Press* [hereafter *CDSP*], vol. 24, no. 39, p. 6.)

reminder of an otherwise outmoded and retrogressive institution. (Furthermore, in relation to present policy, the attempt to give the soviets an increasing role in the transitional phase could be considered merely a means of shifting the pressure for democratization into more easily controlled channels.) There is thus a logical theoretical requirement for redefining the juridical relationship between the soviets and the state during the transitional phase, a requirement that has not, as yet, been fulfilled.

The question of juridical relationships is generally a vexing one, since in Soviet theory the entire concept of law is considered a holdover from capitalism, just as the state is. Therefore, the legal (*pravovyi*) norms of socialist society must gradually give way to social (*obshchestvennyi*) norms. More precisely: "In the process of communist construction there will occur a dialectical transformation, a development of legal norms and legal relationships into the unified, non-juridical norms and ideological relationships of communist society."[20] However, close examination of the new, non-juridical norms reveals that they do not differ intrinsically from current norms, but rather that they differ *extrinsically*, in the context of their application to a presumably different social situation. For example, there is now a law which prohibits theft of state property, and this law is enforced by certain governmental organs such as the militia, the procurator, and the people's courts. The function of these state organs and legal norms is to prevent a particular act from occurring. If we take the same situation at a time when non-juridical norms and public organization are the dominant features of society (and this does not necessarily mean full communism), we see that theft of the people's property is still forbidden, but now by the less formal means of non-juridical norms; and the apprehension and punishment of the wrongdoer is carried out by public rather than state organs. Indeed, the punishment might take a different form, involving community pressure and public confession rather than court procedures and incarceration. The essential difference, then, is not that the norms themselves are drastically changed, but rather that the social context—according always to the theory—has been transformed.

This leads directly to a further observation that the one area of social life which has received the most attention from Soviet theory on the transfer of state functions has been crime prevention and law enforcement. Such public organizations as the *druzhina*, the comrade's courts, and the apartment committees have been either created or reinvigo-

---

[20] V. M. Lesnoi, *Gosudarstvo, pravo i kommunizm* (Moscow: Izdatel'stvo Moskovskovo Universiteta, 1964), p. 68. See also P. S. Romashkin, "O roli ubezhdeniia i prinuzhdeniia v sovetskom gosudarstve," *Sovetskoe gosudarstvo i pravo*, 1960, no. 2, p. 27.

rated, in order to take over certain law enforcement, or policing functions. In some cases, a state agency has actually been abolished and its entire function passed on to a public organization, as has happened in the sports and propaganda fields. In other cases, a public organization has been established within the structure of an existing state organ, as with the standing committees of the soviets. In still other instances, the state institution has been retained and performs functions "parallel" to those of the public organization. This is the case, for example, with the people's courts and the comrade's courts. The *druzhina* and militia are also considered to perform parallel functions. In neither of these cases has the state organ divested itself of any of its essential functions; rather, the public organization has formed, in effect, an auxiliary of the state organ to carry the latter's operations into new areas of social life. The general guiding principle of this parallelism seems to be, at least for the present, that the public organization handles the less important matters, while the state organ reserves jurisdiction in more important cases. However, doctrine holds that the situation will gradually be reversed in the future, and indeed this reversal is often mentioned as one of the leading characteristics of the transitional process.[21] The trend toward a greater role for public organizations is taken as a prime indicator of the increased "consciousness" of the masses, one of the most important attributes of the transition process.

In speaking of increasing the consciousness of the people, we are once again faced with what is, by orthodox Marxist standards an essentially artificial situation. As noted in chapter I, the socialist revolution itself was supposed to be the harbinger of the realm of consciousness, the beginning of an era in which men, prepared by the previous course of history and the changed social system, would naturally achieve an understanding of the basic laws of social development. The new material conditions of socialist society would give rise, of themselves, to this understanding (or "consciousness"), and there was little expectation that this understanding would have to be taught, painstakingly and sedulously, over an extended period of years. However, the Bolsheviks inherited a backward peasantry and a none-too-conscious working class. The achievements of the Soviet leaders in the fields of traditional education have been considerable, but their attempts at inculcating consciousness have had a mixed result. They have, without question, been successful in molding public opinion in many approved directions, but

---

[21] For one of many, many articles along these lines, see N. G. Aleksandrov, "Razvitie marksistsko-leninskovo ucheniia o gosudarstve i prave v materialakh XXI s'ezda KPSS," in *Nekotorye teoreticheskie voprosy stroitel'stva kommunizma* (Moscow: Izdatel'stvo "Znanie," 1960), pp. 85–113.

they have fallen short of their own goal, which is nothing less than the creation, through intensive and all-inclusive propaganda efforts, of attitudes which simultaneously support the regime and achieve the consciousness, in somewhat altered form, of original Marxism.

The modern Soviet interpretation of consciousness has two components. On the one hand, it embodies a set of propositions about the real world, about the forces operating in it and the direction of its development. On the other, it contains a set of value judgments, a code of morality, which is intended to harmonize with the set of propositions concerning reality. The problem is that acceptance of the propositions in a general way does not assure that an individual will be guided in his own actions by the corresponding code of morality. The morality of a nation, Soviet or otherwise, can generally be accepted as being within the legitimate concern of its governing bodies; but in this case, we are dealing with an extraordinarily different species of morality, a morality which not only accepts the possibility of perfecting man's nature but which actually demands it. It demands this perfection on the basis of the original Marxian thesis that man is largely a product of his social environment, and that this environment can be perfected through man's conscious use of social laws. In Marx's view, however, man's perfectability was the natural product, the predictable resultant of forces acting in the universe; it was certainly not the result of a massive, long-term campaign of indoctrination. In this sense, then, the Soviets have departed from orthodoxy. However, a good case can be made for accepting this departure as a logical response to the recognition that Marx's predictions "do not descend from the heavens" but must be realized by conscious effort of the leadership. Even if this is not quite good Marxism, it is definitely good Leninism.

In one respect this insistence on perfection has had, an unintended result. When man's final perfection (or close approximation of it) can be confidently awaited as an inevitable result of history, there is no pressure on those who govern to bring it about through government fiat. However, when this perfection is thought to be desirable, and even necessary, but not *inevitable*, then purposeful governmental action must be the logical remedy. The result is an attempt to bring about man's perfection by decree. To the extent, then, that man stubbornly resists being perfected, there is a counter-tendency for governmental action to become more demanding, and it is this sort of action and reaction that can be seen at work in the theoretical discussions (as well as governmental activities) of the past several years in the Soviet Union. For example, it is often stated by the regime's spokesmen that their increased concern for the elimination of crime is not connected with an actual increase in the crime rate, but rather with the fact that, as society approaches ever closer to communism, the people can less and less afford to show tolerance toward the occasional violator. As an editorial in *New Times* (the English edition of *Novoe vremia*) put it: "Building communism implies refashioning human character. And this requires intolerance of everything that obstructs our forward movement, intolerance of all the old survivals that mar the life of society and its members."[22] This intolerance, which has been demonstrated by increasingly severe punishments for certain crimes in recent years, is partly a manifestation of the process just described. The differences between the actual Soviet man and the theoretical, ideal man of communist society become more apparent when communism is brought forward from a distant to an immediate goal. When awareness of these shortcomings is combined with a tradition of social engineering and paternalism, the result is an increasingly severe and disciplinarian attitude on the part of those who set policy in these matters.[23]

The refashioning of human character is one of the main processes of the transitional period. On the theoretical side, as we have seen, the problem involves a comparison between the existing Soviet citizen and a hypothetical ideal citizen of communist society, a model we will describe in detail in chapter IV. On the practical side, however, certain measures have been taken to bring about the desired result. Education has been stressed, and meets with particular approval when a citizen takes courses after working hours.

The major refashioning, however, will take place in the workers' attitude toward labor. Since we are here dealing with an attitude, it would be natural to expect that Soviet theory would place primary emphasis on the material conditions which give rise to it—since all attitudes are part of the "superstructure." In actual fact, however, contemporary doctrine is quite ambivalent on this score. When the primary focus is on a comparison of labor under capitalism and socialism, or a comparison of present and previous working conditions in the Soviet Union, the tendency is to make great claims for Soviet working conditions and for the Soviet workers' attitudes toward their work. The following is a typical example:

> The characteristic feature of a socialist society that makes it fundamentally different from a capitalist society is the fact that labor is not considered a purely personal matter. Labor acquires direct social significance. It is a matter of honor and a sacred patriotic duty of Soviet man. The consciousness that his labor is needed by society and that it serves an

[22] "They Will Live in Communism," *New Times*, 1959, no. 1, p. 3.

[23] The application of increasingly severe penalties for economic crimes such as "parasitism" and "speculation" and the introduction of capital punishment for embezzlers and counterfeiters can be seen as examples of this process.

elevated end—the prosperity of the motherland and the building of a comminist society—greatly enhances the dignity of Soviet man and is a true source of inspiration in work.[24]

Such statements attempt both to relate a theoretical principle of the social system—common ownership of the means of production—with the workers' attitude in practice and bring in such extraneous emotions as patriotism and righteousness.

> *Everything that has been achieved today is the fruit of your truly golden hands, dear comrades, of your inquiring minds and creative efforts.* At mine stopes, oil derricks and rolling mills, in factories and plants, in institutes and laboratories, in fields and livestock sections—in every city and village, Soviet people worked selflessly on the fulfillment of plan assignments and the pledges and counterplans they had made, thereby strengthening the might of the socialist homeland.[25]

Fundamentally, these oft-repeated declarations claim that the workers are motivated by the knowledge that they are part-owners of state property and that this knowledge leads to feelings of altruism and fellowship and, more important, to highly productive labor.

This, however, is only one side of the picture. When the doctrinal argument shifts to the theoretical justification for certain practical measures taken by the government, or to a discussion of the differences between socialist and communist labor, a more pessimistic note enters the argument. For example, the idea of wage payment for labor performed has been well established and theoretically justified by the Soviet writers as the proper labor system for the socialist stage. The statement of this principle generally runs as follows:

> The principle of distribution according to work under socialism is conditioned not only by the level of development of production, but by the level of consciousness of the workers themselves. The importance of this principle is concluded from the fact that it creates material self-interest of the workers in the results of their labor, and increases their desire to raise the productivity of labor. If we had retreated from this principle and begun to give to each equally, then the interest of each worker in raising his qualifications, and in increasing the output of products would have disappeared. Levelling would denote crying injustice, because it would permit loafers to evade work, to do nothing and to receive all goods equally with those who labor honestly.[26]

[24] G. Glezerman, "Talks about Communism: Labor Becomes First Vital Need," *Izvestiia*, May 20, 1959 (*CDSP*, vol. 11, no. 20, p. 22).

[25] "The CPSU Central Committee's Appeal to the Party and the Soviet People," *Pravda* and *Izvestiia*, January 4, 1974 (*CDSP*, vol. 26, no. 1, p. 3).

[26] V. Platkovskii, "Formirovanie kommunisticheskikh obshchestvennikh otnoshenii," *Kommunist*, 1962, no. 15, p. 27.

This sort of statement can be taken as an admission that, despite theoretical common ownership of production facilities, the Soviet worker under socialism does not differ in any notable way from his capitalist brother, who is also motivated by "material self-interest," and who also receives wages for labor performed. None other than "V. I. Lenin taught that in economic construction it is impermissible to rely solely on [the workers'] enthusiasm."[27] This principle of material self-interest is constantly stressed, and is defended against those who propose to introduce the communist principle of distribution according to need prematurely. In fact, a few collectives which had decided to pool their wages and distribute them equally were roundly criticized in the pages of *Voprosy filosofii*.[28] In a similar vein, the idea of competition is also supported as a necessary feature of socialist production.

Competition and material self-interest are certainly effective means of increasing the individual worker's incentive to produce, but the insistence on doctrinal support for these principles places the Soviet theorists squarely in the midst of another ideological paradox. Both of these labor techniques are based on an essentially individualistic conception of human relations. In a very real sense they play one man's interests against another's, for they create situations where some gain at the expense of others. Since these principles would seem profoundly antithetical to the communist ethic of fellowship and shared rewards, the assertion that "the chief means of education for the new, communist characteristics in work is competition"[29] would seem to contain a logical inconsistency, even though competition in the Soviet Union is often conducted between groups rather than individuals. There is some recognition among Soviet writers that the notion of material self-interest is contrary to communist morality. In a rather guarded statement, one such writer acknowledges both the dilemma and the psychological dangers of material rewards for work:

> In socialist society, a man's working activity is objectively connected with material self-interest. The Party and state are constantly improving the

[27] A. G. Kulikov and V. P. Kamankin, eds., *Ekonomicheskaia reforma v razvitii* (Moscow: Izdatel'stvo "Misl'," 1971), p. 15.

[28] D. S. Avraamov, "Brigady kommunisticheskovo truda i vospitanie molodëzhi," *Voprosy filosofii*, 1959, no. 10, p. 135. There is an excellent discussion of the concept of material self-interest and whether in Soviet society it causes a contradiction with the desire for economic equality, in *Voprosy stroitel'stva kommunizma v SSSR* (Moscow: Izdatel' stvo Akademii nauk SSSR, 1959). See especially the articles by Ia. A. Kronrod, G. A. Prudenskii, and the rebuttals by P. N. Fedoseev and K. V. Ostrovitianov.

[29] P. I. Kuznetsov, "V trude vospityvaetsia chelovek budushchevo," in *Moguchaia sila kommunisticheskoi ideinosti*, ed. A. P. Filimov (Leningrad: Lenizdat, 1961), p. 88.

system of material stimulation of workers' production. However, under well-known conditions, personal material self-interest does not strengthen the moral stimulus and ideological motivation [of workers], but becomes, through consumerism, a means [for the development of] the psychology of individualism and egoism.[30]

The Soviet explanation of this problem depends on the notion that under socialism the level of production is insufficient to guarantee each person's needs, but that as the transition to communism progresses and these needs are successively met, the new communist principles will emerge. This explanation is plausible to a degree, since the intensity of competitive drive is related to the prevailing level of supply and demand, but it does, at the same time, raise some interesting implications. First of all, it makes a worker's attitude toward work essentially dependent on the expectation of rewards, since only the security of abundance will suffice to abate the competitive drive. Secondly, this explanation implies that the attitude toward work is more dependent on supply levels than on the social system, an obviously heretical view from the standpoint of Marxist orthodoxy.

This improvement in the average worker's attitude toward labor is envisioned as part of a general transitional process of raising the "cultural level" of the Soviet worker and peasant. The definition of "cultural level" (sometimes referred to as "cultural-technical level") variously includes such factors as one's productive capabilities, literacy, appreciation of the arts and literature, creative artistic talent, manners, and general conduct. All of these characteristics are to be developed by purposeful effort during the transition so that the present Soviet citizen will be a fit subject of the future communist society. Soviet theoreticians generally claim that the Soviet citizen of today is already quite highly "cultured" according to all these criteria, although much remains to be done before communism can be attained. One Soviet study, for example, claims that "at present there exists in the countryside a new type of peasant, a man with a secondary education, cultured, literate, and with a deep understanding of music, literature, and technology."[31] Despite this, evidence is occasionally published which indicates that present educational levels are quite low by existing standards, to say nothing of the standards which must be established for a transition to communism.[32]

---

[30] Kh. P. Pulatov, *Kommunizm, gosudarstvo, kul'tura, lichnost': stroitel'stvo kommunizma i problemy kul'turno-vospitatel'noi funktsii obshchenarodnovo sotsialisticheskovo gosudarstva* (Tashkent: Izdatel'stvo "Uzbekistan," 1971), p. 71.

[31] *Izmenenie klassovoi struktury obshchestva v protsesse stroitel'stva sotsializma i kommunizma* (Moscow: Izdatel'stvo VPSh i AON pri TsK KPSS, 1961), p. 258.

[32] A comparison of the 1959 and 1970 census data indicates that while Soviet

As already pointed out, the Soviet term for education (*vospitanie*) implies not only instruction in the standard repertoire of academia but the inculcation of a set of attitudes, a specific moral and ethical code. Indeed, the Soviet theoreticians tend to emphasize the latter aspect in discussions of raising the cultural level. As part of this emphasis, they have published and widely disseminated a "Moral Code for the Builder of Communism," which contains a group of twelve altruistic and goal-oriented guides to action with a format similar to that of the original Ten Commandments.[33] Labor brigades have been formed in factories with the aim of encouraging these new attitudes and increasing production. Because of this emphasis on instilling an ethical code, the brigades represent something of an innovation in Soviet labor organization. As in former times, the brigades pledge themselves to certain production norms, but, in addition, they bind themselves to a code of conduct which applies both on the job and off. Similarly, the brigades enter into competition with other brigades. This is a long-established procedure of Soviet labor organization, but in this case the brigades compete for the "banner of communist labor," a brilliant red affair awarded not only on the basis of productivity but also as a sign that they have learned to work and *live* in a "communist manner." As the published diary of one brigade member indicates, living in a communist manner apparently involves spending practically all of one's leisure time in collective self-improvement and recreational activities with other brigade members.[34] The involvement of brigade members in each other's personal lives is further indicated in the following comment of another brigade member: "We pay great attention to the struggle for a healthy life. If earlier the workers regarded with patience those who drank, now such conduct is considered inadmissable. Earlier no attention was given to how com-

---

education has made some strides in raising the average level of workers and peasants, achievement still lags behind the claims that are often made. The 1959 census showed that 3.3 percent of the working population had achieved a completed higher education, and 43.3 percent had at least some secondary education. By 1970, 6.5 percent had a completed higher education and 65.3 percent had some secondary schooling. However, the 1970 census revealed that 25 percent of the working population had less than eight years of schooling, and 10 percent had less than six years. Since these figures are undoubtedly higher for peasants than for urban workers, there are obviously some formidable tasks ahead of the Soviet educational system before the Soviet working force is brought up to the level required in the transition period. Census figures were published in *Pravda*, April 17, 1971 (*CDSP*, vol. 23, no. 16, pp. 14–18).

[33] See V. Kolbanovskii, "Moral'nii kodeks stroitelia kommunizma," *Kommunist*, 1961, no. 15.

[34] See V. Anisimov and G. Kalugin, "Kommunizma zrimye cherty," in *K pobeda kommunisticheskovo truda: Ob opyte raboty partiinykh, komsomol'skikh i profsoiuznykh organizatsii s brigadami kommunisticheskovo truda* (Moscow: Izdatel'stvo VPSh i AON pri TsK KPSS, 1961), p. 173.

rades behaved toward their families but now the collective reacts severely to incorrect behavior of workers in life and in the family."[35] This collective involvement in the totality of daily life, together with the brigade slogan, "one for all and all for one," and an additional individual pledge to improve oneself through additional education and specialized training, summarizes the distinctively novel features of the brigade movement.

On the theoretical level, the brigades are viewed as forerunners of communistic labor organization, or as "genuine schools of communism" which "daily educate [the workers] in the high moral qualities which are necessary for men preparing to enter the communist tomorrow."[36] They are thus part of the general process of upgrading the workers' cultural level and communist consciousness. In this theoretical respect, they bear a certain resemblance to the public organizations and soviets.

In all of this purposeful effort to improve upon contemporary Soviet man, there is an underlying, usually covert, appraisal of his present faults. As mentioned above, the programs adopted for the transitional period often point clearly to the deficiencies they are intended to correct. The program for improving attitudes toward labor and for improving "cultural levels" is an obvious example of this phenomenon. A closely related problem area, that of changes in the work process itself, is a perhaps less obvious but equally interesting example.

The Soviet theorists have taken literally the original Marxian notion that differences between town and country and between mental and physical labor are grounded in the presocialist modes of production, although they have had to acknowledge that the lingering effects of these divisions carry over into the socialist stage. Since these differences are identified with capitalism and continue to exist in Soviet society only as survivals of a decadent system, it is naturally important that they be eliminated during the transitional period. The authoritative textbook, *Fundamentals of Marxism-Leninism* (English edition of *Osnovy marksizma-leninizma*), makes the distinction that, although there is still a difference between mental and physical workers under Soviet socialism, "the antithesis of the interests of these two categories of workers, which is characteristic of the exploiting system, is already being eliminated under socialism."[37] Since this antithesis is already being eliminated, the task of the transitional period is to overcome

[35] A. Pozdniakov, "V bor'be za kommunisticheskii trud rastët novyi chelovek," in *K pobede kommunisticheskovo truda*, p. 213.
[36] V. Shimanskii, "Razvedchiki budushchevo," in *K pobede kommunisticheskovo truda*, p. 84.
[37] *Fundamentals of Marxism-Leninism*, 2nd ed. (Moscow: Foreign Languages Publishing House, 1963), p. 666.

gradually the difference between these two categories of labor. However, the Soviet theorists have wisely retreated from the untenable position that *all* differences between mental and physical labor will cease, claiming only that the *essential* differences will be abolished. Certain nonessential differences connected with differing working environments will continue, even under communism, but these differences will have no harmful social consequences, as they now have by implication.[38]

There are several aspects of this process of overcoming differences in the laboring process. One is the gradual change in the working force which results in a higher proportion of predominantly non-physical occupations each year. One Soviet study claims that the number of mental workers is growing at a rate four to six times greater than the general increase in the working force.[39] This development is directly related to the upgrading of the Soviet worker's production qualifications, and is largely responsible for the great emphasis on additional vocational training for semi-skilled workers. The goal of this reeducation program is to raise "the cultural-technical level of physical workers to the level of engineers, technicians and agronomists."[40]

The increase in the proportion of mental to physical workers in the total working force is not only a product of intensive vocational training but is also a natural result of rapid technological advances in industry. Education supplies the needed specialists, but the need for these specialists is created through an advance in the level of technology. This advance, like its counterpart in America, brings with it an increase in the complexity of each specialty and a general shift away from physical toward mental activity.[41] The Soviet view, illustrated by the following quotation, looks to automation as the culminating step in this direction:

> With the complex mechanization and automation of production processes, physical labor is infused with intellectual content, new professions arise demanding mastery of the scientific foundations of production, and knowledge of new techniques; that is, mental labor begins to play a predominant role. Consequently, automation has a direct influence on the cultural-technical level of the workers, demanding of them a knowledge of mechanics, electronics, and other sciences, bringing to them a significantly greater share of mental labor.[42]

---

[38] See L. N. Kogan, "Ot truda sotsialisticheskovo k trudu kommunisticheskomu," *Voprosy filosofii*, 1960, no. 2, p. 18.

[39] *Izmenenie klassovoi struktury*, p. 314.

[40] *Ibid.*, p. 306.

[41] The controversial question of the division of labor under these circumstances will be discussed in detail in the next chapter.

[42] *Izmenenie klassovoi struktury*, p. 342. See also *ibid.*, p. 274.

This outlook sees each individual job category being "infused with intellectual content" to an ever-increasing degree, thus demanding increasingly qualified workers.[43]

On the other hand, some Soviet writers view the elimination of the mental/physical distinction not so much as the infusing of greater mental content into each specific job, but rather as the increasing tendency for a single worker to combine several diverse specialties, some predominantly physical, some predominantly mental, within his general capabilities (or "work profile"). This is a very different, almost diametrically opposed, point of view, for it does not look to technology for a basic change in the content of work, but rather to the worker for a basic change in his mental and physical capacities. The humanistic basis of this view is well typified in the following example:

> Today there is already being brought up a new type of worker of wide background who has mastered functions of physical and mental labor, thus manifestly overcoming the past. As in the case of engineers and teachers, the labor of these workers does not exclude wide specialization and separation of functions. But these functions already are not limited to the dimensions of an isolated profession. Today the worker fulfills one function, tomorrow another.[44]

There are several rather obvious difficulties with this outlook. In the first place, it assumes that all, or very nearly all, workers have a high potential capacity for absorbing the intricacies of several diverse specialties. This is a highly dubious proposition for the present, but it is always subject to the Marxist counter-argument that the very nature of man will change in the future as his social surroundings change. A second objection to this view is that it fails to deal adequately with the increasing complexity of modern production processes, which in turn leads to greater specialization of labor.[45] This observable trend in modern production processes would certainly tend to dim the prospects for the "poly-specialization" that would be required of each individual worker. Perhaps the most important difficulty with this position, however, is that it really does not solve the problem of differences between mental and physical labor at all—it simply recognizes that such differences exist and will continue to exist, and then tries to mitigate the

[43] This view, incidentally, is also widely held in the United States, where automation is more advanced.

[44] S. G. Strumilin, *Problemy sotsializma i kommunizma v SSSR* (Moscow: Izdatel'stvo ekonomicheskoi literatury, 1961), p. 296.

[45] This point, as will be seen in the detailed discussion in the next chapter, is a central one in the Soviet debate over the future of the division of labor under full communism.

effects of this continuing difference by ensuring that every worker will at different times be engaged in both types of activity.

Certain qualifications, however, are necessary here. This last objection is, of course, based upon the premises of the doctrine itself, upon an evaluation of a solution offered by Soviet theoreticians for a problem which only they wish to solve.[46] While the point has been made that this solution is doctrinally unsound, on a practical level it might indeed prove to be beneficial, since it could conceivably operate to relieve monotony on the job, utilize more of the average worker's potential, and reduce (or eliminate) the tendency toward social stratification based upon a status differential between blue-collar and white-collar occupations.

It should also be mentioned that, in all of this discussion among Soviet theoreticians, there is a general recognition of the rather basic fact that all human activity contains both mental and physical elements. The theoreticians, therefore, are concerned with a *predominance* of one element over another in each particular case. The proponents of the first-mentioned view—the infusing of all physical labor with mental content —would logically expect, therefore, a future situation in which all laboring activity would be predominantly mental, since they do not speak of the possibility of a counter-tendency—the infusing of mental work with an increasing physical content.[47] This proposal is therefore tantamount to eliminating the difference between mental and physical labor by *eliminating physical labor itself*. It is thus surprisingly similar to proposals often advanced in the West in somewhat less extreme forms, but it is certainly a vast mental distance away from the original Marxian vision of "poly-specialization" in terms of hunting, fishing, cattle-breeding, and critically criticizing.

The increasing mental content in all productive activities will apparently affect the special position of the intelligentsia during the transitional period. Soviet theory holds that "the intelligentsia is a social stratum [*sloi*] which arose as a result of the distinction between mental and physical labor,"[48] and which has a "class character" without itself being a class. The conclusion based on this definition, is that the intelligentsia will disappear as the difference between mental and physical labor is gradually overcome.

[46] The real situation, naturally, is a universal phenomenon, but in non-Marxist countries it is not considered a problem to be "solved."

[47] This does not mean, however, that the future will be devoid of physical activity. The doctrine calls for increased sports activity during leisure time to develop the future men and women of labor physically. It is also recognized that some light physical activity will remain in the work process.

[48] *Izmenenie klassovoi struktury*, p. 299.

The question of class structure is intimately connected with the second set of differences to be eliminated during the transition, the differences between town and country. These can be divided into two categories: differences between the urban and rural physical environment, including labor conditions, and differences between city dwellers (often referred to as "workers" and "employees" [*sluzhashchie*]) and peasants. In other words, as in the case of mental and physical labor, we are dealing with both human and environmental factors. In fact, there is a relationship, occasionally noted by Soviet theorists, between the two dichotomies (mental-physical and town-country). This relationship is the result of identifying the peasant in a very general way with physical labor and the city dweller with mental labor. In a more exact way— concentrating on the environmental rather than personal aspect—we can say that agricultural labor is more physical than modern industrial labor. The interdependence of these two pairs of categories has been expressed by one Soviet study as follows: "In a situation where the country still lags behind the town and where the cultural and technical level of the peasants is lower than that of the workers, it is difficult to speak of the complete conquest of differences between people who engage in mental and in physical work."[49] According to this view, "the two processes develop simultaneously, but they will not be concluded, most likely, at the same time."[50] This rather vague formulation of concurrent development of the two parallel trends has been more specifically defined in the following terms:

> The character of mental labor is differentiated to a much greater degree from that of physical labor than agricultural labor is differentiated from industrial. Therefore, raising the labor of workers and peasants to a level of engineering and agrotechnical labor demands a higher development of productive forces and a much greater increase of the cultural-technical level of the workers and peasants than is necessary for the transformation of agricultural labor into a variety of industrial labor.[51]

From this formulation of the problem, we can expect that the differences between town and country will be eradicated at some time prior to the elimination of differences between mental and physical labor.

As in the case of mental-physical labor differences, the Soviets have stopped short of the claim that all differences will eventually be abolished, recognizing that some *nonessential* differences will remain even

---

[49] *Ibid.*, p. 253.

[50] *Ibid.*

[51] V. Semenov, "Na puti k besklassovomy obshchestvu," *Kommunist*, 1962, no. 1, p. 45.

under full communism. This qualification is also meant to offer a contrast with the present situation in which *essential* differences are still in existence. Essential differences are felt to have certain sociological consequences, such as class differentiation, whereas nonessential differences are seen as arising from disparate elements in the immediate working environments of factory and farm.

As previously mentioned, the class structure of Soviet society is closely related to this topic. According to theory, the differences between town and country in present-day Soviet life are expressed by the existence of two "fraternal" classes, workers and peasants, with the workers as the leading element. Therefore, on the day when such differences are finally reduced to their nonessential traces, the two classes will have coalesced into a unified, classless, communist society. Even at the present time, according to the theory, the interests of peasant and worker coincide, so that there are no antagonisms and no conflict between them.

In order to bring about this merger, the peasant must be raised in cultural-technical level until he is the equal of his city-dwelling comrades, a process that involves the entire gamut of educational techniques generally expressed by the word *vospitanie* (upbringing). Living conditions in the country must also be brought up to city standards. From a doctrinal point of view, however, the most important difference between town and country at present is the existence of two forms of property, cooperative (*kolkhoz*) property in the rural areas, and all-people's (*vsenarodnyi*) property in the urban areas.[52] *Kolkhoz* property is defined as cooperative in a juridical sense; that is, the members of the *kolkhoz* formally own the property in common and lease the land, which belongs to the state, in perpetuity. *Vsenarodnyi*, on the other hand, is simply the Soviet term for state property, and expresses the oft-stated formula that state property is the property of all Soviet citizens in joint ownership. The second type of property is naturally considered a higher form by the Soviet theorists, and, therefore, the trend during the transition must be toward merging cooperative property with all-people's property until the former is eliminated. This kind of reasoning simply amounts to an assertion that the amount of communist content in property is directly proportional to the number of people who share in its possession. It seems inevitable that the subjective feeling of ownership will be diluted as more people are included as owners, but this is entirely appropriate as preparation for full communism, where property-owning—or more properly speaking, the desire to

[52] See A. K. Kurylev, "K voprosu o preodolenii sushchestvennovo razlichiia mezhdu gorodom i derevnei," *Voprosy filosofii*, 1959, no. 4.

possess objects—will not be an attribute of man. Because of this goal, the transition period is designed to effect a dilution of the very concept of property by enlarging the sphere of property that belongs to everyone (i.e., all-people's property) and thus in effect belongs to no one.

The practical side to this elimination of cooperative property is the elimination of the *kolkhoz* itself. It is well-established doctrine that the *kolkhoz* is a temporary form of rural organization and an expression of the relatively backward condition of the Soviet peasant. Like Lenin's New Economic Policy, it is a useful, transitory arrangement expressing an existing relationship that is considered an unfortunate necessity. The timetable for the elimination of the *kolkhoz* has not been established yet, but because of the doctrinal necessity of having a single form of property under full communism, it is generally concluded that the *kolkhoz* will disappear "earlier than the full transition to communism, prior to the final solution of other problems of communist construction."[53] The problem is complicated by the fact that the *kolkhoz* is the embodiment of not only cooperative property but private property as well. The private plots of ground on which the peasants grow money crops to supplement their incomes are the last vestiges of "private economy" and are thus incompatible with the theoretical demands of a society building communism. Since private property (*chastnaia sobstvennost'*)—as distinct from personal, nonproductive property (*lichnaia sobstvennost'*) such as clothing and household articles—is considered a lower form of property than cooperative property, the private plots are marked for more immediate elimination than the *kolkhoz* itself. According to one source: "The time has already come for the gradual dying away of the *kolkhoznik's* private economy. Because of differences in the economic development of the *kolkhozy*, this time has already arrived . . . for some of them, while for others it will come only in the future."[54] On the other hand, another source reports:

> The time has . . . not arrived for the merger of *kolkhoz*-cooperative and all-people's property. The *kolkhoz* structure contains within itself great possibilities for the development of productive forces in the country, for the inculcation of advanced techniques and the improvement of the cultural living conditions of the village population. It fully conforms to the present level of agricultural production.[55]

[53] *Izmenenie klassovoi struktury*, p. 254.
[54] *Ibid.*, p. 248.
[55] Moroz, *Dialekticheskii materializm*, p. 62. An interesting prospect is raised by G. T. Kovalevskii, "Ob ekonomicheskoi sushchnosti nedelimykh fondov," in *Voprosy stroitel'stva kommunizma v SSSR: Materialy nauchnoi sessii otdelenii obshchestvennykh nauk Akademii nauk SSSR* (Moscow: Izdatel'stvo Akademii nauk SSSR, 1959), p. 342: "It is difficult to say at present whether the merger of

As for the more immediate prospects of the collective farmer losing his private garden plot, there are three necessary prerequisites. The first is the "growth of production in the *kolkhoz* to such a degree that not only gives the state a sufficient quantity of products and not only guarantees the *kolkhoz* social requirements, but also fully satisfies the needs of the members of the *artel* for these products."[56] Similarly, the other two requirements are "general growth of the *kolkhoznik*'s income received from the *artel*, so that he no longer needs an additional source of income (private economy)" and "the understanding of the collective farmers themselves that such a measure is necessary and needed in order to improve their entire lives."[57] Increasing the collective farmer's understanding of the inevitable is, of course, a problem for *vospitanie*, while the other two points are related to the program for increasing agricultural productivity during the transitional period.

In the Soviet view, however, the two problems are interrelated. It is currently acknowledged that in a certain sense the peasants' private property sets his interests against those of the worker, for the peasant "as owner of private property still enters the market as a seller and therefore is interested to some degree in raising market prices,"[58] while the worker as consumer has, naturally, opposed interests. However, when the day arrives that the peasant can have his normal needs fulfilled through the *kolkhoz* exclusively—in other words, when *kolkhoz* productivity is raised to a very high level—then he will voluntarily give up his private plot as an unprofitable and time-wasting diversion from his work in the collective. The collective farmer's "understanding" of the problem is thus directly tied by Soviet doctrine to the level of agricultural productivity.

The question of property relations in the Soviet countryside brings up an interesting side issue in contemporary doctrine. As is well-known, the Soviet peasant has received payment for many years through the system of computing the number of "labor-days" he has contributed to the *kolkhoz* during the year. This computation, done by the *kolkhoz* bookkeeper, is based on both the quantity and the quality of the work he has performed. In most cases, the collective farmer receives a certain portion of the produce left after the *kolkhoz* makes its state deliveries, and his share is based upon the number of labor-days he has accumu-

---

*kolkhoz* and all-people's property will take place under socialist or communist conditions. It is completely possible that such a merger will take place sooner than the entry into full communism. In this case we will have a socialist structure based on a single all-people's property. . . ."

[56] *Izmenenie klassovoi struktury*, p. 249.

[57] *Ibid.*

[58] *Ibid.*, p. 230.

lated. In some cases, however, the collective farmer receives a supplementary cash payment.

This situation contains certain paradoxical elements in terms of the doctrine. On the one hand, money payment of the peasant corresponds to money payment of the industrial worker, who is regarded as the leading element in Soviet society, and it tends to reduce the "essential difference" between town and country. From this standpoint, the introduction of money wages for the peasantry can be considered a progressive step. On the other hand, it is an explicit tenet of Marxist doctrine that money is a capitalist market device and therefore has no place under communism. From this point of view, then, the introduction of money wages must be considered retrogressive. This, in turn, implies that the labor-day system used by the peasants is more progressive than the money wages system used by the workers—a conclusion that certainly places the leading position of the workers in jeopardy. In a sense, it makes the peasants the vanguard of society, since, as one Soviet writer put it, "through the labor-day [they] may move directly over to the principle of distribution according to needs"[59]—the distribution system of full communism.[60]

Certainly, there is a definite logical basis for the opinion that the labor-day system more closely resembles communist distribution than does the money wage system inherited *in toto* from capitalism. Therefore, a call for transition from the labor-day to wage payment for the peasants, a step suggested by some writers,[61] is, in effect, a call for a step backward in the hope that the practical results in terms of peasant incentives may produce two steps forward.

In order to bring living conditions on the *kolkhoz* up to urban standards, a considerable increase in social services and housing construction is planned for the transitional period. As apartment houses gradually replace individual dwellings and social services gradually replace many domestic functions of the family, Soviet theory expects that the peasant will be drawn from individualistic, family-oriented feelings to a feeling of collectivism which will embrace the entire *kolkhoz.*

[59] G. M. Andreeva, "Ob izmeneniakh v klassovoi strukture obshchestva v period razvërnutovo stroitel'stva kommunizma," in *Zakonomernosti perekhoda ot sotsializma k kommunizmu,* ed. D. I. Chesnokov (Moscow: Gosudarstvennoe izdatel'stvo "Vysshaia shkola," 1961), p. 89.
[60] It has also been held that wage payments are retrogressive because they would only obstruct the necessary transition away from the *kolkhozik's* private economy. See K. Orlovskii, "Kolkhozy—shkola kommunizma dlia krest'ianstva," *Kommunist,* 1961, no. 11, p. 111.
[61] See, for example, N. A. Aitov, "Stiranie razlichii mezhdu krest'ianstvom i rabochim klassom v bytu i kul'ture v period razvërnutovo stroitel'stva kommunizma," *Voprosy filosofii,* 1961, no. 12, p. 107.

The precise course of future development for the collective farm has apparently not been determined, although the necessity for its disappearance, as we have seen, is well-established. One Soviet author rather hazily predicts that "in the future, through a series of transitional forms, the *kolkhoz* organizations will gradually combine with state economic organizations and organs of power in a single system of social management."[62] Another predicts that the *kolkhoz* will be gradually drawn into the state by the advances of technology and the need for larger capital outlays in order to introduce advanced techniques.[63] It is also stated that the elimination of the *kolkhoz* "does not at all mean simply the nationalization of the *kolkhoz*, transforming it into a *sovkhoz* [state farm]. Of course, the creation of *sovkhozy* on the foundation of the *kolkhozy* has a place in some cases . . . but as a whole [this] does not seem to be the chief method."[64] The most likely future course for the *kolkhoz* is thus placed in doubt without an alternative being offered, and the net result is to leave the procedure by which the *kolkhoz* will be removed from the scene open for future party consideration.

Soviet writers look forward to a great increase in social services not only in the *kolkhoz* but in the rest of society as well. One major result of this program will be a fundamental change in family structure and family relations, and a consequent change in the status of women in Soviet society. Domestic work will be assumed to an ever greater extent by a network of service establishments, such as public dining halls and laundries, thus lightening the considerable load of housework which Soviet women now bear. A similarly widespread network of boarding schools will be provided so that women will be freed from the daily worry of child raising and will be free to engage in productive labor and cultural recreation. The goal of this program would be to bring about the day when "each family would have the opportunity, if desired, to place the children and adolescents in children's institutions without charge."[65] Based upon estimates of increased boarding-school construction, Soviet writers expect that separation of parents and children will become more and more common as the transitional period progresses, although they are careful to point out that this will never be accomplished through "administrative" or compulsory measures.

[62] Platkovskii, *Politicheskaia organizatsiia*, p. 126.

[63] Andreeva, "Ob izmeneniakh v klassovoi strukture," p. 85.

[64] *Izmenenie klassovoi struktury*, p. 255. The Party Program states, however, that "as the kolkhozes and state farms develop, their production ties with each other and with local industrial enterprises will grow stronger. The practice of jointly organizing various enterprises will expand." *The Road to Communism*, p. 531.

[65] V. Platkovskii, "Formirovanie kommunisticheskikh obshchestvennykh otnoshenii," *Kommunist*, 1962, no. 15, p. 33.

The increase in social services such as these naturally calls for a corresponding increase in expenditures, and in the Soviet Union these expenditures for the service industries are lumped under the heading of the "indivisible [*nedelimyi*] fund of public consumption." This "fund" is a catchall term for all undifferentiated expenditures on the public-at-large, rather than an actual sum of money administered by a single governmental agency. According to Soviet statistics, the fund has shown a rapid increase in the past two decades from a total outlay of 4.2 billion rubles in 1940 to 24.5 billion rubles in 1960. By 1980, the indivisible fund is expected to provide half the total requirements of the working population.[66] In the eighteen-year period ending in 1961, the percentage of free goods and services used rose from 23 to 33 percent of total consumption, and this trend is expected to continue during the transition.[67] It would be difficult to overestimate the importance of this fund in the theoretical literature, since it is very often viewed as the single most important indicator of the country's progress toward creating the necessary material preconditions for the entry into full communism. Through the fund's gradual expansion, the average Soviet citizen is expected to achieve an understanding of a higher principle of distribution, "the principle that the greatest part of social wealth is distributed through a social fund, independently of the quality and quantity of labor, without wages."[68] It is therefore expected that "the [indivisible] social fund will lead directly to the communist principle of distribution according to needs."[69]

Despite the unique qualities claimed for it under Soviet socialism, the indivisible fund is strikingly similar to public expenditures of nonsocialist countries, especially some of the advanced welfare states of Western Europe. Only its predicted future would seem to distinguish it really clearly from the welfare programs of these countries. One rather large qualification, however, must be added. In the Soviet scheme of things, the indivisible fund is considered a *replacement* for private property rather than an augmentation of it. As the fund expands into more areas of economic life, private property, and even some forms of personal property, will shrivel away and die. In reality, the demise of private property cannot be left to chance, but must be assured by state action and an unrelenting campaign. In the words of one eminent Soviet theoretician:

---

[66] I. N. Gavrilenkov, "Sovetskoe obshchenarodnoe gosudarstvo v period razvёrnutovo stroitel'stva kommunizma" (candidate's dissertation, Voenno-politicheskaia ordena Lenina Krasnoznamennaia Akademiia imeni V. I. Lenina, 1962), p. 109.

[67] Nikitin, *Chto takoe kommunizm*, p. 85.

[68] Platkovskii, "Formirovanie kommunisticheskikh," p. 28.

[69] *Ibid.*

The new public forms of satisfaction of steadily growing and reasonable needs, disclosing their superiority more and more fully, are inexorably squeezing out the old individual forms of the use of material and cultural goods. But this process cannot take place spontaneously, of course. Only by ensuring the preponderant development of public forms and gradually restricting individual forms is it possible to accelerate the complete victory of communist methods of satisfying the needs of the entire population and of each individual.[70]

The same author makes this point a bit firmer in declaring that "by force of the law, which expresses the will of a united and monolithic Soviet people, it is necessary to close all loopholes through which private owners crawl. In this case it is a matter not of restricting and squeezing out private-property tendencies but completely eliminating them."[71] Even such items of personal use as *dachas* (country homes), which are not necessarily used as a source of private, "unearned" income, are to become public property. This sort of development is tied to growth of the indivisible fund in the following manner:

It is to be assumed that . . . when the public forms of satisfying needs both in terms of quantity and especially of quality of service reveal their advantages, people will begin voluntarily to give up their *dachas* and society will be able on the basis of reasonable payment or without compensation to acquire and improve them for use by all the people.[72]

The growth of the indivisible fund is looked upon not only as a harbinger of heightened communist economics and individual consciousness but also as a part of the general drive to establish the "material-technical base of communism." The material-technical base is a general term which combines all the necessary material preconditions for the entry into the stage of full communism. The highly respected Soviet economist, S. G. Strumilin, has defined this term as follows: "The material-technical base of communism means a level of development of productive forces of society, sufficient to guarantee abundance of material and spiritual welfare, indispensable for the full satisfaction of all the growing needs of the people."[73] The Party Program states that an "abundance of material welfare" will be achieved by an increase of not less than 500 percent in total industrial output, and 250 percent

---

[70] Ts. Stepanian, "Communism and Property," *Oktiabr'*, 1960, no. 9 (*CDSP*, vol. 12, no. 42, p. 19).

[71] *Ibid.*

[72] *Ibid.*

[73] S. G. Strumilin, *Slovar' semiletki* (Moscow: Gospolitizdat, 1960), p. 157. It should be noted that in good materialist fashion, this definition links the "productive forces of society" with a *guarantee* of "spiritual welfare."

in agricultural output (with 1960 as the reference base).[74] In terms of both per capita industrial output and labor productivity, establishment of the material-technical base will mean the total eclipse of the United States as world production leader, a point which obviously has great psychological significance for the Soviet leaders.

No great change is expected in the development of relations between the nationalities of the Soviet Union during the transitional phase. A trend toward gradual merging of the smaller nationalities and their assimilation into the mainstream of Russian culture has been observed, and officially approved, during the entire Soviet period. This process is expected to continue during the transition. It is an observed tendency for some non-Russian parents to encourage their children to study the Russian language, since this opens up new career possibilities and in general is considered a mark of "culture."[75] The fact that Russian has become the lingua franca of the Soviet nationalities is expressly approved because use of the Russian language permits each nationality to become familiar with the culture of the others and also with "world culture."[76]

A related problem is the relationship among the various socialist countries during the transition. Khrushchev made something of a contribution to the literature of Marxism-Leninism in this area by formulating the theory of the "more or less simultaneous entry" of the socialist countries into the stage of full communism. His theory is based on the fact that "new laws of development, laws unknown to humanity in the past, operate in the economic system of socialism."[77] The specifics of these new laws were not spelled out by Khrushchev himself, but several other Soviet theoreticians have attempted to make these laws more definite. One Soviet study has drawn the obvious inference from Khrushchev's thesis by stating that simultaneous entry for all countries of the socialist camp means, in effect, that "the process of building socialism and communism in the countries of peoples' democracy will be accelerated compared to the process in the Soviet Union."[78]

In contrast to the law of uneven development of capitalist countries, attributed to Lenin, the new formula for the socialist camp is embodied in the phase "planned, proportional development." By this is meant that the socialist countries, not being engaged in blind and intense competi-

---

[74] *The Road to Communism*, pp. 515, 524.

[75] Platkovskii, "Formirovanie kommunisticheskikh," p. 34. The author's own observations in Soviet Georgia and Armenia would tend to confirm this point.

[76] D. M. Kukin, "Vdokhnovliaiushchee znamia bor'by za kommunizm," *Voprosy filosofii*, 1961, no. 8, pp. 36–37.

[77] Khrushchev, "Kontrol'nye tsifry," pp. 107–8.

[78] *Izmenenie klassovoi struktury*, p. 287.

tion with each other, are able to plan their economic development to the mutual advantage of all. Fraternal aid is given by the more developed to the less developed, based on the long-standing principle of proletarian internationalism, and the less-developed countries are able to take advantage of the experience of the other, more advanced socialist countries. Furthermore, Soviet theory holds that rational planning techniques (established in the Council for Mutual Economic Aid) lead to the efficient allocation of economic tasks on an international level or, in other words, the "international division of labor." This principle allows each country to develop its own resources in the most economically advantageous manner without incurring the danger of exploitation by the other fraternal countries. The difference between this system and capitalist international economics is explained by one Soviet writer in the following terms:

> The forms of economic co-operation between the socialist countries are varied. An important part is played by forms which are also used in the capitalist world: foreign trade, credit agreement, etc. But under socialist conditions these forms have acquired a qualitatively new content, corresponding to the principle of fraternal aid and proletarian internationalism. These relations have become genuinely equal and disinterested, wholly free from the desire to profit at each other's expense.[79]

Since the forms of these international economic arrangements are conceded to be the same as those of capitalism, while the content or spirit has fundamentally changed, one would expect that the transitional period will not see any radical innovations in international economic cooperation between the socialist countries, but rather a further development of the "fraternal spirit."

Another area in which startling innovation is not expected is the area of Communist party control. All spheres of economic, political, and social life are expected to be firmly under the broad, and in fact expanded, control of the Party apparatus. The idea of expanding Party control has been given a very important place in plans for the transitional period and has been the subject of countless brochures and books, generally written in a very predictable pattern.

Justification for the expansion of the Party's role in guiding Soviet society toward communism is given in several ways. On the most abstract level, the long-held theory of the Party's function in dealing with the "objective laws" of historical development is given a new interpreta-

---

[79] Sh. Sanakoyev, "The 21st Congress on the Socialist Countries' Transition to Communism," *International Affairs* (Moscow), 1959, no. 5, p. 36. The more recent difficulties with Rumania over the course of her economic development would tend to cast considerable doubt on this assertion.

tion. As previously discussed, the importance of the human will in the building of communism has been stressed by Soviet doctrine for some time, thus differing in this respect from the original Marxist classics to some extent. Within this framework, it is the Party's function to control social laws—without being able to change them—so that society can use them to its own advantage. As one Soviet writer put it:

> Economic laws do not lose their objective character in the conditions of planned building of socialism and communism. However, skillfully utilized by the Communist Party, they are transformed from the demonic authorities that they were under capitalism into powerful allies of the working classes and of all society.[80]

Since it is universally recognized that only the Party can perform this function of controlling objective laws, the Party thus becomes the embodiment of the "conscious factor" in historical development. During the transition, the "conscious" or "subjective" factor is expected to play an increasing role, i.e., the role of human ("subjective") will, consciously directed, is to grow in importance as compared to the objective, immutable laws of social development. Putting these two doctrinal tenets together results in the proposition that "at the present stage, the growth of the role of the subjective factor, of the awareness and organization of the masses in communist construction, means above all the further intensification of the guiding activity of the Communist Party."[81] The central point is that "mankind is not moving toward this great goal [of communism] blindly, automatically" but is being consciously directed toward it by "the working class, headed by the Communist Party."[82]

Since the Party is the "vanguard of the people," and the people are to increase their active role during the transitional phase, the active role of the vanguard is also to increase. This is to be done by "directing the activity of the masses with increasing skill, promptly seizing upon and widely disseminating their initiative, increasing their political awareness, organization and discipline even more and considering and satisfying their growing requirements as fully as possible."[83]

On another level, support is given the concept of increasing the Party's role by identifying the Party with the corrective technique of "persuasion" (*ubezhdenie*), a growing technique, rather than with

[80] V. Ivanov, V. Pchelin, and M. Sakov, "The Party's Growing Role in the Building of Communism," *Kommunist*, 1960, no. 17 (*CDSP*, vol. 12, no. 1, p. 3).
[81] *Ibid.*
[82] *Ibid.*
[83] *Ibid.*

"compulsion" (*prinuzhdenie*), a method which is disappearing. To quote a typical source:

> To the degree that our Motherland advances closer to communism, the organization and persuasion of the masses will acquire ever more significance and, on the other hand, compulsion and administration . . . will become all the less significant. The Party, as is well known, bases its guiding role on persuasion. Therefore, the Party itself represents the ideal instrument of communist society. Consequently, the further along the road to communism our country advances, the stronger will grow the guiding role of the Party in the life of our society.[84]

It is quite apparent, however, that the "persuasive" methods of the Party are to be directed primarily toward convincing the populace of the Party's own vital role. In the present Soviet definition, an important part of "consciousness" is the conscious understanding that the Party's ever-growing role in communist construction is inevitable. In one Soviet writer's words: "The more conscious the masses become, the better they understand the necessity of their own organization and the more passionately they accept the Party's guidance, seeing in this the primary condition for the most rapid building of communism."[85] Similarly, as a result of the Party's persuasive efforts, "they adopt the domestic and international politics of the Party as their own politics, as an expression of their fundamental interests and therefore give it their unlimited trust and support."[86] Since there is always complete identity of the Party's and the people's interests in Soviet doctrine, the necessity of increased Party activity can be seen as resulting from the growth of the people's activity, the two being viewed as two sides of the same process.

There are many specific references in the Soviet literature to the necessity for increased Party activity in various spheres of public life, such as ideological work, supervision of the arts, production control, and the like. In all of these cases, increased party involvement is considered a sure-fire remedy for a present shortcoming, regardless of the particular shortcoming under consideration. In this manner, *party involvement becomes a generalized solution* to the increasingly complex problems anticipated during the transitional period. Indeed, the very fact that the complexity of these problems will increase during the

---

[84] V. I. Evdokimov, *Vozrastaiushchaia rol' partii v stroitel'stve kommunizma* (Moscow: Gospolitizdat, 1960), p. 27.

[85] N. Lomakin, "Partiia Lenina," in *Nekotorye problemy teorii i praktiki stroitel'stva kommunizma: Sbornik statei v pomoshch izuchaiushchim marksizm-leninizm* (Moscow: Voennoe izdatel'stvo Ministerstva Oborony Soiuza SSR, 1961), p. 36.

[86] *Ibid.*

transition has been cited as a prima facie reason for prospective increases in party activity.[87]

The most important task of the Party, however, is that of bringing up a new type of man, one who will be fit and able to live under full communism. This upbringing is a long-term, gradual process that, as already mentioned, increases in importance the closer Soviet society comes to the communistic goal. In their own estimation, the Soviet people have "entered a period in which the education of the man of communist society has become an immediate, actual, concrete task rather than a remote dream."[88] In contradistinction to original Marxism, however, the new consciousness required of Soviet citizens is not expected to arise of itself out of new material and social conditions. It is not, in other words, a spontaneous development, but rather the result of "large-scale, daily political-educational work of the Communist Party."[89] The Party's task in this area is made even more difficult by the theorem—well-supported by evidence from Soviet life—that "social life changes more rapidly than does public awareness."[90]

Since this lag of consciousness behind social development gives rise to the retention of capitalist survivals in the minds of Soviet citizens, the Party's work must be continually enlarged and improved. In this approach, which substitutes purposive Party effort for theoretically predetermined, natural development, we see more the influence of Lenin than Marx—the Lenin, that is, of *What Is To Be Done?* rather than of *State and Revolution.*

### The Khrushchev Timetable

The optimism which distinguished the Khrushchev period and set it off from the greater caution that has characterized Khrushchev's successors is nowhere better illustrated than in their contrasting approaches to the periodization of the transitional period. Under Khrushchev, the near future was viewed as a relatively short and direct step into a fully communist society, and Khrushchev himself led the way with heady projections and assurances that communism would be achieved by the current Soviet generation. This hopeful prospect, however, has been dimmed by the post-Khrushchev team, which has eschewed definite time-

---

[87] See, for example, Evdokimov, *Vozrastaiushchaia rol'*, p. 6.

[88] Ivanov, Pchelin, and Sakov, "The Party's Growing Role in the Building of Communism," (*CDSP*, vol. 12, no. 1, p. 3).

[89] M. P. Sakov, *Osnovnoi printsip kommunizma* (Moscow: Gospolitizdat, 1961), p. 18.

[90] Ivanov, Pchelin, and Sakov, "The Party's Growing Role in the Building of Communism," (*CDSP*, vol. 12, no. 1, p. 3).

tables and predictions and retreated to a more traditional vagueness.

Nevertheless, Khrushchev's timetable is still of considerable interest, even without Khrushchev on the scene to push it along. The timetable is enshrined in the 1961 Party Program, still an authoritative document used by Brezhnev et al. for hortatory purposes. Although the timetable cannot be considered "binding" on Khrushchev's heirs, they must contend with the demoralization that would inevitably flow from a direct denunciation of the Khrushchevian projections. They cannot attack Khrushchev's timetable frontally but must rather engage in a game of delicate "doublethink" in order to stretch and distort it. They must rely primarily on the short memory of the Soviet public to accomplish this sleight-of-hand, but those who do not forget so easily will recall that Khrushchev left a very formidable legacy of goals to be achieved in specific, and rather short, time periods.

In fact, the Party Program and Khrushchev's speeches at the Twenty-second Party Congress constituted a twenty-year plan for the economic and social transformation of Soviet society. These goals were either placed within the framework of the timetable or left for solution in the period beyond the vision of that Party Program. Generally speaking, the twenty-year transitional period was divided into two ten-year stages. Interestingly, the crucial event which was to separate these two periods was not the accomplishment of some important internal transformation of society but rather the final victory of the USSR over the United States in international economic competition. This event should have occurred in about 1970, at the end of the first stage. In Khrushchev's vision, the decade of the 1960s should have seen the Soviet Union draw ever closer to the per capita production of the United States, until the fateful and historic day when the Soviets would have been able to claim the world's highest living standards. The Party Program describes what that would mean:

> Everyone will live in easy circumstances; all collective and state farms will become highly productive and profitable enterprises; the demand of Soviet people for well-appointed housing will, in the main, be satisfied; hard physical work will disappear; the U.S.S.R. will have the shortest working day.[91]

[91] *The Road to Communism*, p. 512. Of course, Khrushchev's timetable was grossly overoptimistic, as indicated by the fact that 1970 passed into history with the Soviet Union still lagging significantly behind America in its standard of living. This is, in itself, sufficient reason for the regime to drop further references to the specific timetables of the program, but it also demonstrates the fundamental dilemma of the regime: it cannot afford to denounce the program, and, in fact, prints new copies every year with the now false predictions standing as an implicit indictment of the regime's failures.

Aside from the fact that the Soviet Union has not achieved the predicted superiority over American production, the Soviet choice of standards by which to measure their own progress is quite instructive. The crucial dividing line between the first and second stages of the transitional period was derived from a competition between two countries, one of which was almost totally beyond Soviet control. (One assumes!) If Khrushchev had set some absolute production figures as the goal, he would have had to contend only with the difficult problems of the Soviet economy. But by insisting on measuring Soviet accomplishments against the ever-changing external standard of American economic growth, he took on the added problem of forecasting the American growth rate and made an uncontrollable variable a decisive indicator of Soviet progress. Khrushchev was, in effect, saying that the American economy has a maximum growth rate considerably lower than the natural and predictable increase of the Soviet economy. This kind of reasoning springs from the doctrinal view of the capitalist world, which is seen as being chaotically driven by social laws that the capitalists are unable to manipulate and, ultimately, unable to understand.

Since the maximum possible American growth rate is more or less fixed at its present rate by the inherent limitations of the capitalist system, states the doctrine, the date on which Soviet production will surpass that of the United States should be predictable by a simple extrapolation of the recent performance of both systems. Furthermore, the doctrine permits the socialist system to optimize its own productive capabilities through willful, purposive party activity, while the capitalist world can only struggle in vain against the "objective" limitations of its obsolete "relations of production." Thus the outcome of the economic competition between the two systems is the inevitable victory of Soviet socialism, and it is in this context that Khrushchev outraged his American hosts by saying with bland assurance, "We will bury you."

The importance which the Soviet theorists have given to the competition with the United States indicates the extent to which they search for visible verification of the doctrine. Soviet Marxism-Leninism is true to its forebears in being a doctrine of this world, constantly subject to the supreme test of comparison with reality. Whereas other doctrines may depend on certain unverifiable absolutes or "necessary truths," Marxism-Leninism stands or falls on the basis of its ability to describe reality coherently, especially its course of development. It is in this spirit that initial Soviet successes in space flights and in overtaking American economic standards were constantly credited to the purported superiority of the Soviet social and economic system.

Later American demonstrations of superiority in space technology were a severe blow to the doctrinal optimism purveyed by Khrushchev. Khrushchev, who identified himself most directly with this optimism, was particularly vulnerable to demonstrations of American superiority, such as the U-2 overflights, the Cuban missile crisis, and the energetic and eventually successful American efforts to overcome the initial Soviet lead in the "space race." The post-Khrushchev leadership has learned the lessons of Khrushchev's mistake and has taken a more cautious position on the question of peaceful economic competition between the two systems. Whereas the ultimate outcome is still un-questionable, post-Khrushchev analyses have stressed the "protracted" nature of the competitive process, thus avoiding the potential disillusion-ment that could ensue from unequivocal invalidation of a central thesis of Marxism-Leninism. The essential point, however, is that Marxism-Leninism, in order to be true to its self-definition as a "science," must always be subject to verification by empirical evidence. Disconfirming evidence must be incorporated into a new set of confirming rationaliza-tions, so that the core beliefs of the ideology remain intact. In fact, disconfirming evidence seems to increase the efforts of the theoreticians to provide an appreciation of the new facts consistent with the theory.[92]

It is for these reasons that the Khrushchev timetable became enor-mously disquieting to his successors. It contained a plethora of victory predictions in economic competition with the United States, predictions which rapidly turned sour. For example, total industrial output was planned to increase within the first decade by "150 percent, thus ex-ceeding the level of U.S. industrial output," and at the end of the second decade (approximately 1980) by "not less than 500 percent, thus leav-ing the present overall volume of U.S. industrial output far behind."[93] Even in agriculture, where the Party Program is more circumspect, it was claimed that in the first decade the Soviet Union would outstrip the United States in per capita output of essential agricultural products.

The program also established some other material goals for the first decade of the transition. Labor productivity was to increase by 100 percent, and agricultural productivity was to be raised by 150 percent. The national income was similarly to rise by 150 percent and between 900 and 1,000 billion kilowatt hours of electrical energy were to be available per year by the end of the 1960s. At the same time the work week was to have been reduced to 35 or 36 hours.

Although the Soviet economy made measurable progress during the

---

[92] The same sort of phenomenon has been observed and studied with respect to millenarian sects in *When Prophecy Fails* by Leon Festinger, Henry W. Riecken, and Stanley Schachter (New York: Harper & Row, 1964).

[93] *The Road to Communism*, p. 515.

1960s, it fell short of the program's euphoric predictions in almost every respect. The average work week in 1969 remained at 40.7 hours,[94] about five hours more per week than predicted; electrical energy production in 1971 was 800 billion kilowatt hours,[95] about 100 billion kilowatt hours less than predicted; labor productivity in industry increased by 76.7 percent from 1960 to 1971,[96] almost 25 percent less than the goal set by the program. Perhaps most important, the gap between Soviet and American living standards seemed to widen rather than diminish. While the Soviet gross national product per capita increased by 39.8 percent from 1960 to 1969, the American gross national product per capita increased by 64.5 percent during the same period.[97] In roughly equivalent dollar figures, the difference between the two increased from approximately $1,625 to $2,962.[98] Thus, even though the Soviet Union did overtake the United States in total production of concrete, steel, and some other basic commodities, the disparity in the visible standard of living widened rather than narrowed. Khrushchev's dream of the Soviet Union energetically striding past a gasping and demoralized United States had been dashed, and his timetable for the first decade stands as a monument to his grand illusions.

Even more grandiose are the program's forecasts for the 1970s. It states that, by the end of this decade, labor productivity will rise by 300 to 350 percent, and electrification of the entire country, the subject of a slogan that goes back to Lenin, will "in the main be completed."[99] There will be a gradual transition to free public catering, and a sufficient number of free boarding schools will be constructed to accommodate all children whose parents wish to enroll them. At the same time, the work week will be shortened to less than 35 hours, and an entire month of paid vacation will be provided for all Soviet working people.

By the end of this decade, in 1980, the program foresees that the "material-technical base of communism" will have been built. This will mean, among other things, a yearly consumption of between 2700 and 3000 billion kilowatt hours of electrical energy and 250 million tons of steel.[100] Automation will have been introduced on a mass scale, and

---

[94] Ellen Mickiewicz, ed., *Handbook of Soviet Social Science Data* (New York: Free Press, 1973), p. 70.

[95] *Narodnoe khoziaistvo, 1922–1972* (Moscow: Statistika, 1972), p. 158.

[96] *Ibid.*, p. 149.

[97] Percentages were calculated from figures published by the Department of Commerce, and in Mickiewicz, *Handbook*, p. 93.

[98] Mickiewicz, *Handbook*, p. 93.

[99] *The Road to Communism*, p. 516.

[100] Based on 1971 production figures, this would mean an increase of 350 percent in electrical energy production and slightly more than 200 percent in steel production during the 1970s.

vast networks of water and road transportation will have been constructed. Agricultural productivity will have increased five to six times over 1961 and the national income will be 400 percent of the 1961 level, with a corresponding increase in real per capita income of 250 percent. Everyone, "including newlyweds," will be provided with a "comfortable flat conforming to the requirements of hygiene and cultural living."[101] The "indivisible fund" of public consumption will equal half the aggregate real income of the population, thus making it possible to provide the following services at public expense:

1) Free maintenance of children at children's institutions and boarding schools (if parents wish)
2) Maintenance of disabled people
3) Free education at all educational establishments
4) Free medical services for all citizens, including the supply of medicines and the treatment of sick persons at sanatoria
5) Rent-free housing and free communal services
6) Free municipal transport facilities
7) Free use of some types of public services
8) Steady reduction of charges for, and partially free use of, holiday homes, boarding houses, tourist camps and sports facilities
9) Increasingly broad provision of the population with benefits, privileges, and scholarships (grants to unmarried mothers, mothers of many children, scholarships for students)
10) Gradual introduction of free public catering (midday meals) at enterprises and institutions, and for collective farmers at work[102]

All of these free public services are considered forerunners of a communist society, and their introduction by 1980 would mean that by that time "a communist society will in the main be built in the U.S.S.R."[103] The implications of this prediction are quickly qualified, however, by the statement that "the construction of communist society will be fully completed in the subsequent period."[104]

In searching for the difference between a "communist society in the main" and a "communist society," we find that the differences lie for the most part outside the sphere of material production. Of course, Soviet writers fully anticipate major advances in the national economy after 1980, but these increases will only have the effect of carrying forward a trend begun during the transitional period, namely, the trend toward superabundance of material goods. The really important differences between "communism in the main" and full communism lie in the

[101] *The Road to Communism*, p. 540.
[102] *Ibid.*, p. 545.
[103] *Ibid.*, p. 512.
[104] *Ibid.*

related areas of social institutions and social psychology. These are complex areas, and Soviet theoreticians have recognized the probability that considerably more time will be needed to effect marked changes in them than is required for planned advances in social production, even though the latter are quite phenomenal. It has been acknowledged, therefore, that even after the material-technical base of communism has been completed, "not a little time and collective creative effort will still be required" for the "final realization" of communism.[105]

During Khrushchev's time, the specific timetable for entry into "communism in the main" generated, it would seem, a degree of enthusiasm and optimism too excessive even for Khrushchev. At the Twenty-first Party Congress, he was constrained to issue cautions to "some comrades [who] may say that the principle of communism should be introduced sooner."[106] He warned that "to pass prematurely to distribution according to needs when the economic conditions for this have not yet been created . . . and when people have not been prepared to live and work in a communist way would harm the cause of communism."[107] The dangers to which he was pointing were nicely illustrated by the reminiscences of another delegate to the Twenty-first Congress, one of the "ordinary workers" who regularly appear at these meetings:

> "When will we build communism?"—such a question I frequently heard at the meetings, in public and at home. It was found that we have many "experts" who firmly determined to the year and month the "date" of the construction of communism. . . . Of course, it is impossible to determine by calendar the day and hour of the entry into communism.[108]

Events since 1961 have shown that not only "some comrades" were overoptimistic: the whole Khrushchevian program was based on an exaggerated confidence in the Soviet economic system's ability to make unprecedented advances into the realm of plenty. Faced with hard and bitter facts, with the continued necessity of buying foreign technology, managerial expertise, and many tons of wheat, the Soviet leadership and the corps of ideological specialists have modified the timetable by stretching it out beyond the immediate future, but they have not significantly altered the nature of the process.

The retreat from Khrushchev's untenable but rather clear picture of the immediate future, without the substitution of an equally clear alternative, has left considerable room for differences of opinion to arise.

[105] Strumilin, *Problemy sotsializma i kommunizma*, p. 409.

[106] Khrushchev, "Kontrol'nye tsifry," p. 94.

[107] *Ibid.*

[108] V. I. Gorbunov, *Dumy o s"ezde: Rasskaz rabochevo delegata XXI S"ezda KPSS* (Moscow: Gospolitizdat, 1959), p. 24.

However, most of the debate in ideological circles in the last ten years has concerned rather minor disagreements over the correct periodization of past Soviet development. Defining periods of development correctly has always been considered a vital activity by Soviet ideologists, and the assumption of rationality in socialism makes periodization even more crucial. Under full socialism, according to one Soviet theorist, "it not only has extremely important theoretical and practical significance, but also becomes a matter of political interest."[109] Thus even seemingly trivial distinctions in defining the stages through which the Soviet Union has passed and will pass on the road to communism loom large in the Soviet ideological world.

Disputes over periodization of the past need not concern us, since the two important questions connected with the building of communism are defining the present stage of development and predicting the future stages that will be required to achieve full communism. In regard to the first question, recent ideology has provided a more conservative interpretation of contemporary Soviet development than was given by Khrushchev. He defined the "current stage" (i.e., that of the early 1960s) as the period of "full-scale" (*razvërnutoe*) building of communism. Obviously this suggested both an all-out effort and a short time span before the process would be completed (or at least completed "in the main"). The Brezhnev formulation, enunciated at the Twenty-fourth Party Congress (March 1971), was that the Soviet Union is presently in the stage of "fully developed socialism."[110] This, of course, refers to an already completed process, and implies no dynamic force at work within present society that is pushing it into being something else. The difference in terminology is highly significant, and surely not accidental. Phrases about the building of communism have not been dropped, but the emphasis is on the accomplishments of the past and the rather long time span which will be required to achieve what Khrushchev thought was around the corner.

The precise significance of the phrase "fully developed socialist society" has not yet been clarified by Brezhnev or the theoreticians. It should be remembered that the "victory" of socialism was declared in 1936, so it would seem that the thirty-five years required for the progress from socialism's "victory" to its "full development" could not have been a period of many rapid advances. Although Soviet data indicates that the "private sector" of the economy has significantly declined in importance in recent years, the *kolkhoz* private plots nevertheless

---

[109] Kh. P. Pulatov, *Kommunizm, gosudarstvo, kul'tura, lichnost'*, p. 11.
[110] L. I. Brezhnev, "Otchetnyi doklad TsK KPSS XXIV S'ezdu KPSS," *Kommunist*, 1971, no. 5, p. 31.

provided four percent of the total income from foodstuffs in the country in 1971.[111] Until the private economy of collective farmers is eliminated entirely, it would not seem proper to speak of a fully developed socialism.

Although the features that distinguish fully developed socialism from earlier stages have yet to be defined, some features of the concept are fairly clear from recent commentaries. The conservative implications of Brezhnev's terminology have not been overlooked in ideological circles. For example, P. Fedoseev, a "distinguished" ideologist writing in the "distinguished" theoretical journal *Kommunist*, declares that "socialism is not a brief stage but a comparatively prolonged phase of economic, social and political development en route to communism."[112] According to Fedoseev, the socialist phase consists of two periods, the first leading up to the full development of socialism (completed in 1971), and the second leading up to the development of full communism. This second period, in which the Soviet Union is now situated, Fedoseev calls the "period of direct (*neposredstvennoe*) building of the material-technical base of communism." Lest this be confused with Khrushchev's "full-scale (*razvërnutoe*) building of communism," Fedoseev introduces two significant cautionary distinctions. First, he asserts that this period "is represented by a prolonged process" and involves a "gradual transition." Second, he refutes the Khrushchevian notion that communist elements would increasingly appear within the fabric of socialist society during the transitional period. Instead, Fedoseev maintains that the process of transition is "dialectical" and "is accomplished within the limits of developed socialism." He continues:

> It is impermissible to represent the matter as if during the transition to communism to an ever greater extent the effects of the fundamental principles of socialism are reduced, and instead there is produced, so to speak, a blending of them with communistic elements. . . . The essence of the matter is that the movement toward communism proceeds by way of the development and perfection of socialism, and on that foundation, new forms of social relations, communist forms of consumption, and the new traits of the man of the future will take shape and develop. This is the living dialectic of the transformation of socialism into communism.[113]

Although he does not mention Khrushchev's theories or timetable directly, Fedoseev demonstrates the sad fate of Khrushchev's optimistic

---

[111] *Narodnoe khoziaistvo*, p. 390. It is likely that the figure is understated, and it must be kept in mind that it does not include the privately-produced food that is consumed by the farmers or bartered locally.

[112] P. N. Fedoseev, "Postroenie razvitovo sotsialisticheskovo obshchestva v SSSR—torzhestvo idei Leninizma," *Kommunist*, 1974, no. 2, p. 22.

[113] *Ibid.*, p. 23.

forecasts when he mentions that current efforts to prepare a long-range plan covering the period up to 1990 will provide for a "qualitatively new stage in the construction of the material-technical base of communism."[114] This obviously means that by 1990 there will still be other "qualitatively" different stages of building the material-technical base ahead, before communism, even communism "in the main," is reached. Other sources indicate that during this prolonged period of development, the role of the state will intensify and expand and "will not, of course, exclude the possibility of using methods of compulsion when necessary."[115]

Of course, none of these recent themes are new, and the notion of a "dialectical" development (from greater activity of the Soviet state during the transition to an eventual "withering away" under communism) was already sanctioned under Khrushchev. Without introducing any elements of novelty, however, the recent discussions of transition to communism have changed the contextual meaning by elongating the time perspective. The "future" for the average Soviet citizen extends as far as his expected lifetime. Even if he inwardly rejoices at the thought of his great-grandchildren living under full communism, the idea does not (we can assume) lift his spirit quite as much as the prospect of enjoying his own retirement years in a communist society. As a motivational factor, energizing the current working generation, the appeal of communism is no doubt vitiated by pushing it beyond the foreseeable future.

Thus the regime has already come up against the ironic paradox of basing its legitimacy on a utopian goal. It has been forced by necessity to take a step back from utopianism, but it cannot afford to surrender, totally and irrevocably, its ultimate utopian pretensions. "Building communism" remains the *raison d'être* of the entire party-state machine.

In seeking reasons for the comparative decline (though not the demise) of utopianism in recent times, one must put at the top of the list the relatively modest performances of Soviet agriculture and industry. The Soviet theory of "scientific communism" has always been grounded in the practicality of the "material-technical base." The failure of this base to materialize on schedule has had many more immediate consequences, but hardly a more significant one than the loss of

---

114 *Ibid.*, p. 27.
115 AN SSSR, Institut gosudarstva i prava, "Razvitoe sotsialisticheskoe obshshestvo i demokratiia (Vozrastanie roli gosudarstva v usloviiakh razvitovo sotsialisticheskovo obshchestva)" *Sovetskoe gosudarstvo i pravo*, 1973, no. 2, p. 5.

the Khrushchevian self-assurance that propelled communism into the forefront of the regime's goals.

What was that communism to be? In the next two chapters we examine the physical landscape of the projected communist society and the character of the "new communist man" who is destined to inherit and inhabit that society.

# CHAPTER III  THE FUTURE COMMUNIST SOCIETY

While discussions of the transition to communism are entirely legitimate, according to the doctrine of Marxism-Leninism, there is an inherent prejudice in the doctrine against "premature" speculation about the future communist society. Such speculation, in doctrinal terms, is unscientific and "subjective," since it attempts to jump ahead of the objective material conditions from which sound theoretical principles must emanate. As one Soviet ideologist put it: "The classics of Marxism-Leninism contain many warnings that one cannot avoid falling into utopianism if one seriously tries to formulate concrete details of the future, the more so since the tempo and possibilities of communist development are not comparable to the tempos and possibilities for development of any other pre-communist society."[1] This hesitancy is even further heightened in the present case by the previously mentioned fact that the Marxian image of communism bears certain embarrassing similarities to Thomas More's original utopia and to other dreams of social perfection like the society portrayed by Edward Bellamy in the nineteenth century.[2] Furthermore, the authoritative party documents on the subject have been rather vague in their descriptions of communism, thus making a detailed analysis by a rank-and-file theoretician a risky venture on several counts.

It is not surprising, therefore, that such detailed descriptions are fairly scarce in the Soviet literature. It is perhaps more surprising that there is, nevertheless, a sufficient number of generally fragmentary portrayals from which to piece together an adequate, although often incon-

---

[1] A. N. Gerasimov, "Unichtozhenie protivopolozhnosti mezhdu fizicheskim i umstvennym trudom v SSSR i protsess preodoleniia sushchestvennovo razlichiia mezhdu nimi" (candidate's dissertation, Ministerstvo Vysshevo Obrazovaniia SSSR, Moskovskii Gosudarstvennyi Ekonomicheskii Institut, 1956), p. 48.

[2] See Edward Bellamy, *Looking Backward* (New York: New American Library, Signet, 1960). The original edition was published in 1888.

sistent, picture of this society as it is presently envisioned by Soviet theoretical writers. The inconsistency is mostly due to the absence of official party dicta on the specific questions of communist society, but, as a positive side effect of this lack, there is more genuine difference of opinion, even debate, in this area than in most areas of Soviet theory.

## Social Relationships

The primary social unit of all societies is the family, and Soviet society does not differ from the general rule in this respect. Based upon Engels's well-known analysis of the presocialist family and its evolution, contemporary Soviet theory emphasizes the economic aspects of bourgeois family relations and often denies the possibility of normal human emotions arising from marriage under capitalism. Socialist marriage is viewed as infinitely superior because it is not based on mere monetary considerations; wives and children are freed from their bourgeois status as chattels, and the entire family is considered coequal in rights.

The communist family is yet another matter. It is seen as being liberated from a number of present restrictions which still cause difficulties under socialism. First of all, the role of women as wives and mothers will be drastically changed. For one thing, the full-time job of housework will be eliminated so that all women will be able to engage in socially useful, productive work along with their husbands. It is said that "under communism the transitions will be completed from the presently-existing, separate household economies and individual services to a collective economy and social satisfaction of the daily needs of the people. Collective forms of social economy and communal services will predominate."[3] Communal services will apparently include housecleaning (or rather, apartment-cleaning), laundry service, and food preparation. It is predicted that "communist society will have a well-arranged system of social feeding. Individual preparation of food in domestic conditions will disappear of itself, as domestic weaving, for example, did in the past."[4] It is anticipated that a widespread network of public dining halls will free the communist wife from "kitchen slavery" and permit her to develop her talents with the same freedom as her husband. It has also been pointed out, however, that some amount of domesticity will still be available to the communist citizen:

[3] *O kommunizme: Kniga dlia chteniia* (Moscow: Gospolitizdat, 1963), p. 380. According to the preface of this collective work, the chapter under discussion was written by M. I. Lifanov.
[4] *Ibid.*, p. 386.

Communism . . . will not mean the compulsion in every instance to use social institutions for the satisfaction of the daily needs of society. Domestic dinners, lunches, domestic evenings and receptions undoubtedly will be preserved in that degree to which they will be necessary for the family in the satisfaction of its needs for "domestic happiness" and socializing with friends in a home-like atmosphere.[5]

Although freeing women from "kitchen slavery" certainly is a noble and laudable goal, it would be well to point out here that there are two arguments that run through Soviet writings on the subject. There is the humanistic argument, which focuses on the advantages which will accrue to women when they are finally able to devote their time to the development of their highest potentials—but there is also the social engineering argument, which views women as simply an input for the social machine, an input that must be utilized as efficiently as possible. The primacy of efficiency as a yardstick for conscious social organization is apparent in almost all of the Soviet literature on the communist society, although there is often an attempt to show that efficient organization necessarily leads to maximizing "the free development of the personality" of each member of society.

The Soviet point of view on the question of child-rearing and the position of children within the family is a good example of this rather subtle mixture of humanism and efficiency orientation. As a matter of fact, there is an apparent difference of opinion among various Soviet writers on this topic, and there are grounds for suspecting that this division is the result of an inherent contradiction between humanism and "efficiency" in the process of child-rearing itself. One school of thought, which we will characterize as efficiency-oriented, predicts that under communism children will be separated from their parents and will be brought up by the community in a public boarding school. These boarding schools will permit "relatives, particularly mothers [to be] freed from the daily care of children."[6] This method is efficient, not only from the point of view of the mother (who would be freed for socially useful labor), but also with respect to the child and the community, since the latter desires a generation of model citizens. This point is made quite clearly by S. G. Strumilin, a well-respected Soviet economist and, in his later years, a leading contributor to the literature on the future society. He starts with the observation that "many [mothers] are filled with maternal egoism, are jealous of others and really

[5] A. Kharchev, "Sem'ia i kommunizm," *Kommunist*, 1960, no. 7, p. 60.
[6] *Ibid.*, p. 61.

love their own children exclusively."[7] He then goes on to describe the harmful social consequences of this maternal egoism:

> Such a mother regards her child, even if he is an ordinary dunce, as a miracle of nature and the apex of perfection. She protects him from his playmates, from the heat, cold and fresh air, filling him with sweets and medicines, heaping toys and nicknacks on him, protecting him from all extra mental strains.
>
> As a result, mother's little boy, unless subject to other influences, will grow up to be a self-adulating individual sneering at all that surrounds him, in short, a useless individual, a *stilyag*, a good-for-nothing who will never find his place in Soviet life.[8]

It is quite clear that Strumilin objects to maternal upbringing of children because it may lead to an exaggerated spirit of individualism, a spirit alien to communism. On this basis, he shows the superiority of collective upbringing:

> The children's collective, particularly if not under pressure and guided by the experienced hand of an educator, can do more to inculcate the best social habits than the most sympathetic and loving mother. Prompt and effective reaction on the part of such a collective to all anti-social manifestations prompted by the egoistic disposition of the child are sure to nip them in the bud.[9]

In Strumilin's view, then, the child must be subjected to strong collective influences from the beginning if he is to develop the "correct" social disposition for communist society. The education of children is too important to *society* for it to be left in the inexperienced, inefficient hands of the mother; instead, trained, carefully selected specialists, using uniform and tested techniques, will develop "all the inborn social instincts [of the child] . . . by means of the new conditioned reflexes created through comradely relationships" with the peer group. Strumilin, utilizing this Pavlovian, efficiency-oriented approach, proposes a system of collective upbringing "from the cradle to the graduation certificate":

> Emerging from a hospital every Soviet citizen would be assigned to a nursery, then to a kindergarten maintained day and night, then to a boarding school from which he would enter independent life—taking a job in production or continuing his studies in his chosen profession.[10]

---

[7] S. G. Strumilin, "Communism and the Worker's Daily Life," *Novyi mir*, 1960, no. 7. (As translated in *The Soviet Review*, vol. 2 (1961), p. 10.)

[8] *Ibid.*

[9] *Ibid.*

[10] *Ibid.*

Such a dispassionate characterization of communist upbringing is, of course, open to the humanist objection that it neglects the normal maternal and paternal instincts and breaks the bonds of affection between parents and offspring. To this objection, Strumilin replies that "the public organization of upbringing is not aimed at the complete separation of children from their parents" and that no one "will prevent them [the parents] from visiting their children after working hours, when they will be able to visit the children's premises . . . as often as the rules permit."[11] Another Soviet writer claims that "feelings of love between relatives will not die out, but on the contrary will be strengthened" even with the widespread introduction of boarding schools and consequent separation of parents and offspring at an early age.[12] The mechanism by which separation of parents and offspring would bring about deeper emotional ties between them has never been explained by the efficiency-oriented school, and one would suspect that such a mechanism does not, and could not, exist. On the other hand, this separation might indeed be a potent method of uniformly instilling socially-approved character traits at an early age.

This efficient approach to the problem of child-rearing under communism has been opposed by other Soviet writers, who maintain that the family will remain the best agent for inculcating the proper attitudes in future citizens of communism. It is said, for example, that "nothing can replace parental warmth toward children, and parents without children will not receive the full joy of love and family happiness. The influence of the family on a child is determined to a significant degree by the fact that within it he receives his first impressions of life around him, and these impressions are, as a rule, the strongest and firmest, forming the habits and character of the grown man."[13] Another writer, in answer to a reader's question, maintains that "in the future the majority of children will continue to live at home and will go to school only to study."[14] As for the efficiency-oriented argument that the family is not a reliable instrument for the stringent moral upbringing required of the communist citizen, this last writer predicts that "the negative blemishes found in some homes will disappear" as a natural result of the general increase in communist morality during the transitional period.[15] He thus concludes that the communist family, as opposed to the socialist

---

11 *Ibid.*

12 Kharchev, "Sem'ia i kommunizm," p. 61.

13 *O kommunizme*, p. 395.

14 I. Metter, "Saturday's Mail: They Left School," *Literaturnaia gazeta*, January 13, 1962. (*Current Digest of the Soviet Press* [hereafter *CDSP*] vol. 24, no. 3, p. 8).

15 *Ibid.*

family, will be as efficient a teacher of approved moral precepts as any boarding school and will, in addition, provide healthier emotional attachments for communism's children.

There is no difference of opinion concerning a similar social problem: the care and treatment of the aged and others unable to work. All people incapable of working for society will be cared for by society, which will relieve the family of this burden. The general feeling is that such care will be provided by special institutions specifically designed to handle the various categories of citizens who require help. Strumilin, himself an octogenarian, declares that the aged "may render inestimable aid to society despite their lesser ability to work" and finds that "this is a real labor reserve as yet insufficiently tapped."[16] This raises the prospect that in the future society increased use will be made of the elderly in auxiliary functions. This shift is based upon the communist moral value that honest labor is the foundation of a man's self-respect, and that it is, in a sense, inhumane to deprive an elderly, but capable, man of the satisfaction attached to useful activity.[17]

If the family were in fact reduced to husband and wife, and children were placed under the direct supervision of the collective from "the cradle to the graduation certificate," this would indeed represent a major revolution in the social structure. It is far from certain, however, that this will actually be the approach selected by the Soviet leaders of the future. Although top Party people, including Khrushchev, have called for increased construction of boarding schools, the conservative, traditional argument in favor of preserving the present family structure undoubtedly carries much weight among the people. However, public opinion is offset to a degree by the tendency toward smaller family units in modern, increasingly urbanized, increasingly affluent societies. The decrease in size of the modern Soviet family and the decreased attachment of offspring to the family as the primary economic and social unit would probably make the transition to institutional upbringing less traumatic. It should be kept in mind that a large proportion of Soviet women at present have full-time employment and already entrust their children's care to one of the many day-care centers and nurseries provided by the regime. The question is thus left open for the future to decide.

Under the assumption that the primary family unit, the husband and wife, will be freed from the burdensome care of dependents (or at least a good share of it) and time-wasting domestic chores, it will be involved

---

[16] Strumilin, "Communism and the Worker's Daily Life," pp. 12–13.

[17] The same sort of reasoning can be seen behind the increasing tendency in present-day Soviet society to use old-age pensioners in advisory and auxiliary functions, both in production and social control.

only with important and socially valuable matters. Husband and wife, therefore, "will not have occasion for annoying discord and empty wrangling" and this will mean that "the marriage union under communism will be fuller, firmer and happier than it ever was in the irretrievable past."[18] It is predicted that the family will be much more closely drawn into the collective, and this will be especially true if the family is actually reduced to husband and wife. During leisure hours, "family life will be all the more closely connected with the workers' clubs, libraries, sports organizations and creative, artistic collectives."[19] Combining the effects of this increased participation in the wider collective and decreased (or possibly eliminated) involvement in housekeeping and the care of dependents, we can draw the safe conclusion that the family itself will occupy a less important place in the life of the communist citizen. Several functions of the family will be performed by the collective; children, if not actually separated from their parents, will at least be drawn away from them by various children's organizations and intensified schoolwork, and the parents themselves will be drawn out of the home environment to merge their interests with those of the larger community. Despite Soviet assertions to the contrary, these steps, if actually carried out, could not but reduce the significance of marital ties, even if the most conservative approach to these problems eventually prevailed.

There is general agreement that sexual promiscuity will have no place under full communism, and that monogamy will be the general rule. Free love is today considered a survival from bourgeois morality.[20] There is apparently some feeling, however, that marriage certificates or other formalities may not be necessary, much as with common-law marriages in the English tradition. One writer has drawn a fine distinction which indicates a certain ambivalence:

> Communist morality is in principle against extramarital ties when they are the result of [moral] dissolution and frivolity, but motherhood of an unmarried woman often comes about through other motives having nothing in common with amorality, but rather the wish to have and to raise one's own children. The state assists such mothers, and the most important form of such help is the boarding school.[21]

Since the same writer has declared communism to be "a period of consistent monogamy," one would imagine that the problem of unmarried mothers would rarely arise in the future. Despite all the emphasis

---

[18] S. G. Strumilin, *Rabochii den' i kommunizm* (Moscow: Profizdat, 1959), p. 32.
[19] Kharchev, "Sem'ia i kommunizm," p. 61.
[20] *O kommunizme*, p. 392.
[21] Kharchev, "Sem'ia i kommunizm," p. 61.

given to the idea that communist marriage and love will be stronger and truer than ever before, there is an awareness that marital problems do arise from personal incompatibilities that might still occur under communism. One work admits this rather candidly:

> All this hardly means that under communism there will not be any conflicts in family life. For example, the love of one spouse may evaporate as a new love arises, but such cases will become much rarer than at present.[22]

Although conflicts are to be expected, there is some reason to believe that marital difficulties will be less of a problem than they are now. Dissolution of a marriage will apparently be a rather simple matter. Since there is a good possibility that the significance of the marriage bond itself will be diluted by "freeing" it and merging it more fully in the collective, the opportunities for discord will probably be reduced. There can be no doubt, however, that the direct influence of the collective on the individual would be enhanced if the cohesiveness of the family unit—as a potential competing influence—is reduced.

Within the wider collective, social relationships are expected to be generally harmonious, since there can no longer be any basic conflict of interests. There can be no such conflict simply because everyone will find that personal and social goals are two aspects of the same thing. This identity of interests is not only the result of the inherent perfection of the social system: the citizen of communism will himself contribute to social harmony by thinking instinctively in terms of the general welfare. Since there will be no classes under communism, only a "monolithic association of workers occupying an equal position in society,"[23] there can be no class struggle, or even difference in class interests.

At this point we meet one of the central difficulties of the theory. While it is at least conceivable that all, or nearly all, communist citizens would carry the interests of the entire society closest to their hearts, it is considerably more difficult to imagine a society in which all the citizens would agree in all cases on the practical steps to be taken in furthering those interests. Even if the slogan of communist society truly becomes, as the Soviet theorists aver, "Man is a friend, comrade and brother to man,"[24] one can still imagine a fraternal disagreement over policy

---

[22] *O kommunizme*, p. 397.

[23] "Programma postroenniia kommunizma," (editorial), *Voprosy filosofii*, 1961, no. 8, p. 13.

[24] V. Platkovskii, "Formirovanie kommunisticheskikh obshchestvennykh otnoshenii," *Kommunist*, 1962, no. 15, p. 35. This is nicely contrasted with Khrushchev's slogan for capitalism: "Man is a wolf to man."

issues. Some sort of decision-making machinery to resolve such disputes would therefore seem a necessity for communist society.

## Economic and Political Organization

The Soviet theorists have recognized the fact that no society, not even communist society, can survive without some form of organization. They have tried, however, to draw a distinction between the organization of communist society and that of all others. As a starting point, they have drawn on the Marxian idea that politics and political institutions are expressions of class struggle or class differences and are thus concepts relevant only to particular historical stages. This definition hinges on the semantic identification of politics with a particular kind of conflict and would not merit our further attention if it were all that the Soviet theoreticians offered in support of this aspect of the doctrine. It certainly seems like a meaningless quibble, for example, to state that under communism "the need for political election campaigns will disappear . . . while, on the other hand, there will most likely be a need for non-political elections."[25] Insofar as such statements are based on the disappearance of classes under communism and the consequent need for a change in terminology, they tell us nothing about the real changes that we should expect.

There is another side to the Soviet argument, however, and it contains much that is both serious and provocative. Although the first Soviet definition of politics confines it to the expression of a particular type of conflict, this second definition recognizes the wider scope of the term as an expression of all types of conflict where competing goals are resolved to the advantage of some and the disadvantage of others. It is simply the statement that politics will disappear because under communism *conflict itself will disappear*. Lack of conflict, in turn, is a measure of the high level of consciousness which the members of communist society will attain. The importance of the term consciousness is once again apparent from still another point of view. Here consciousness means that everyone will recognize the need for organization in society, will wholeheartedly assent to any particular choice of leadership, will obey both general social norms and particular directives of the leadership, and will take his inevitable turn at the helm when the opportunity arises. This attitude is nicely summed up in the following remark of a Soviet theoretician:

[25] A. I. Denisov, "O sootnoshenii gosudarstva i obshchestva v perekhodnyi ot kapitalizma k kommunizmu period," *Sovetskoe gosudarstvo i pravo*, 1960, no. 4, p. 38.

> Of course, even under communism, power will exist, although deprived of its political, specifically governmental features, and even direction [*rukovodstvo*] will exist within definite limits. However, it will be such power and such direction to which all will submit voluntarily and consciously, as in a good orchestra the musicians submit to the direction of the conductor.[26]

The analogy is quite apt. In both the orchestra and communist society, organization is based on the principle of *voluntary submission*. In both organizations, there is a *conscious* recognition by the led of the leader's authority, based on the knowledge that subordination is necessary for the accomplishment of certain recognized tasks. In a purely formal sense, then, the orchestra analogy holds up well. However, in real life, politics exists even within the best of orchestras, and one would imagine that even the most conscious and willing members of communist society would find occasion to disagree, to find support for their own points of view, and thus to form opposing groups within society, even if on a temporary basis. This point the Soviet theorists have not considered, and it is possible to infer from this silence that consciousness in the Soviet definition may have yet another meaning: submission *without question and without exception* to all decisions of the leadership. If this submission were born of an inner, well-indoctrinated belief that the leadership at all echelons is infallible, then certainly politics, as both we and the Soviet theorists understand it, would be truly dead.

If we assume that men will be thus convinced and will amount to mere instruments in the hands of the leadership, we can more easily understand the modern Soviet interpretation of Engels's remark that under communism "the government of persons is replaced by the administration of things." It is not at all unfair to the Soviet theoreticians to point out that by carrying the logic of their own argument a bit further than they have done the conclusion is unavoidable that people, as well as material goods, would be included in this "administration of things."

Behind the Soviet argument there is the rather remarkable assumption that the correct course of action will always be unambiguously clear to all right-thinking citizens of communism; right and wrong will be clearly distinguishable, and for those who do not immediately see the correctness of a particular decision, an explanation will suffice. Therefore, the Soviet theorists imagine communist decision-making to be a purely technical matter, based on scientific, economic criteria rather

---

[26] Iu. P. Smirnov, *Gosudarstvo i kommunizm* (Minsk: Izdatel'stvo vysshevo, srednevo spetsial'novo i professional'novo obrazovaniia BSSR, 1962), p. 83.

than value judgments. Other Soviet writers have not taken notice of
D. I. Chesnokov's heterodox remark that "insofar as questions of economic and cultural construction are at the same time political questions,
the activities of mass public organizations will have a political character."[27] On the contrary, the general Soviet opinion holds that economic
and cultural matters will be decided scientifically, and that politics has
no place in such calculations. In the standard Soviet view, therefore, the
communist citizen will be voluntarily submitting himself to the requirements of rational, scientific, and invariably correct decisions—in other
words, to *necessity*—and this, as we have seen, is the well-established
Marxian definition of true freedom. In another perspective, it is also a
continuation into the future of the equally well-established rule that the
Party, in the final analysis, is always correct.

One Soviet legal expert, drawing on this sort of reasoning, has suggested that norms of communist behavior may be quite a bit simpler
than present legal norms:

> A part of the legal and organizational norms presently in force are being
> transformed into the unified principles and rules of communist self-
> management, but a significant part will be eliminated, since relations of
> social authority will be considerably simpler than [present] relations of
> political power.[28]

This simplification of social rules is a result of the fact that "participation in self-management will be transformed into the habitual and universal social activity of each citizen."[29] In other words, the fact that all
will have equal positions in society and will share in the responsibilities
of management means that present rules defining the power of some
citizens over others can be eliminated in the future.

The idea that all citizens will take an equal and active part in communist social self-management—the official phrase for self-government
under communism—has been qualified and restricted by numerous Soviet writers. For example, Strumilin says that "*the most able and qualified* persons will take turns in positions of leadership,"[30] a statement
which raises the possibility of a rotating "collective" leadership of a
relatively few men. This oligarchical tendency is also apparent in the
following remark of another Soviet theoretician:

[27] D. I. Chesnokov, *Rol' sotsialisticheskovo gosudarstva v stroitel'stve kommunizma* (Moscow: Izdatel'stvo sotsial'no-ekonomicheskoi literatury, 1959), p. 60.
[28] L. S. Iavich, *Pravo i kommunizm* (Moscow: Gosudarstvennyi izdatel'stvo
iuridicheskoi literatury, 1962), p. 88.
[29] *Ibid.*
[30] S. G. Strumilin, "What Communism Is: Thoughts about the Future," *Oktiabr'*,
1960, no. 3 (*CDSP*, vol. 12, no. 15, p. 13). (Emphasis mine.)

> Workers, selected for one or another managerial post, will carry out their functions during the course of a definite period, and will then once again return to their former place or take a new position in accordance with their knowledge and interests. Only in the central (branch) organs of planning, accounting, distribution, etc., where direct and uninterrupted accomplishment of definite functions particularly important for society must be guaranteed, does there arise, of course, the need for preserving strong organizational abilities, great experience and knowledge.[31]

This sort of system could accurately be described as oligarchy at the top and democracy at the bottom—a system that could hardly remain stable without the strong influence of thoroughly inculcated consciousness to smooth over the apparent contradiction. The idea of democracy at the bottom has also been supported by Chesnokov, who proposes the following elective principle:

> For any elected position a worker can be elected only for one time. All elective social work by an individual is carried out voluntarily after he has discharged his obligation to society by creating material and spiritual wealth side-by-side with the remaining members of society.[32]

Although there is unanimous agreement that all members of communist society will participate in some sort of managerial role at one time or another, there is an evident assumption that most of this participation will be at the bottom of the managerial ladder, thus preserving some kind of distinction between the leaders and the led. Although this difference between the "decisive" individuals and the others will decrease in the future, it will nevertheless remain.[33] It is apparent that communist society, like all other societies, will be composed of men and women of varying talents and abilities, some destined to lead, and others to follow. While all will share equally in obedience to social rules, some will share more equally than others in the responsibility—and power—of leadership. This contention is supported first of all by the inarguable fact that people are unequal in native abilities, and they will continue to be so, even if all achieve their full potential under the communist principle of "the full flowering of the personality." Undoubtedly, some will be more qualified to fill the complex role of future technocrat than others. Secondly, it is held that the complexities of an advanced economy—as distinguished from the simplicity of social relations—will require a representative form of self-government:

---

[31] Smirnov, *Gosudarstvo i kommunizm*, p. 85.

[32] D. I. Chesnokov, *Ot gosudarstvennosti k obshchestvennomu samoupravleniiu* (Moscow: Gospolitizdat, 1960), p. 20.

[33] P. I. Nikitin, *Chto takoe kommunizm* (Moscow: Izdatel'stvo Moskovskovo Universiteta, 1961), p. 126.

In communist society, power, in all its fullness, will belong to the people. However, this does not mean that every practical question will have to be decided solely by a country-wide vote following national discussion. There is no necessity for this. Moreover, if each more or less important question would be put to a vote, society would hardly have time left for anything else. Furthermore, even the most detailed and thorough advance discussion will not be able to foresee the many changes in conditions that will occur in the course of practical activities, and will be unable to remove the necessity for direct, daily management. This management, and consequently the direct realization of the people's power, must be delegated to certain individuals—to representatives, fully empowered by the people and answering for the success of [public] affairs. . . . Obliging an individual to fulfill managerial functions, society must, for a definite period, give him the right to issue directives to other members of the collective. In this manner, society takes on itself the obligation to submit to the instructions issued by the leader [*rukovoditel'*], keeping for itself the right to name (or elect), remove and control him.[34]

The foregoing quotation sums up the gist of countless fragmentary remarks in the literature, defending the idea of delegated power under communism. It is remarkable chiefly in its near identity with the commonplace explanation of representative democracy in the Western political tradition. But, while the idea that direct democracy is not practicable in modern society has long since been accepted in the Western tradition, this realization is a bit more difficult to square with the Marxist theoretical tradition. It seems that even under communism Engels's "administration of things" remains, despite all expectations, a "government of people." Soviet doctrine, faced with an embarrassing similarity between the formal structures of communist self-government and bourgeois democracy, has tended to emphasize the new "spirit," or content, of this familiar form of government. Thus, we find that the "high consciousness and culture [of ordinary workers] will permit them constantly and knowledgeably to control the artivities of any leader, and in cases of necessity, to correct him."[35] This will be accomplished not only through elections and periodic accountability of the leaders but through "daily control, [and] direct participation of the population in management."[36]

As we have seen, it is only the notion of consciousness that rescues the theory from logical or conceptual difficulties. Although "consciousness" will be discussed in the following chapter in terms of individual

---

[34] G. S. Grigor'ev, *Obshchestvennaia vlast' pri kommunizme* (Perm': Permskoe knizhnoe izdatel'stvo, 1961), p. 56.
[35] *Ibid.*, p. 57.
[36] *Ibid.*

psychology, a word is in order here concerning its relation to the theory of self-government just discussed. There seems to be a general consensus among Soviet theoreticians that the common member of communist society will play an active role in its administration, although this participation may be apparent only in the lower echelons. On the other hand, the theoreticians have recognized the need for a hierarchical administrative structure and some form of representative government. None of this precludes the development of democratic institutions, provided that consciousness does not mean total acquiescence in, or even indifference to, decisions of the people's representatives. If consciousness, in other words, were merely unquestioning obedience to authoritative decisions, the only democratic feature of communist society would be the rotational basis of leadership—a feature that is limited by many practical considerations. But, as previously mentioned, there is more than a hint in present Soviet doctrine that this is precisely the intended meaning of consciousness. We have, on the one hand, the typical statement that "developed, non-state communist society is unthinkable without organs of self-management and definite social norms regulating productive and social actions of its members," with the proviso that "observation of these norms will be voluntary and habitual."[37] On the other, we find both numerous comments to the effect that "communist society, by its very nature, excludes the slightest manifestation of disorganization or unsystematic behavior in any sphere of human activity"[38] and a penchant for emphasizing discipline above all else, as in the following:

> Communist society will be based on large-scale, automated industry, demanding from society great coordination, discipline and accuracy. Such orderliness and coordinated activity will be characteristic of the entire life of the harmoniously developed worker of communism.[39]

If we combine these two elements of the theory, we arrive at the inevitable conclusion that observation of the strictest discipline and orderliness in all spheres of life will become habitual for the member of communist society. From the human point of view, it creates the rather terrifying picture of Orwell's society of compulsive automatons, and from the institutional point of view it makes democracy an impossibility. The irony of the situation is apparent if we recognize that it is precisely *consciousness*—the focus of the Soviet vision—which makes the communist society seem rather more akin to Orwell's *1984* than to

[37] Iavich, *Pravo i kommunizm*, p. 82.
[38] Smirnov, *Gosudarstvo i kommunizm*, p. 85.
[39] A. P. Butenko, "Gosudarstvo i kommunizm," *Voprosy filosofii*, 1962, no. 12, p. 141.

Marx's communism. If we eliminate consciousness from the picture, we can see that communist society does, in fact, contain many features that are democratic in a formal sense, such as widespread participation in government and representative government based on elections. When consciousness enters the picture, however, it becomes perfectly natural, to convince oneself as did one Soviet writer, that secret ballots will no longer be necessary, and that leadership will not carry with it any advantages.[40]

Despite the visible flaws in the foundation of Soviet "democratic communism," a great deal of attention is given by Soviet theorists to the particular institutional forms which will prevail. As a matter of fact, there is some disagreement on this score, with some writers standing behind the soviets as the logical model for communism and others supporting the public organizations. Khrushchev himself was apparently a supporter of the public organizations.[41] He is on record as having said the following at the Thirteenth Congress of the *Komsomol*:

> We say that under communism the state will wither away. What sort of organizations will remain? Public. They may be called *komsomol*, unions or something else, but they will be public organizations, through which society will regulate its affairs.[42]

Nevertheless, the two most authoritative theoretical documents of the post–Stalin period, the Party Program and the textbook called *Fundamentals of Marxism–Leninism*, steer a careful course midway between both points of view by calling for the further development of both types of organization; they also look forward to some variety of amalgamation of the soviets and public organizations under communism. The textbook merely mentions in passing that "it is quite possible that in future a new type of public organization will arise which will incorporate the best elements accumulated in the work of party, governmental, and trade-union organizations."[43] The program similarly looks forward to "communist self-government of the people which will embrace the

---

[40] L. M. Karapetian, "Politicheskaia organizatsiia obshchestva v period razvërnutovo stroitel'stva kommunizma" (candidate's dissertation, Akademiia obshchestvennykh nauk pri TsK KPSS, Kafredra filosofii, 1962), p. 300.

[41] The reader's attention is once again directed to the article by Solomon M. Schwarz entitled, "Is the State Withering Away in the USSR?" in *The U.S.S.R. and the Future: An Analysis of the New Program of the CPSU*, ed. Leonard Shapiro (New York: Frederick A. Praeger, 1963), pp. 161–70.

[42] As quoted in V. Platkovskii, *Politicheskaia organizatsiia obshchestva pri perekhode k kommunizmu* (Moscow: Gospolitizdat, 1962), pp. 68–69.

[43] *Fundamentals of Marxism-Leninism*, 2nd ed. (Moscow: Foreign Languages Publishing House, 1963), p. 674.

soviets, trade unions, cooperatives, and other mass organizations of the people."[44]

With the lack of a clear-cut and authoritative position on this question, the field has been left open for speculations of various sorts. There is thus no single "Soviet view" on this subject, but many, some of which appear diametrically opposed. Taking the future of the trade unions as an example, we find in the literature many different predictions of their future fate. In one place we can read that the trade unions in the distant future will be transformed into the "fundamental unit of the economic apparatus," resembling the *sovnarkhozy* (Regional Economic Councils).[45] Another writer suggests that there will be no need at all for unions under communism, but that it would be useful to form an organization "of the type of the Academy of Sciences," uniting workers of the same field over the entire country and acting as a transmission belt for the exchange of technical information.[46] Yet another writer pictures the following course of development for the trade unions:

> In the distant future, when the principle of elective representation is widespread both for managerial posts in enterprises and in other economic organizations, the role of the trade unions will become, in essence, decisive, for it is precisely they, under the direction [*rukovodstvo*] of party organizations, that will decide questions concerning the formation of production-management organs. However, this will coincide, in all probability, with that period when the unions themselves will begin to wither away, when the place of professional organization of workers organized by branch of industry will be taken by an all-inclusive organization of workers at each enterprise—the production collective.[47]

Because of this general confusion concerning the future roles of not only the trade unions but the *komsomol*, cooperatives, and other Soviet "public organizations," it is not possible to characterize a single plan as the general consensus. There is, however, a tendency to resolve the issue in general terms by calling for a vaguely defined merger of state and public organizations in the future, the possibility raised by the Party Program.

The soviets have been given a central role in the organization of communist society by many Soviet writers. It is said that "amongst all

[44] *The Road to Communism: Documents of the 22nd Congress of the Communist Party of the Soviet Union* (Moscow: Foreign Languages Publishing House, n.d.), p. 555.

[45] V. V. Nikolaev, "O razvitii sotsialisticheskoi gosudarstvennosti v kommunisticheskoe obshchestvennoe samoupravlenie," *Voprosy filosofii*, 1960, no. 12, p. 34. The Economic Councils were abolished after Khrushchev's ouster.

[46] Grigor'ev, *Obshchestvennaia vlast'*, pp. 566–67.

[47] Platkovskii, *Politicheskaia organizatsiia*, p. 122.

the state and public organizations guided by the Communist Party, the basic core of the organization of communist self-management will consist of . . . the soviets,"[48] and that they are "the model of power in communist society."[49] It is not quite clear whether the soviets under communism will remain as they are now, or whether they will undergo some form of transformation. One view which suggests the necessity for a change in the soviets is that "under communism the soviets will be retained not merely as one of the possible forms of the organization of self-management, but as the predominant foundation on which the best features of management contained in professional, cooperative and other mass organizations will be combined and crystallized."[50] The one proposal that may serve as a compromise between the supporters of the soviets and the public organizations predicts that the soviets "will be ever closer joined with other social organizations, and the difference between them will become constantly less noticeable."[51] The logical conclusion of this development is that "in the end, the soviets will be united with other mass organizations of workers,"[52] thus forming the structure of communist self-management. However, a highly regarded standard textbook on Soviet law ignores the soviets entirely, emphasizing instead the importance of the production collective and envisioning the establishment of "operating organizations" that will be elected by representative assemblies on a territorial basis and coordinated with a second set of organizations based on industrial branches.[53] This proposal is also a compromise, for there is a secondary difference of opinion between those who stress territorial organization for communist self-management, and those who stress industrial-branch organization. The territorial organization is described by D. I. Chesnokov as follows:

> Inevitably there will exist organs of self-rule in the village, town and district. Delegates selected by general meetings of the collective will gather in district (borough) and town sessions to select collegial organs of administration. In communist society even after the victory of communism on a world-wide scale, after overcoming the remains of national divisions, there will be preserved divisions into large zones which will be able fundamentally to guarantee all the material and spiritual needs of the

[48] Karapetian, "Politicheskaia organizatsiia," p. 289.

[49] Grigor'ev, *Obshchestvennaia vlast'*, p. 60.

[50] Kh. P. Pulatov, *Kommunizm, gosudarstvo, kul'tura, lichnost': stroitel'stvo kommunizma i problemy kul'turno-vospitatel'noi funktsii obshchenarodnovo sotsialisticheskovo gosudarstva* (Tashkent: Izdatel'stvo "Uzbekistan," 1971), p. 61.

[51] N. P. Farberov, *Gosudarstvo i kommunizm* (Moscow: Obshchestvo po rasprostraneniiu politicheskikh i nauchnykh znanii RSFSR, 1961), p. 22.

[52] Farberov, *Gosudarstvo i kommunizm*, p. 22.

[53] A. I. Luk'ianov and B. M. Lazarev, *Sovetskoe gosudarstvo i obshchestvennie organizatsii*, 2d. ed. rev. (Moscow: Gosiurizdat, 1961), p. 317.

population. In connection with these zones will arise the necessity for district organs of self-rule able to coordinate the activities of all parts of society in the various divisions of the given zone. Consequently, district sessions of the people's representatives will be called to select district collegial organs.[54]

On the other hand, N. P. Farberov suggests that the *sovnarkhozy* will remain as the basic economic directing units of communist society although "their structure, form and methods of action" will be further perfected.[55] Actually, the difference of opinion is more apparent than real, for the territorial approach is generally taken by those interested in "political" and nationality problems, while the industrial branch approach is used in several discussions of the future communist economy.

It is a curious fact that Soviet explanations of communist economic organization invariably stress centralization and strict methods of conrol to a far greater extent than descriptions of other phases of communist organization. There has never been any doubt among Soviet economists that centralized planning is the most efficient way, indeed the only permissible way, to achieve economic growth. This method is now advanced into the communist phrase as the overall solution to the many problems that would arise from the phenomenal rates of growth that are anticipated. The Soviet image of communism is quite clear on this score. It starts from an awareness that highly advanced production requires a great deal of coordination of various related processes. Labor allocation and scheduling of working time will also be complicated by the introduction of mechanization and automation, since, as Khrushchev once put it: "Production by machine has a definite rhythm that is impossible without a corresponding scheduling of people's work."[56] The job of the planning agency under communism, as it is pictured by Soviet planners today, is truly staggering. The agency will be concerned not only with the allocation of capital, machinery, and labor in all branches of a highly diversified economy, but it will also be involved in construction, communication, transportation, scientific research, and all other fields of endeavor that have economic significance. It will have to be sensitive to consumer demand so that the needed assortment of goods is always available, and at the same time, it must distribute raw materials to the various enterprises in exactly the correct proportions to avoid bottlenecks. The task is so immense that one pair of writers has

[54] Chesnokov, *Ot gosudarstvennosti*, p. 21.
[55] Farberov, *Gosudarstvo i kommunizm*, p. 17.
[56] N. S. Khrushchev, "Kontrol'nye tsifry razvitiia narodnovo khoziaistva SSSR na 1959–1965 gody," in *Vneocherednoi XXI S"ezd Kommunisticheskoi partii Sovetskovo Soiuza: Stenograficheskii otchet*, 2 vols. (Moscow: Gosudarstvennoe izdatel'stvo politicheskoi literatury, 1959), 1:100.

suggested that the central organs will solve "basic questions of economic and cultural development, [but] will not be able, of course, to serve all areas, without exception, of the many-sided life of communist society."[57] Because of this, they predict that other more or less independent organs on a smaller scale will undertake certain subsidiary social tasks.

Other Soviet writers, however, do not shrink from the implications of this massive effort at total planning and control of a complex economy. In fact, they embrace the idea with enthusiasm:

> Communism finally concludes the transition to planned organization of the entire social production. Under communist conditions, all production will function like a single coordinated mechanism. Thus communism will finally conquer spontaneity in the development of society.[58]

We have already mentioned in another context that the desire for social efficiency tends to produce a demand for model citizens who are cooperative and as easily controllable as other factors in the social equation. This desire is even more crucial in the field of economics, where Soviet planners feel that the entire success of the economy depends upon "each participant in production submitting all his activities to a single, general plan."[59] In the name of economic efficiency, Soviet theoreticians have given the central planning agency enormous, all-encompassing powers, and they have placed the individual worker in a position where his social responsibility requires constant submission to "the plan," in the name of the general welfare. Under such conditions, the technical specialists would have vast powers. Their decisions would have the authority of scientific necessity, and the populace would be predisposed to accept their policies as such without too much questioning. As one Soviet writer remarked, in a bit of an understatement: "No economy can do without economists, planners, and statisticians. . . . Therefore, the roles of these groups of the technical-economic intelligentsia . . . will be particularly important."[60] The great importance of economic decisions should be apparent to anyone, and especially to a Marxist. Regardless of whether productive activity is the single most decisive factor in social development, as Marxism claims, there can be no doubt that there are no "purely economic" decisions which do not, in reality, have an effect on other areas of social life. It is, therefore,

[57] Luk'ianov and Lazarev, *Sovetskoe gosudarstvo*, p. 318.

[58] A. Kovalev, "Kommunizm—nachalo podlinnoi istorii chelovecheskovo obshchestva," *Kommunist*, 1962, no. 3, p. 105.

[59] Grigor'ev, *Obshchestvennaia vlast'*, p. 47.

[60] M. S. Azhenov, "Izmeneniia v rabochem klasse i intelligentsii Kazakhstana v protsesse stroitel'stva sotsializma i perekhoda k kommunizmu" (candidate's dissertation, Akadamiia nauk SSSR, Institut filosofii, 1963), p. 184.

quite meaningless to classify a government as "non-political," as has
one Soviet writer, because "it is occupied with exclusively economic
questions."[61] In fact, economic, or so-called bread and butter, issues
are often crucial political problems for a government. This would be
especially true under communism, where planned direction of the economy would define the entire life of society. The overwhelming powers of
the planning agency and the acquiescent "consciousness" of the average
citizen combine to give the following picture of economic decision-
making under communism:

> Regulation of such questions of social life as planned development of
> production, distribution of the labor force and material resources, sched-
> uling of working time and the arrangement of successive participation in
> organs of self-government will be carried out on the basis of social norms
> and normative acts. They will be established by organs of self-govern-
> ment, and based on the authority of these organs, their social influence
> will be guaranteed.[62]

The assumption here is that these decisions are "scientific," and thus
above question. As Chesnokov put it: "Planning and estimating organizations under communism neither command nor direct production; they
secure universal calculations and plans, scientifically based on estimates
for development of the economy and culture."[63] This approach lends
to economic policy a neutral, noncontroversial aura which it is hardly
likely to have in any society. G. S. Grigor'ev, in the provocative and
rather original work referred to earlier, recognizes this problem and
offers the following solution:

> Even in the future, in communist society, there may arise different points
> of view, for example, on the question of where to construct a certain
> factory or whether to construct it at all, or whether or not to begin
> exploiting a certain natural resource—such will be the highly important,
> major tasks of definite enterprises or society as a whole. Although the
> answer to these and similar questions will be based on a thorough scien-
> tific study, it is impossible to expect that in all cases there will be only a
> single answer possible. There may be several conclusions, the correctness
> of which it will be impossible to check immediately. From this, however,
> it does not follow that people in the future will refuse to undertake any
> practical action until all sides are convinced of the correctness of one or
> another conclusion. Practical accomplishment of the decision adopted by

---

[61] Platkovskii, *Politicheskaia organizatsiia*, p. 101.
[62] Karapetian, "Politicheskaia organizatsiia," p. 278.
[63] Chesnokov, *Ot gosudarstvennosti*, p. 14.

the majority of votes will be obligatory for each [citizen], irrespective of whether he agrees with this decision or not.[64]

This solution, apparently based upon a referendum and subsequent acceptance by the minority of the majority decision, seems basically sound when isolated from the other aspects of communist society (even though, incidentally, it is formally identical to the existing theory of democratic centralism). There is good reason to doubt whether a genuine choice would be given the electorate under communism, however, if we recall the past and present Soviet voting procedure and the meaning generally attached to "communist consciousness."

Although the possibilities of future conflict over economic policy are rarely considered by Soviet theoreticians, a great deal of attention is given to the future roles of the Soviet state and the Communist party. As mentioned in the previous chapter, the state is due to begin the process of withering away during the transitional period, while the Party will remain for an undetermined period even under communism. The state will not be needed under communism because its functions, (administration and compulsion, for example) will be either unnecessary or better handled by new forms of self-management. The single exception to this rule is the qualification that if "the danger of imperialist attacks" remains, the defense functions of the state will be retained into the period of full communism.

As for the Party, it is a curious fact that its future leading position is well-established, while its specific role is not. It will unquestionably have the chief responsibility for keeping "consciousness" and social organization on a high level, but its organizational relations with the central planning agency, the public organizations, or the transformed soviets are unclear. However, the general outlines of its activities and a justification of its continued existence are given in the following excerpt:

> Communism is the most organized society man has ever known. It is a society founded on the conscious and voluntary submission to rules worked out by the members of society themselves and the habitual observation of these rules as a regular norm of conduct. This assumes an exceptionally high level of consciousness which, naturally, can not be achieved in a haphazard social order but requires great ideological political work amongst the masses. With the construction of communism, society does not cease to need organizations which carry out cultural and ideological education of the masses. . . . Methods of persuasion, social opinion, and comradely influence will occupy an ever larger place in the

[64] Grigor'ev, *Obshchestvennaia vlast'*, pp. 48–49.

life of Soviet society and under communism these methods alone will regulate relations between people. In connection with this, the role of the Party will grow ever greater because its guidance of the masses is wholly founded on persuasion, based on the power of authority and on propagation of the great ideas of Marxism-Leninism.[65]

This approach suggests that the Party will have a primarily ideological function and will leave the important administrative decisions to other organizations. However, other writers state that the Party is necessary under communism to "guarantee the coordinated functioning of all links of social self-management"[66] and to "direct and coordinate the activities of the ramified organizational system of communist self-management in [society's] interests.[67] These descriptions of the Party's future sound suspiciously close to those of the Party's present. They also raise the question of what functions would be left to the central planning agency if the Party "directs and coordinates" the communist organizational setup. If the Party did indeed retain control over the direction of the communist economy, we might be able to take at face value the remark of Chesnokov mentioned earlier that the planning agency would "neither command nor direct production" but would simply "estimate," since the Party would presumably continue in approximately its present role. We might also assume, in this case, that the central planning agency would be simply an enlarged and highly complex version of *Gosplan* (the present Soviet state planning agency).

However, the matter is complicated by the firmly established theoretical principle that the Party must eventually disappear. It seems fairly certain that Soviet discussions of the role of consciousness and central planning refer to a more distant phase of communism than does the commentary on the future Party. According to this interpretation of Soviet doctrine, the Party would remain in control during the initial stages of communism, while the planning agency grew in complexity and efficiency. At some later stage, as the generally high level of consciousness made its continued functioning unnecessary, the Party would disappear. At this point, the planning agency would assume full control of the economy. We find some support for this interpretation in remarks like the following: "The Party is an historical organization; it arose at a definite stage of man's development called forth by the needs of the class struggle. . . . After the Party has completely carried out its tasks, it

[65] N. Lomakin, "Partiia Lenina," in *Nekotorye problemy teorii i praktiki stroitel'stva kommunizma* (Moscow: Voennoe izdatel'stvo Ministerstva Oborony Soiuza SSR, 1961), p. 67.

[66] Karapetian, "Politicheskaia organizatsiia," p. 305.

[67] Nikolaev, "O razvitii sotsialisticheskoi gosudarstvennosti," p. 36.

will pass from the arena of social life."[68] Further clarification of the conditions necessary for the disappearance of the Party is given by Chesnokov:

> It will take many years and decades of life for the people under communism to work out fully and to become adapted to the new organization of society—and to create, finally, the conditions for the dying off of the Party. This process is lengthy and gradual. It will occur to the degree that *all members of society are raised to the same level of consciousness and organization as the members of the Party.*[69]

As Chesnokov later states explicitly, this would mean that the Party, far from disappearing, would "be transformed into an all-inclusive organization, merged with organs of self-management."[70] Chesnokov and others also make clear that this will not occur until communism is victorious over the entire world, in contrast to the earlier hypothesized demise of the state, which required only the great preponderance of communism on a world-wide scale. The essence of this viewpoint is that the Party, as another writer put it, will "be joined with the people, will combine with them,"[71] and that this will occur when the entire society is composed of model party members—model communists living in a model communist society.

## The Economics of Superabundance

The economics of communism will be characterized by three major features: superabundance of all material goods, distribution of these goods according to needs, and lack of a market system using money as the medium of exchange. In actual fact, however, everything hinges on the first of these characteristics: material superabundance. Soviet theory more or less acknowledges this by giving great stress to the importance of material production in the building of communism and by constantly asserting that full communism will be impossible without an abundant supply of goods to satisfy the great and expanding needs of communist society. Khrushchev, during his period of leadership, was a constant and vigorous exponent of the primacy of material abundance. In typically down-to-earth fashion, he once explained communism thus:

> Communism as we understand it means abundance. . . . If communism is proclaimed when there is, say, only one pair of pants to ten people, and

---

[68] Lomakin, "Partiia Lenina," p. 69.
[69] Chesnokov, *Ot gosudarstvennosti*, pp. 25–26. (Emphasis mine.)
[70] *Ibid.*, p. 26.
[71] Karapetian, "Politicheskaia organizatsiia," p. 305.

that pair of pants is divided equally into ten parts, then everyone will be going around without pants altogether. We reject this sort of trouser-less communism. It would be a perversion.[72]

At another time, he declared: "The bowl of communism is a bowl of abundance, and it must always be full."[73] The problem lies, however, in the fact that the "bowl of communism" is in reality many bowls—in fact, an ever-increasing number of them—each of which must be kept filled at all times. In addition to having a crucial significance in the individual psyche of the communist citizen (as we shall see in the next chapter), the concept of material abundance is responsible for a host of economic problems. Leaving aside for the moment the formidable problem of establishing rational consumption levels for the population, we can see that a rapidly advancing economy is one in which products are constantly changing, and the assortment is constantly growing. In a static situation, it could be rationally determined that a certain number of a particular item of consumption was required. A simple formula, based on past experience, could be used for this purpose. However, in the ever-changing communist society, where new technology will be more rapidly and continuously used to benefit the people, there would be a constantly recurring interval between the introduction of a new device and the filling of warehouses. In other words, there would be constantly occurring—albeit temporary—shortages, unless discoveries were kept closely guarded secrets until sufficient supply levels had been achieved. Of course, this solution is not suggested by the theoreticians, and it is extremely doubtful that it would be feasible in any case. Barring secrecy, there does not seem to be any method of preventing consumer demand for new items from exceeding the initial supply unless the consumer himself becomes so highly conscious that he does not *feel*, or at least does not indulge, a personal desire for anything which is not available in superabundant quantities at the local warehouse, a solution that is indeed proposed by present Soviet theory.[74]

The elimination of money is closely related in Soviet doctrine to the achievement of an abundant economy. Abundance is necessary in order to introduce the communist principle of distribution according to needs, and the latter principle makes money essentially superfluous. The reasoning behind this assertion is quite straightforward. Money is used

[72] Interview with Gardner Cowles, *Pravda*, April 27, 1962 (*CDSP*, vol. 14, no. 17, p. 18).

[73] N. S. Khrushchev, "On the Program of the Communist Party of the Soviet Union: Report to the 22nd Congress of the C.P.S.U.," p. 195.

[74] See chapter IV for a discussion of this problem, as well as the related problem of calculating "reasonable needs" for a wide assortment of goods. Also see Strumilin, *Rabochii den' i kommunizm*, p. 41.

under capitalism and socialism as a means of exchange, and under socialism in particular it represents earned income and, consequently, socially useful labor performed. Under socialism, money in effect becomes a certificate attesting to the fact that the holder has performed a certain quantity of labor for society. This certificate is then converted into a certain equivalent quantity of goods or services provided by society in return. Under communism, however, there is no exchange of social labor for equivalent goods and services, but rather a distribution of equivalent shares of unlimited quantities of such goods and services with the understanding that each member of society performs "according to his abilities." Calculation of work performed becomes unnecessary, and money, which is simply a convenient means of making this calculation, becomes superfluous. Instead, the needs of each individual are computed on the basis of criteria like physical characteristics, type of work, geographical location, and individual tastes. With this calculation in hand, each citizen draws from the social supplies a quantity of goods commensurate with his scientifically-determined needs. This system is described by Chesnokov in the following terms:

> Under communism, items of consumption . . . lose the form of goods on sale for money. People will use apartments, cultural institutions, means of transportation and communication, laundries, tailor shops, etc., without paying. Stores will be converted into general warehouses where the workers of communist society will be able to obtain items for personal use.[75]

A somewhat more sophisticated approach is offered by Strumilin, who suggests that a certain basic supply of free goods and services will be supplemented by a free choice of luxury items in the following manner:

> In addition to the entire free supply of goods in kind, all consumers will be given the right to acquire by coupon book, let us say, any additional goods in the social stores within limits established each month according to the goods' full value.[76]

As for the difficulties inherent in planning the production of such items, subject, as they would be, to the personal preferences of roughly 300 million consumers, Strumilin claims:

> Insofar as each in making his selection will follow his tastes and requirements even in the area of secondary needs [luxuries] and scarce goods, the necessary planning proportions will be determined after a time.[77]

---

[75] Chesnokov, *Ot gosudarstvennosti*, p. 11.
[76] Strumilin, *Rabochii den' i kommunizm*, p. 61.
[77] *Ibid.*

Such coupon books would not represent money since they would be distributed on the basis of needs calculated for each citizen rather than as wage payments for labor performed. Strumilin's suggestion has not been taken up by any other Soviet writer, although it is the only one that offers a reasonable outlet for consumer preferences, short of programming them in an enormous electronic computer.

Other Soviet writers in addition to Strumilin, however, have indicated that the monetary exchange system will not disappear immediately when the Soviet Union enters the period of full communism. Such respected theorists as the academician K. S. Ostrovitianov have declared that money relations will be necessary "for a given period of time" under communism, even if only to permit continuation of trade between capitalist, socialist, and communist countries.[78] Another writer declares that "even when all working people will be guaranteed a sufficiency of the most important items of consumption free of charge through the social fund, for a certain time there will still remain a need for material encouragement of the best workers through wage payments."[79] Implicit in this statement is the assumption that complete conversion to communist distribution requires not only abundance but also full achievement of communist consciousness, a more prolonged process. This point is made explicit by yet another theoretician in the following formula: "The transition to distribution by needs will be realized . . . when abundance of all necessary consumables is achieved and when all people, voluntarily and irrespective of the material goods received, will work according to their abilities, understanding that it is necessary for society."[80]

This dual insistence on abundance plus consciousness once again creates something of a doctrinal paradox. Surely, a truly conscious person, one who would work "irrespective of the material goods received," would not need *abundance* of these material goods as an incentive to continue working. We can safely assume that such a person would be satisfied by mere *sufficiency* of food, clothing, and shelter in order to keep alive and ready to work according to his fullest abilities.

---

[78] K. S. Ostrovitianov, "Nekotorye problemy stroitel' stva kommunizma v SSSR i zadachi obshchestvennykh nauk," in *Voprosy stroitel'stva kommunizma v SSSR* (Moscow: Izdatel'stvo Akademii nauk SSSR, 1959), p. 28. For an English-language summary of this report and the meeting at which it was presented, see "Economic Problems of Building Communism," in *Problems of Economics* (Moscow: January 1959), vol. 1, no. 9, pp. 46–67.

[79] V. S. Naidenov, "Printsip material'noi zainteresovannosti—printsip stroitel'stva kommunizma," *Voprosy filosofii*, 1962, no. 5, p. 16.

[80] P. N. Fedoseev, *Kommunizm i filosofiia* (Moscow: Izdatel'stvo Akademii nauk SSSR, 1962), p. 246.

This supply level has unquestionably been achieved in the Soviet Union already, and we can therefore assume that a truly conscious individual in the present Soviet milieu would function in a genuinely communist manner. This line of reasoning brings us to the inevitable, if startling, conclusion that the Soviet insistence on superabundance is made completely irrelevant by the assumption of communist consciousness.

The reverse proposition is also both true and revealing: the Soviet insistence on communist consciousness would be completely irrelevant under conditions of true superabundance. In fact, each requirement, of itself, is sufficient to create an ideal communist society of sorts, although the picture of this society would not be identical in both cases. If we postulate a genuinely superabundant society, a society, that is, in which the material, artistic, and intellectual output is so vast that all needs of all citizens, short of the most outrageously frivolous whims, could be met without creating any scarcities, we then have an economic model of communist society. Such a society would not need "communist consciousness" to keep consumption at relatively austere levels, and might, in fact, need to stimulate consumption in order to prevent the public warehouses from overflowing. If, on the other hand, we postulate a society of men and women thoroughly imbued with communist consciousness, we have a psychological model of communist society that could exist on *any* economic level from bare subsistence to outright affluence.

The fact that the Soviet theorists have insisted on both superabundance and communist consciousness can be attributed to several underlying factors. The first of these is the implicit Soviet acceptance of the term "abundance" as basically psychological, rather than economic. Abundance implies that a certain level of individual *satisfaction* is substantially exceeded. Satisfaction, however, is a purely subjective term which indicates that one's expectations are fulfilled. We can see, therefore, that people's expectations, thus their "satisfaction level," depend on their past experience and environments. In more concrete terms, we can say that abundance for a Chinese peasant would probably be considered mere subsistence, or worse, by an Iowa farmer, simply because ideas of abundance are dictated by past consumption patterns. Since satisfaction—and thus, abundance—are such subjective terms, we can see that the Soviet insistence on communist consciousness is predicated on the idea that the socially-conscious individual will be needed in order to keep the "level of abundance" within feasible limits.

Another aspect of the dual insistence on superabundance and consciousness is also of interest. As noted, the Soviet theoreticians insist on material abundance as a necessary precondition for the consolidation of communist consciousness. The implication seems to be that no man, not even communist man, can be expected to work without direct compensation unless he is guaranteed a very high consumption level. In fact, judging from the forecasts of the Party Program, he would require a consumption level more than twice as high as that now prevailing in the United States. It would not be unfair to suggest that, at this high level of guaranteed consumption, the concept of divorcing labor from the expectation of material rewards loses a great deal of its significance. It would seem to be more a guarantee of economic security—similar in form and intent to the aims of labor unions in the West—than a departure from the traditional psychology of the workingman.

There is yet another logical complication. On the surface it is quite supportable, from a Marxist viewpoint, to claim that communist consciousness can be fully developed only under conditions of superabundance. This can be taken as a specific formulation of the Marxist idea that the superstructure depends on the material base. However, as we have just seen, the concept of superabundance is not an objective, physically defined term. It is actually a dependent variable, a function of the material environment. We thus are faced with a logical "vicious circle" in which consciousness depends upon superabundance and superabundance depends upon consciousness. The former statement is an explicit part of Soviet doctrine; the latter is implicit in the Soviet insistence on consciousness as a prerequisite for communist distribution. The mutual dependence of these two variables, however, has never been formulated in Soviet doctrine. The Soviet theoreticians treat abundance as though it were a definable part of the material environment, rather than as an *idea*, and thus a component of the doctrinal superstructure.

Soviet theorists have also been quite concerned with the ethics of communist distribution. It would seem that they are rather anxious to show that distribution according to need does not mean distribution of equal shares to each person, and, furthermore, that distribution of equal shares would be less equitable than a formula taking individual requirements into account. Thus, it is iterated and reiterated that although "communism does not mean equality in consumption, or leveling [*uravnilovka*]," it does mean that "everyone's needs will be satisfied with *identical fullness*, that is, people will be equal in their standard of living."[81] By this is meant that the computation of each person's needs will not be accomplished by establishing an average quota for each object and ignoring individual variations. Citizens will draw *unequal*

---

[81] P. Mstislavskii, "Kommunizm i ravenstvo," *Kommunist*, 1961, no. 15, p. 33.

*amounts* of goods from the public warehouse, but they will receive *equal benefits* from the goods obtained. In the computation of these various amounts of goods for each person, we once again, presumably, find the central planning agency, whose responsibility will include the planning of consumption as well as production. One can deduce from the theory that, by bringing both basic economic functions under one roof, communist society will be able to avoid the dislocations noted in the contemporary Soviet economic system. Indeed, this added responsibility and power lends additional force to the earlier observation that the central planning agency will virtually control the mainsprings of communist society.

## Property Relationships

Under communism, only two types of property will remain: all-people's and personal. Cooperative property as embodied in the *kolkhoz*, cooperative dwellings, and other present legal forms of cooperative ownership will be abolished at some date prior to the advent of full communism. It is firmly established that all-people's property will include many articles which are at present in the hands of private owners. In fact, personal property is expected to include only those objects which are not usable by more than one person simultaneously and possibly some articles of small value which could conceivably be utilized by more than one person but which would not represent a large outlay of funds.

As already mentioned, it is generally acknowledged that "there will still be personal property, but it will be limited to objects of individual use. Personal ownership of other material . . . goods loses whatever economic meaning it ever had and disappears."[82] Such "objects of individual use" will include wearing apparel, books, and other like items that are used continually in the course of daily living. One writer, however, has raised the possibility that even such personal articles as these may become all-people's property on "permanent loan" to individuals:

> One would think that even the most far removed of our descendents will . . . lay claim to personal linens, personal clothes, footwear, etc. Concerning such items, it would be strange to talk of their being reserved only for temporary use. But it is sometimes said thoughtfully that such things may be set aside [by society] for permanent use. They point to the fact that

[82] M. P. Sakov, *Osnovnoi printsip kommunizma* (Moscow: Gospolitizdat, 1961), p. 55.

although land is given to the *kolkhoz* in perpetuity, it is not the *kolkhoz*'s property, but remains the property of the state.[83]

If such a proposal were adopted, it would probably amount to a mere formal distinction, since the individual would retain such articles until they had worn out. However, the idea that everything, including one's own underwear, belongs to the collective would certainly go a long way toward impressing the individual with his dependence on the collective in every respect.[84] Even if these articles remained personal property, the fact that each individual would draw his supplies from the social warehouse in accordance with the *collective's* calculation of his particular needs would have something of the same effect.

Thus, such articles as automobiles and *dachas* are to become the property of society and will be used by individuals on a temporary basis. One argument that is used to support this enlargement of all-people's property is the assertion that "rental" (presumably free of charge) will be more convenient for the individual than outright ownership:

> Every automobile enthusiast would prefer to use cars, as required, from a public rental point, rather than waste money on a purchase, and free time on maintenance of it in addition. And who does not acknowledge that it is more convenient to rent a *dacha* from the state or to use a rest home rather than waste time and energy on maintaining one's own *dacha*?[85]

It is also quite clear, however, that added convenience for the individual also means added efficiency for society as a whole, and efficiency is one of the main considerations in building a communist society. Maintenance of automobiles and individual dwellings can be arranged "in serial" (i.e., on a mass production line) by central organizations of trained specialists (or rather, "poly-specialists") who will do the job with far fewer man-hours of labor expended. Another writer lists three advantages of this "social satisfaction of individual needs": (1) it is

[83] G. Gak, "Kommunizm i lichnaia sobstvennost'," *Kommunist*, 1961, no. 1, p. 69. For the argument that individual consumption of certain articles does not necessarily lead to the retention of personal property, see M. V. Kolganov, *Sobstvennost' v period perekhoda k kommunizmu* (Moscow: Ekonomizdat, 1963), pp. 72–73.

[84] There is a rather striking similarity here, as elsewhere, between the communist society and the organization of most modern armies. These armies also foster a type of "team consciousness" and offer free social services and clothing in return for purposeful activity and adherence to a rather strict moral code and pattern of behavior. In addition, they centrally plan the production, distribution, and consumption of all goods, which remain the property of the army, not the individual.

[85] K. Sevrikov and Iu. Feofanov, "Lichnaia sobstvennost' i stroitel'stvo kommunizma," *Kommunist*, 1962, no. 13, p. 64.

"incomparably more economical," (2) it "frees the citizen from the nuisances of daily care," and (3) it "develops to a much greater degree than personal property the moral qualities of the man of communist society, develops collectivism and consciousness of the indivisible unity of personal and social interests.[86] The third point is perhaps the most interesting, for it hinges, on the familiar concept of consciousness. In a superabundant society, there would presumably be cars available for all who needed them. Despite this abundance of automobiles, however, the individual would have to requisition a car through "channels," which would entail, in turn, creation of another bureaucracy—a bureaucracy with at least the *potential* power to control the use of a vast amount of social property. Under the assumption that consciousness will prevail, however, the individual would "understand" when his request was refused, because he would be convinced of the "indivisible unity of personal and social interests." Such a system would indeed "develop collectivism" by making the desires of the individual once again dependent on the decision of the collective, through its bureaucratic machinery.

As for all-people's property, we are assured that it will include everything not consumed on an individual basis. It will certainly include all the productive forces of communist society and will signify the emergence of a single-class social structure and the resolution of all essential differences between town and country. Although the productive forces will belong to all the people, these forces can never belong to a single group of the people or be divided in any way that would limit joint ownership by the entire society. Thus, it is stressed that "the anarchistic demand to make enterprises the property of the 'direct producers' [i.e., the workers] is a step backward . . . to the middle ages."[87] The necessity for centralized planning of the economy also leads directly to the insistence on centralized ownership of all the means of production.

*Automation and the Nature of Work*

Present theory has inherited from Engels the idea that labor will be a "primary necessity of life" for the healthy citizen of communism. Indeed, the idea of the fundamental importance of labor in human history is deeply embedded in Marxism. Under communism, however, the former impediments to the derivation of genuine satisfaction from work will be eliminated, and labor will actually become a "source of pleasure" for the first time in the history of mankind. Work could not be a

[86] R. O. Khalfina, "O prave lichnoi sobstvennost' v period razvërnutovo stroitel'stva kommunizma," *Sovetskoe gosudarstvo i pravo*, 1960, no. 12, p. 32.
[87] Platkovskii, *Politicheskaia organizatsiia*, p. 108.

pleasure under capitalism because of the exploitation of the workers, and even under socialism, heavy physical labor and dull, repetitive labor tended to rob the working process of its basic creativity. Only under communism can creativity become an inherent part of work in all its aspects.[88]

This point of view, although dominant in present theoretical discussions, is not accepted by all Soviet writers. In fact the whole question of the nature of work under communism remains one of the chief battlegrounds for Soviet theoreticians, and has produced the most lively, if not the most enlightening, debate in the entire literature on the future society. The debate is concerned with two closely related concepts which must be distinguished from the beginning.

First of all, there is the well-accepted idea that the essential differences between mental and physical labor will be eliminated under full communism. Despite all the ambiguities which this statement implies, the general premise that mental and physical labor will somehow be brought more closely together, both by the advance of technology and by conscious design, is feasible. Subsumed under this process of amalgamation will be all but the nonessential differences between different working environments.

The process of overcoming essential differences takes place during the transitional period. In this respect, it differs from the second, closely related concept of the division of labor, which will be overcome only during a later period of full communism. This second concept has wider implications, since it includes not only divisions into mental and physical tasks (such as design and production) but also divisions in the actual production process itself, which are the results of modern mass production techniques. This issue is at the very heart of Soviet theory, for it is derived from genuine Marxist sources, in which the division of labor is viewed as a specifically capitalist feature. The problem for the theoreticians arises from the fact that the entire course of modern technological advance has served to increase, rather than decrease, the specialization of skills and professions. Consequently, the division of labor is likely to be accentuated in the future, regardless of the economic system.

The continuing division of labor puts the Soviet theorists on the horns of a doctrinal dilemma. In effect, they have inherited an error originally made by Karl Marx, and they must now find some way of resolving the contradiction between theory and practice without admitting—probably even to themselves—that Marx did in fact err. Marx's mistake lay in identifying the division of labor, and consequent aliena-

---

[88] See Nikitin, *Chto takoe kommunizm*, pp. 89–90.

tion, with the capitalist system rather than with the demands of modern technology for efficiency-maximizing production. The very facts that knowledge increases, that production processes become increasingly complex, that the variety and complexity of material goods constantly expands all make it less and less likely that the relatively fixed capacities of the individual human brain will be able to span more than a tiny portion of the totality of human knowledge and experience.

Faced with this problem, the Soviet theorists have responded in various ways. As in the discussion of differences between physical and mental labor, some theorists have proposed that the work process itself will be generalized, so that the division into separate operations, each performed by a separate worker, will be abolished. This sort of approach generally looks to automation as the means by which labor will be despecialized. Thus we have the statement that "the complex automation of production will free man from narrow operational and detailed specialization and will create conditions for work of a wide scope, which takes in an entire production cycle."[89] Even though automated equipment is seen as becoming increasingly specialized, it is contended that the worker will become a generalized repairman and controller, able to stand at the control panel of many different types of automated assembly lines.[90] The relationship between man and machine is of crucial importance in this approach. Since this school of thought is committed to eliminating the division of labor, despite all the evidence of modern production, the automated machine becomes a useful dialectical tool—it can always be claimed that present trends will be reversed by the widespread introduction of automated equipment. The machinery will become more specialized while the men who control it will become more widely qualified. In fact, Strumilin, one of the foremost proponents of this view, sees a new type of division of labor, not between men, but between machines:

> In these new conditions the old divisions of work lose all their distasteful *specific features*. The old professions will simply be blended one into the other, but the new universal functions of control and direction of the entire system under automation can hardly be called a profession, for within it will be combined the entire *complex* of specialized knowledge and work functions. . . . Under conditions of the highest specialization of machines and utilization of technology, communism will affirm a *new*

[89] Sakov, *Osnovnoi printsip kommunizma*, p. 20.
[90] See *Izmenenie klassovoi struktury obshchestva v protsesse stroitel'stva sotsializma i kommunizma* (Moscow: Izdatel'stvo VPSh i AON pri TsK KPSS, 1961), p. 198.

*division of labor* not fundamentally between people but between machines.[91]

There are many difficulties in the approach of what we may call the school of "doctrinal optimists." The optimists look forward to the elimination of the division of labor because they see automated machines as somehow being less varied in fundamental principles of design of operation than present-day production machinery. In this view, "the development of technology causes an uninterrupted growth not only of the differences, but also of the common elements of construction in the machine technology of all branches of production."[92] This makes it possible for the individual engineer-worker "to broaden his professional profile," or working qualifications, to include a wide variety of skills. If we assume that the problem is purely technological and does not have any direct relationship to the form of property ownership in society, the American experience, as a more advanced case of the same process, can offer some interesting guidelines. In the United States, technological and scientific advances have led to two diverging trends in technical education. On the one hand, the vocational training of technicians, skilled workers, and clerical personnel has become increasingly diversified, and there has been a general upgrading of skill levels. On the other, the education of scientists and engineers has tended to become less specialized, responding to the increased need for broadly qualified scientists who can cope with problems that increasingly cut across the old demarcations of specialities.

Assuming that the American experience has some relevance to future trends in the Soviet Union (and Soviet scholars have tacitly admitted this), we can see that there may be some merit in the argument of the Soviet school of doctrinal optimists. Decreasing specialization and division of labor may well be the future path for *creative* technological endeavor, i.e., in the fields of research, design, and development. However, in the actual process of production, even in automated plants, the trend is toward increasing complexity of operations, hence, increased specialization. Even if fewer workers are needed for the sequence of operations in a particular production process, the greatly expanded variety and complexity of products calls forth an increase in the aggregate quantity of production specialities. The Soviet optimists, however, introduce a point of confusion by equating the upgrading of working skills with the eventual creation of a single category of engineer-work-

[91] S. G. Strumilin, *Problemy sotsializma i kommunizma v SSSR* (Moscow: Izdatel'stvo ekonomicheskoi literatury, 1961), p. 296. (Strumilin's italics.)

[92] G. I. Shemenev, "Inzhenerno-tekhnicheskaia intelligentsia v period razvërnutovo stroitel'stva kommunizma," *Voprosy filosofii*, 1960, no. 8, p. 31.

ers, who will apparently be as qualified to engage in technological research as in daily production chores. Even if this were possible—and
there remains considerable grounds for skepticism here—the result
would still be the same. We would have simply an occupational "split
personality," with broad theoretical knowledge but relatively narrow
operational qualifications. It would be a rare individual indeed who
would be able to master the complexities of a wide variety of sophisticated equipment and still have time left for the other demands on his
capabilities made by communist society. Since his talents would no
doubt be spread too thin for him to make any lasting contribution in
any one field, it would be inefficient from a social production point of
view to train a man with such unusual gifts in so many fields of endeavor. This would certainly be antithetical to the fundamental values
of communist society.

Opposed to this group of optimists is the school of "doctrinal pessimists," those who foresee a continuation and even an increase in
specialization and separation of production functions. Although the difference between these two groups is not so great as appears at first glance,
the pessimists emphasize the necessities of modern production rather
than the necessities of the doctrine. The following remarks by G. E.
Glezerman, a distinguished Soviet theoretician, are typical of this approach:

> It is deeply mistaken to represent automation as lowering a worker's labor
> in any branch of industry to button-pushing, and to think that he could
> push those buttons with equal success in a metallurgical plant, electric
> power station or bread-baking plant. . . . In actuality the workers in an
> automated plant . . . are highly qualified controllers [naladchiki], who
> must deeply study the particular technical processes and the construction
> of the mechanism in order to be able to correct a malfunction if neces-
> sary. Such workers must be specialists in their field.[93]

Others have attempted to rephrase the doctrinal requirement for an end
to the division of labor in such a way as to make it conform to the
demands of modern production and knowledge. While admitting that
specialization is bound to continue, even under communism, they tend
to explain this away by claiming that the harmful effects of the division
of labor will be eliminated, and that each particular speciality will be
broadened and made less fragmentary. P. Iudin, another well-known
Soviet theoretician, analyzes the problem as follows:

[93] G. E. Glezerman, "Kul'turnyi rost obshchestva—neobkhodimoe uslovie
perekhoda k kommunizmu," *Voprosy filosofii*, 1957, no. 3, p. 16.

It seems to me that the liquidation of the existing division of labor is not at all equivalent to the liquidation of labor division in general. Workers of communist society will not cease to be specialists in various fields, but on the contrary will be transformed into specialists of a higher class. However, this specialization does not mean narrow, one-sided development of professional interest, knowledge and habits.

Does this mean that the man of communist society will know and be able to do everything? . . . In our day, one may meet not a few people who have combined different, highly distinct forms of activity. Under communist conditions, even further possibilities in this respect will be opened up. However, this does not mean that each man will be able to work at everything or that specialization will disappear. A surgeon may also be a pilot, an athlete, a musician and a remarkable gardener, but in order to perform a surgical operation, he must be, above all else, a surgeon. In order to reach the heights in any area of art, science, or production, it is necessary to make one type of activity primary, devoting to it the major portion of one's time.[94]

Evidently, Iudin believes there are two processes which will take place under communism. One is the continuing, and perhaps increasing, specialization of work and expertise, and the other is a *limited* broadening of man's capacities so that *some* people may be engaged in two or more diverse fields. He is careful to point out, however, that most of this widening of interests will be avocational rather than vocational. There seems to be wide support among Soviet theorists for this approach, although some give more emphasis to the genuine possibilities of poly-specialization. In fact, this group, whom we have termed the doctrinal pessimists, are more firmly wedded to the idea of poly-specialization and frequent job changes than the optimists, since these latter see the very process of work becoming less specialized. The pessimists need the so-called law of periodic job changes in order to avoid the doctrinally unsound conclusion that the division of labor will actually become more evident under communism.

There is some justice in picturing the pessimists as realists who recognize the world-wide trend toward specialization and who seek to overcome its harmful consequences by instituting a conscious program of poly-specialization and job shifting. The pessimists view the idea of making all jobs under communism both stimulating and rewarding as too utopian, and they insist on a realistic evaluation of present technological trends. Typical of this approach is the following attack on the optimistic viewpoint:

[94] P. Iudin, "Zakonomernyi kharakter perekhoda ot sotsializma k kommunizmu," *Kommunist*, 1961, no. 12, p. 50.

Some economists and philosophers consider that the future society in general will not know [the division of labor] and that under communism . . . all work will be creative. Unfortunately, this is not so. This statement is, most likely, one of those examples of wishes being presented as reality.[95]

Also typical is the same writer's suggestion for solving this problem: "It is quite possible that communist society will organize a continuous combination of creative work with less interesting, non-creative, but highly useful and necessary work."[96] The basis of this point of view is the realization that "universalism is impossible under conditions where the complexity of each field of knowledge is ever increasing. But along with his speciality, the worker of communist society will master yet other professions."[97]

It should be made quite clear, that the pessimists actually foresee a continuation of the division of labor under communism, and this is definitely a heretical point of view from the standpoint of orthodox Marxism. The original concept of the division of labor saw man being divorced from the results of his own labor, and man's labor being segmented into separate, meaningless operations. Although the pessimists look forward to increasingly broad specialization and more inclusive work functions, they do not foresee any end to the segmentation and separation of labor functions, despite all the claimed virtues of automation and mechanization.

While acknowledging that the division of labor will continue under communism, the pessimists often refer to a new, communist division of labor which will be cleansed of all the harmful side-effects of the old capitalistic and socialistic division of labor. The new division of labor is generally described as follows:

The communist division of labor will be represented by the harmonious organization of people, distributed according to various spheres of productive, and other social activities in conformity with the needs of society and the abilities and interests of each man. The dynamics of social life demand the constant planned change of the entire system of distribution of labor resources; its obligatory element will become a change of work to a succession of different socially useful activities in conformity with the many-sided abilities of mankind.[98]

---

[95] E. L. Manevich, "O likvidatsii razlichii mezhdu umstvennym i fizicheskim trudom v period razvërnutovo stroitel'stva kommunizma," *Voprosy filosofii*, 1961, no. 9, p. 27.
[96] *Ibid.*, p. 28.
[97] *Ibid.*
[98] Sakov, *Osnovnoi printsip kommunizma*, p. 20.

Thus, the communist division of labor will be distinguished from its predecessors by a careful consideration of each worker's abilities and interests—although the "needs of society" may be considered first—and by frequent shifting of jobs to make work more interesting and stimulating for the average worker. For such a worker, this will mean that "the attachment of a man to a single profession will forever disappear; each will be able to choose for himself an occupation according to his abilities and inclinations."[99] Judging from the general trend of discussions in other contexts and the admitted difficulty of any man realistically estimating his own abilities, it would seem more likely that the collective will help each worker decide which job is most suitable for him.

Whereas both the doctrinal pessimists and optimists agree that the "law of frequent job changes" will take effect under communism, the pessimists are considerably more ambivalent on this score. On the one hand, they tend to stress its importance because it is the sole defense against the embarrassing conclusion that the communist division of labor will be more truly divided than the labor of any previous social system. On the other, they must admit, as realists, that progress in all fields of knowledge and production makes it increasingly difficult, if not impossible, for the average man to master more than one or perhaps two complex specialities. While both schools of thought envision a great increase in the capacities of the masses under communism, the pessimists do not agree that a mere change in the social system, plus the widespread application of automation, will enable each man to keep abreast of the accelerated pace of research and development in more than one or two specific fields. The ambivalence of this position is indicated by the fact that the pessimists generally agree that future specialists will have "broad detailed knowledge" of several fields in addition to their own. This leads to the following observation on future changes in production leadership and management:

> The workers' level of general and specialized knowlege will be so high that in our view the necessity will disappear for retaining some sort of group of people whose "speciality" would be the management of production and other social functions. These functions, of course, will remain even under full communism, for machine production is impossible without a corresponding ordering of working people. . . . But these functions will be carried out by different people, primarily those having great experience of life and production.[100]

[99] Platkovskii, "Formirovanie kommunisticheskikh obshchestvennykh otnoshenii," p. 26.
[100] Manevich, "O likvidatsii razlichii," p. 23.

At the same time, the pessimists attack the ideas of such optimists as Strumilin and V. P. Kornienko (of the Leningrad Institute of Precise Mechanics and Optics), who has written that "the division between different branches of production will result in a division between different automatically operating and controlling . . . machines, and not between collectives of people," and that each man "will be able to take on any work in any place of work."[101]

The rather subterranean disagreement between the pessimists and optimists took on the form of a sharp public debate in the pages of *Voprosy filosofii* during 1962 and 1963, a debate which revealed both the substantive and the purely semantic differences between the two groups. The stimulus for this public discussion was an article by A. K. Kurylev in the November 1961 issue. Kurylev, who can be categorized as a doctrinal pessimist, declared:

> The rapid progress of socialist economics, science, technology and culture is accompanied by two tendencies. On the one hand, the results of scientific-technical progress create the desire to acquire diversified knowledge and to develop wide-ranging abilities. Practical realization of this task would require of a man a significant part of his conscious life. Under such conditions, little time would remain for a man to apply his knowledge in practice. And on the other hand, the complication of social production processes and the colossal growth in the volume of knowledge calls forth the necessity for specialization of each individual's working activities, and consequently the necessity for concrete specialized knowledge. Without this, it would be impossible for a man to carry out practical actions.[102]

Eleven months later, the editors of *Voprosy filosofii* decided to devote a large part of their journal to a discussion of the question of labor under communism, apparently because the response from the optimists was so great. Kurylev opened the debate with an attack on those who believe that under communism the division of labor will either completely disappear or will be restricted to a division of labor between machines (an obvious reference to Strumilin). He drew a distinction between the old "professional, capitalist division of labor" and the new "communist system of division and cooperation of labor."[103]

In the following article, V. Ia. El'meev disagreed with Kurylev's thesis that the all-round development of the individual personality—a cardinal feature of communism—is fully compatible with the division of

---

[101] *Ibid.*, p. 24, as quoted by Manevich.

[102] A. K. Kurylev, "O vsestoronnem razvitii lichnosti pri kommunizme," *Voprosy filosofii*, 1961, no. 11, pp. 31–32.

[103] A. K. Kurylev, "Razdelenie truda i vsestoronee razvitie lichnosti v period perekhoda ot sotsializma k kommunizmu," *Voprosy filosofii*, 1962, no. 10, p. 22.

labor between people. El'meev, like Kurylev, attached great importance to the "law of job changes" but, unlike Kurylev, insisted that this law would be incompatible with the division of labor, and would, in fact, *replace* the division of labor. El'meev made a distinction between the "specialization of *labor*" and "specialization of *people*, which is an expression of the division of labor between people, and means the limitation of a man's occupations within the framework of a single speciality."[104] According to El'meev, the specialization of labor cannot be avoided since it is a part of modern production techniques, but the "specialization of people" can be eliminated through the "law of job changes." Thus he admits the necessity of "differentiation (specialization) of forms of human activity" but denies that this will result in a "division of labor between people, between social groups."[105]

E. L. Manevich, one of the more pessimistic of the pessimists, followed with general support of Kurylev's thesis, but criticized the latter for stating that, under communism, people "will be able to change from one job to another, and will be able to change their professions with remarkable ease." Manevich attributes this view to the "socialist-utopians" and declares that only "such a division of labor as is connected with . . . the life-long attachment of people to either physical or mental labor" will be eliminated under communism.[106] The only other noteworthy contribution to this debate was made by A. V. Andreev and Ia. V. Timoshkov, both of whom must certainly represent the most extremely pessimistic viewpoint in the entire debate. These authors criticized both Manevich and Kurylev, the latter for stating that the "law of job changes" will mitigate the effects of the division of labor. Andreev and Timoshkov believe it is "utopian" to talk of workers alternating between different types of work, and they state that it would be correct to discuss not a "new division of labor" under communism, but rather "a new role for the division of labor" under communism. According to these writers:

> Highly productive labor demands of the man of communist society a great amount of knowledge and habits in a defined, narrow field. Only narrow specialization makes it possible to unite mental and physical labor, knowledge and know-how in the working activities of a single man. . . . It

104 V. Ia. El'meev, "Vsestoronee razvitie lichnosti predpolagaet unichtozhenie razdeleniia truda mezhdu liud'mi," *Voprosy filosofii*, 1962, no. 10, p. 28. (Emphasis mine.)

105 *Ibid.*

106 E. L. Manevich, "Sotsial'no-ekonomicheskie osnovy vsestoronnevo razvitiia lichnosti pri kommunizme," *Voprosy filosofii*, 1962, no. 10, p. 36.

is quite obvious that communist society is unthinkable without constantly developing and deepening division of labor.[107]

Of course, this view is squarely opposed to the prevailing opinion of both the optimists and the majority of pessimists, all of whom have supported the idea that "narrow specialization" and "life-long attachment to a single occupation" will disappear in communist society. In fact, Andreev and Timoshkov compound the felony by claiming that there will be an even greater development of "occupational social groups" because "social groups arise as a result of the division of labor."[108] The two fundamental social groups of communism will be the large group of those working directly in production of social wealth and the smaller group of those working in services and direction (*rukovodstvo*) of "all activities of society." According to these theoreticians, therefore, the only difference between labor under Soviet socialism and under full communism would be a freer choice of initial profession and better training in it, along with a constantly "deepening" division of labor. This not only makes them the most pessimistic of pessimists, but also the theorists farthest from the original conceptions of Karl Marx and Frederick Engels.

Several months later, Strumilin offered a rebuttal in the pages of *Voprosy filosofii* in which he criticized Kurylev for, among other things, using an incorrect translation of Marx, dated 1947, in which the terms distribution (*raspredelenie*), and division (*razdelenie*), were confused. Strumilin reiterates his contention that

> the most important difference between the old and new division [*razdelenie*] of labor in conditions of automated production is that the old division and cooperation of labor was carried out between people, but the new specialization and cooperation of productive functions fundamentally is realized between machines and systems of machines, arranged in automatic lines.[109]

Strumilin optimistically predicts that the shortening of the working day to four or five hours and the improvement of educational facilities will enable the average workingman to "master progressively not one but even several types of intellectual activity."[110] Thus Strumilin foresees the division of labor being overcome under communism by constant

107 A. V. Andreev and Ia. V. Timoshkov, "Razdelenie truda i obshchestvennie gruppy pri kommunizme," *Voprosy filosofii*, 1962, no. 10, p. 43.
108 *Ibid.*
109 S. G. Strumilin, "Kommunizm i razdelenie truda," *Voprosy filosofii*, 1963, no. 3, p. 43.
110 *Ibid.*, p. 45.

shifting of each worker's occupation, a view characteristic of the optimists.

In the same issue of *Voprosy filosofii*, however, N. S. Novoselov contends that this division cannot be overcome by the chance combination of unrelated skills in a single individual—as in El'meev's example of the metalworker who teaches history at night—but rather through a change in the "internal content of the labor performed by a worker occupied in a concrete field of production."[111] Novoselov foresees an increase in the division of labor in conformity with increasing technological complexity, as well as an increase in the number of "professional social groups . . . with the appearance of ever newer forms of labor."[112]

The debate continued along these lines in more than sixteen articles and several issues of *Voprosy filosofii*. By this point in the stream of disputation, however, it had become increasingly obvious that, along with a genuinely substantive disagreement, there were a few points of purely semantic controversy. We can see that there is complete agreement on what will *not* be present under communism, namely, the harmful effects of the division of labor. There is also general agreement (with Andreev and Timoshkov standing outside the consensus on this point) that more or less frequent job transfers will occur and will, in fact, be desirable. Furthermore, both pessimists and optimists agree that *jobs* will continue to be specialized, although the optimists see that as a decreasing tendency while the pessimists see it as increasing. The dispute, then, turns on the question of whether *men* in their functions as workers will be specialized, or whether they will be able to surmount this necessity of production by combining diverse skills. El'meev's previously mentioned distinction between "specialization of labor" and "specialization of people" is particularly germane in this respect. On the other hand, there is obviously a purely semantic difference between these two schools of thought that often obscures the real points at issue. For example, the term "division of labor" (*razdelenie truda*) is apparently repugnant to El'meev, who associates it with harmful division under capitalism, while Novoselov and Kurylev feel that the term itself is neutral and merely describes an absolute necessity of modern, technological society. Therefore, the former proclaims the cessation of the division of labor under communism, while the latter see it as actually developing and deepening. The point is that there is really not quite that

[111] N. S. Novoselov, "Razdelenie truda pri kommunizme ne iskliuchaet vozmozhnosti peremeny truda i vsestoronnevo razvitiia lichnosti," *Voprosy filosofii*, 1963, no. 3, pp. 52–53.
[112] *Ibid.*, p. 50.

much difference between the two positions. El'meev's "differentiation (specialization) of forms of human activity" does seem to be rather similar to Novoselov's concept of the division of labor, with perhaps more emphasis on the possibilities of frequent job transfers. In similar fashion, many of the articles in this *Voprosy filosofii* series are merely shallow attacks on the terminology of preceding authors, without any attempt to penetrate below the superficial level of word definitions.

There is only one exception to this increasing formalization of the debate in successive issues of *Voprosy filosofii*, and that was provided by a nonprofessional theorist in the November 1963 issue. In this brief article, Kim Sergeev, identified as a metalworker, took the extreme position that the entire idea of division of labor under communism is unthinkable and would directly contradict the free development of the personality. He wrote that "under communism, social division of labor is completely impossible and in general cannot be reconciled with the idea of free development of the personality," and criticized Novoselov for stating that "the division of labor under communism completely loses its enslaving character."[113] To this he retorted, with apparent feeling: "How can one fail to understand that the division of labor, of and by itself, is already an expression of enslavement?!"[114] Since Soviet theory admits that the division of labor exists at the present time under socialism, one is tempted to make the obvious inference that Sergeev feels the present working situation is "an expression of enslavement." Certainly this position, the only one offered by a present-day worker, indicates that the theoreticians, occupying comfortable and "narrowly specialized" positions in society, may have a much more conservative view of the "egalitarian" social transformations of communist society than do the workers. Sergeev left no doubt whatever concerning the extent to which he is committed to a thorough equalizing of working conditions under communism. He asked:

> What will there be [under communism] instead of division of labor? Under communism there will be a communist organization of labor that is scientifically based and checked in practical life. . . .
>
> In communist society, neither narrow specialization amongst people, nor divisions into narrow forms of social life, nor division of labor will rule, but rather the sum total of laboring activities of the entire society as well as each, separate individual, in the sphere of material production as well as the spiritual life of society. To be only a philosopher or only an historian, legal scholar, economist, etc., will be perfectly unthinkable; such people will be ridiculed with all the severity of communist morality,

[113] Kim Sergeev, "Ostanutsia li professii pri kommunizme?" *Voprosy filosofii*, 1963, no. 11, p. 92.
[114] *Ibid.*

for communism brings about conditions not only for the study of philosophy and history, but also for active labor in production. *Absolutely all members of society*, with the greatest pleasure and enthusiasm, will devote a part of their time to both spheres of laboring activity and also to physical culture and sports.[115]

In this extreme, "radical" view, we have a picture of society as a completely homogeneous entity. It is not quite clear whether Sergeev believes that "all men are created equal" with respect to native intelligence and talents, or whether he simply feels that all men, irrespective of their differing abilities, would really prefer to fill their working days with a wide variety of activities ranging from operating a crane at a construction site to teaching musicology at the local university. He makes it absolutely clear that *every* individual will "actively participate in one or another field of science or the arts" but he does not explicitly state that all of this mental activity will be on the highest level. Although Sergeev can be classified as a radical optimist, he clearly shares the pessimists' feeling that certain work will always be uninteresting, and that the only way to equalize ennui throughout society is to offer it to all citizens in turn.

This conclusion is quite important, for it directly contradicts the general dictum of Soviet doctrine that work under communism will be a "pleasure" and "primary need of life for every healthy person." It is possible to trace this doctrinal tenet back to the original Marxian concept of alienation, although the austere working conditions of past and present Soviet society may also have provided some impetus for this widely acclaimed principle. According to one Soviet theoretician, four conditions are necessary in order for work to become a prime need of life for the citizen of communism: man must consciously work for the good of the entire society; work must answer his tastes and inclinations; each man must be able to work in full accordance with his ability; the worker must receive everything necessary for his work from society.[116] Of these four requirements, the first and last need not detain us, for they are questions of consciousness and material abundance, both previously discussed. The second and third, however, are exactly the points which the pessimists doubt will ever be achieved. The very idea of frequent job changes can be considered a response to the problem, as Manevich put it, that all work will not be "creative," even though all work will be "necessary for society." Even if we assume that the division of labor will be overcome by frequent job changes, the problem still remains that

---

[115] *Ibid.*, p. 94. (Emphasis mine.)
[116] Kovalev, "Kommunizm—nachalo podlinnoi istorii chelovecheskovo obshchestva," p. 103.

work will not be "a pleasure" when it does not answer the worker's tastes and inclinations and when the worker is not using his full potential. The pessimists assume that this will occur fairly often, perhaps when the professor of musicology becomes a crane operator, but almost certainly when the crane operator becomes the operator of a floor polishing machine, or some other menial contrivance. Not all jobs are equally interesting, and therefore not all work will be equally a "pleasure."

It should be added that the attempt to create a society in which all men would work according to their abilities naturally raises the question of how society will determine each man's abilities. Rational testing procedures may be developed in the future, of course, which will give society a true indication of the individual's aptitudes. What will happen, however, if an individual shows remarkably high aptitudes for playing the harp and studying nuclear engineering? A situation like this will require the establishment of a certain order of occupational priorities and thus involves society's values as well as its testing procedures. The individual may, in effect, have his career chosen for him by society since his personal desire to work according to his "tastes and inclinations" will be offset by his conscious desire to work for the good of all.

Part of the emphasis on machine production and automation seems to be a response to the longstanding prejudice, not only Russian but world-wide, against physical labor. One Soviet scholar reports:

> Often in seminars and lectures the question is asked: "Who will do the 'dirty' physical work under communism?" Not facing this situation in contemporary life we do not at once recognize that all such particularly laborious and "unpleasant" work will be done for man by *machines*.[117]

Heavy physical labor is quite definitely considered unworthy of the man of communist society, although some physical work is bound to remain. For example, it is said:

> Even under communism physical work will continue to exist, although non-mechanized, fatiguing work will disappear in the process of introducing complex automation. The most perfected automatic line presupposes the retention of physical labor, for example in controlling and repairing it, but excludes heavy, nonmechanized labor.[118]

---

[117] G. Shakhnazarov, *Kommunizm i svoboda lichnosti* (Moscow: Izdatel'stvo TsKVLKSM, "Molodaia gvardiia," 1960), p. 77.

[118] L. N. Kogan, "Ot truda sotsialisticheskovo k trudu kommunisticheskomu," *Voprosy filosofii*, 1960, no. 2, p. 16.

Thus the communist worker's physical exercise will be limited to repairing machines and to sports and recreation. There are considerable grounds for asking why this must be so, why the worker of communist society would not derive satisfaction from even heavy physical work, as do some workers of present-day society. At least part of this insistence may be ascribed to an academic, intellectual bias, which views all physical work as undignified, unworthy, and uninteresting. There is certainly no a priori reason why physical labor cannot be a genuine pleasure for some people, just as mental labor appeals to others.

The idea that work will become a pleasure also seems at odds with the idea that the working day will be shortened to between four and six hours per day. If work actually became a source of genuine pleasure for the citizens of communist society, there would seem to be no valid reason for such a drastic curtailment of working time. Fear of overproduction could not be the motive, since superabundance is a positive goal of communist society. Even with a somewhat longer working day, there would still be ample time for avocations and recreation. Since Marxism teaches that socially useful labor is one of man's supreme creative acts, there is more than a touch of irony in the Soviet insistence on reducing labor time to the minimum in the workers' ideal community.

The shortening of the working day also brings up the problem of increased leisure time. Soviet theory makes it quite clear that "contemporary production . . . demands the conscious, purposeful use of leisure,"[119] a theme that runs through all Soviet descriptions of the daily communist routine. It is considered ridiculous to expect that "under communism people will be occupied chiefly with amusements and entertainment, that precisely on this they will spend almost all their free time,"[120] or that communism will mean "pressing push-buttons on time and skipping off to free restaurants."[121] On the contrary, people will use their free time "to perfect their knowledge in the most varied fields . . . [and will] study science, production, and be occupied with inventions and rationalization [i.e., labor-saving schemes]."[122] They will also study art, literature, gymnastics and other sports, and will become habitual tourists.[123] Thus, aside from the enjoyment it pro-

[119] "At the Level of the New Tasks of Communist Construction," (editorial), *Voprosy filosofii*, 1959, no. 9 (*CDSP*, vol. 11, no. 46, p. 19).

[120] N. P. Kostin, "O svobodnom vremeni pri kommunizme," *Voprosy filosofii*, 1960, no. 5, p. 145.

[121] "Report of the Y.C.L. Committee and the Young Communist League's Tasks Stemming from the Decisions of the 22nd Party Congress—Report by Comrade S. P. Pavlov, First Secretary of the Y.C.L. Central Committee," *Pravda, Izvestiia*, April 17, 1962 (*CDSP*, vol. 14, no. 16, p. 3).

[122] Kostin, "O svobodnom vremeni pri kommunizme," p. 148.

[123] *Ibid.*, p. 150.

vides, leisure will have the function of improving each member of communist society by making him cultured, physically fit, and more experienced and knowledgeable. It will be pleasure with a purpose, and enjoyment which enriches the mind.

### Social Deviation and Social Restraints

Soviet theoreticians unanimously agree that there is no social basis for crime of any kind in communist society. Under socialism, crime is considered the result of a lag in social consciousness and the influence of bourgeois propaganda, but there is no question in the doctrine of such capitalist survivals tainting full communism. The influence of bourgeois life will be unimportant or even nonexistent, because the Soviet people will have raised their collective consciousness to the level where they will be impervious to such discredited values—and besides, it is optimistically predicted that the imperialist world will have shrunk by that time to the point where it will be unable to propagate its retrogressive ideas effectively. Without capitalist survivals, communist society will be essentially crime-free.

However, as Strumilin has regretfully put it, "No family is without its black sheep," and there is still some expectation that occasional antisocial acts will be encountered. These acts will not be of a serious nature, but will be indicative of a lack of proper social responsibility, and include failure to work correctly, disregard of living regulations, and improper attitudes toward other members of the collective. Communist society will be concerned with the entirety of a member's life and actions; there will be no private matters that are "none of society's business." Actually this total social involvement will not be a radical innovation for Soviet society but rather a continuation and strengthening of trends already evident at present. Take for example the following remarks which refer to the present, but which will be even more true of the future:

> Our society and our social organizations consider it their moral duty to demand an accounting from those who, shutting the door of their apartments, behave disgracefully, who loaf, drink, and in one way or another, make life unbearable for their families and neighbors. Society considers itself justified in interfering in the personal life of those who interfere in the life of society by creating scandals, speculating, becoming parasites or hooligans.[124]

---

[124] F. T. Mikhailov, "Kollektivizm—nravstvennyi printsip stroitelia kommunizma," *Voprosy filosofii*, 1962, no. 1, p. 142.

There is very little doubt, judging from present attitudes of this sort, that the "moral duty" to interfere in the personal lives of citizens will be even more compelling under communism. The obverse of the coin will be the inculcation in each citizen of a sense of responsibility to the collective for his every act, so that it will be felt by all that "one loafer is a disgrace to the brigade, one shirker a blot on everyone, one case of damage is harm for the entire collective."[125] To the degree that this attitude is shared by members of society, antisocial acts could only be the result of an honest mistake, and would be followed by quick confession, repentance, and perhaps remorse.

Because of the primacy of collective responsibility, the freedom of the individual receives a new definition under communism. It, too, is tied in with the communal spirit:

> We are for personal freedom, but not license. . . . Freedom is a definite relationship between people in which each sees his good in the well-being of all, and all are concerned with the well-being of each. And such an attitude inevitably assumes related responsibilities: man for the collective and the collective for man.[126]

This moral code can be reduced to the simple rule that man under communism is free to act for the good of the collective but is not free to act for his own benefit, if it runs counter to the good of the collective. Of course, there is an assumption in the doctrine—mostly a matter of faith rather than analysis—that the interests of the individual are always found in the collective interest, but there is room for considerable skepticism on this score.

The important point, however, is not whether a man's objective interests lie with the collective, but whether he *feels* that they do. When a man gives his life willingly for a cause he believes in, we may feel that this act is not in his own interests, but this will not deter the believer from his sacrifice. In the same manner, the crucial factor for communist self-discipline is a belief in the primacy of the collective interest, and this *belief* is yet another aspect of the all-important concept, *communist consciousness*. It is consciousness which will make the communist citizen a thoroughly integrated member of the collective, submerging his personal, ego-centered desires in the interests of group solidarity. Therefore, the doctrinal precept that crime, will be eliminated rests not only on the assumption that negative influences and survivals of the past will be extirpated but also on the expectation that communist consciousness will eliminate the individual's egocentric drives and make

---

[125] *Izmenenie klassovoi struktury*, p. 179.
[126] Shakhnazarov, *Kommunizm i svoboda lichnosti*, p. 99.

him a totally "social animal." That nothing less would be acceptable is made quite clear by one theoretician:

> Man will become absolutely free in his actions insofar as he deeply understands the confluence of his personal interests with social interests, and *neither sees nor represents any other possible manifestation of personal freedom than in acts which are in harmony with the good of his comrades, the collective, and all society.*[127]

Assuming, as does the doctrine, that such men will inhabit communist society, it will not need the usual institutions to prevent crime, enforce the laws, apprehend, and possibly punish the criminal. Occasionally an imperfectly socialized individual may turn up and commit an anti-social act or behave generally in a manner which calls down on his head the opprobrium of society, but such cases can be handled by society itself through the creation of *ad hoc* investigating committees or courts.[128] Permanent institutions will not be required because good social conduct will become a "habit" of each individual, thoroughly indoctrinated by years of training in boarding schools, isolated from all negative influences. If an individual commits an antisocial act, it will indicate a breakdown or deficiency in the education which he received, and such deficiencies, we may presume, will be speedily corrected along scientific lines.

Despite all these factors preventing even the slightest infringement of communist norms, Soviet theoreticians still expect occasional exceptions to the norm-abiding rule. Soviet doctrine has repeatedly quoted with approval the formula, "He who does not work shall not eat." This rule, which would be applied only to those who were physically able but unwilling to work, gives some idea of the formidable weapons which communist society will have at its disposal in dealing with social deviants. The closely-knit communities of communism will be able to locate the anti-social individual without difficulty because he will not be able to "shut the door of his apartment" and retreat to an area of his life that is "strictly private." He will be constantly involved in public life, and any attempt to withdraw into solitude would be immediately noticed and would become a matter of fraternal concern to the other members of the collective. Furthermore, there is a strong indication in present doctrine that the future collective will be intimately and legitimately concerned with each member's *attitudes*, as well as his actions. Since major, and even minor, crimes will have disappeared, society will be able to turn its attention to correcting slight deviations from the

---

[127] *Ibid.*, p. 95. (Emphasis mine.)
[128] See Grigor'ev, *Obshchestvennaia vlast'*, p. 59.

norm in daily conduct. And the greatest weapon that society will have in making these corrections will be the powerful force of *united public opinion*, bolstered by the elimination of *all* avenues of individual escape into solitude. The point is stated quite succinctly in the following passage:

> Society cannot exist without conscious discipline and if someone does not wish to be subject to such discipline, *he must stand outside of society.* Social opinion and the court of the collective—this is the force which will successfully support social relationships and will restrain violators of social order.[129]

To "stand outside" the collective under communism is to be completely ostracized, a terrifying prospect for anyone reared in such a totally integrated collective. Such measures, however, would probably be utilized only in extreme cases. In less serious instances, the influence of public opinion would be brought to bear on the individual, exerting pressure in the direction of the straight and narrow path. The emphasis would definitely be on rehabilitation rather than punishment, and this, in itself, is quite a commendable approach to the problem of social deviancy. However, there would obviously be such strong pressures on the individual for total conformity that individual character traits might well be buried under an avalanche of "communist norms." It must be kept in mind that the moral code of communism is designed for those who possess idealized, harmonious personalities, and anyone with something less than an ideal personality will certainly fall short in some respects. This suggests that all non-ideal members of society would be under continuous pressure from the collective to reform some aspect of their habitual conduct. One need hardly doubt the oft-repeated Soviet assertion that such social pressure exerts a powerful influence over the individual miscreant. Even under present Soviet conditions in which this force is not nearly as strong as is expected in the future, Soviet sources often report that "many law violators prefer to undergo punishment in a state court rather than appear in a rather unpretty light before the members of their collective."[130] In comparing the current effectiveness of social pressure and governmental punishment through the people's courts, another Soviet theorist writes:

> Social influence, the influence of the collective in which a man works, lives, and studies, possesses great educational power . . . significantly more

---

[129] Shakhnazarov, *Kommunizm i svoboda lichnosti*, p. 61. (Emphasis mine.)

[130] A. F. Kleinman and P. E. Orlovskii, "Rassmotrenie tovarishcheskimi sudami grazhdansko-pravovykh sporov," in *Sovetskoe gosudarstvo i obshchestvennost' v usloviiakh razvërnutovo stroitel'stva kommunizma*, ed. N. G. Aleksandrov (Moscow: Izdatel'stvo Moskovskovo Universiteta, 1962), p. 428.

power than the use of state compulsory measures. . . . The power and advantage of social influence consists in that it is not exhausted by some sort of single [non-recurring] action, but places a man under the permanent control of his environment, manifesting continuous influence over him up to the point of complete correction of his errors.[131]

Under communist conditions, such "permanent control" would surely be felt even more keenly by the individual transgressor and would be even more pervasive in all areas of social life. Since "social probation" and "public censure" will be sufficient to rehabilitate the miscreant, theorists predict that imprisonment will not be necessary.[132] Mere punishment has no place in a perfect society, because it does not necessarily restore the transgressor to the state of perfection theoretically shared by the other members of society. In order for society to be truly perfect, each minor infraction of its rules must end with the guilty party fully reformed, his moral values once again in harmony with the moral code of the collective.

In such a society, the nonconformist would be constantly vulnerable to the benevolent curiosity of the busybody and the morally self-righteous. But, in all the writings on the communist society over the past decade, the Soviet theorists have never suggested that some sort of institutional safeguards for the nonconformist might be necessary or even desirable. The absence of such safeguards does not necessarily mean that nonconformity will be considered antisocial. However, if we consider the significance of the Soviet concept of consciousness, the general characteristics of the predicted communist society, and the intolerance of present-day Soviet society towards nonconformists, we are left with the rather strong indication that conformity in basic attitudes and values, if not in appearance and opinions on topical matters, will be the rule of communism.

Although rehabilitation of the wrongdoer has been considered in present doctrine, the opposite question of social rewards for excellence has not received a great deal of attention. Since material rewards will be based on needs rather than deeds, the extra benefits of outstanding service will probably be restricted to social approbation. Along these lines, one theoretician mentions the "higher principle of encouraging personal talents and service" which will be "social recognition and respect."[133] Assuming that such exceptional citizens will be supremely *conscious* individuals, there would hardly seem to be a need for institu-

---

[131] A. Sakharov, "Rol' obshchestvennosti v ukreplenii sovetskovo pravoporiadka i zakonnosti," in *Nekotorye problemy teorii i praktiki stroitel'stva kommunizma* (Moscow: Voennoe izdatel'stvo ministerstva oborony Soiuza SSR, 1961), p. 267.

[132] Grigor'ev, *Obshchestvennaia vlast'*, p. 54.

[133] Karapetian, "Politicheskaia organizatsiia," p. 300.

tionalizing rewards for meritorious service beyond this recognition. For such a person, reward will lie in the knowledge that his acts have benefited society.

### A Picture of Town and Country

The Soviet theorists have been most reticent in portraying the details of the physical picture of communist society. Part of this reticence is based on the idea that the present historical stage does not yield enough "concrete data" for such predictions, part on the understandable reluctance of Soviet theoreticians to climb too far out on a still untested doctrinal limb. Although nothing authoritative and detailed has yet been written, a few individual speculations have been published which sketch the visage of communist society in reasonable outline.

The most important social principle of communism will be collectivism, and this principle will find expression in the physical plan of society. There is general acceptance of the idea that the physical layout of society must foster and encourage collective ties, interdependence, and constant and close interrelation of the members of the society. It is agreed that the basic organizational building block of society will be the commune with several thousand members and a rather self-sufficient network of social services and facilities.

It is also agreed that citizens will rarely use individual residences— perhaps only for vacations in isolated areas—and instead will live in various forms of apartment dwellings, since if individual homes were required, "the need for housing would grow to colossal proportions."[134] Furthermore, apartment living will better condition the citizen to the requirements of collectivism, in contrast to the individualism fostered by the reigning principle of bourgeois morality, "My house is my fortress." In other words, houses, because of their relative physical isolation and their tendency to encourage "private property psychology," are considered detrimental to the values of communist society. "Togetherness" will apparently be cultivated by the use of large complexes of interconnected apartment houses, with large indoor and outdoor areas designated for public functions.

Looking first at the individual apartment houses and the living quarters within, we see that the requirements for living space per communist person "will not grow by very much in comparison with present accepted sanitary norms."[135] Within the apartment, everything will be

[134] Sakov, *Osnovnoi printsip kommunizma*, p. 37.
[135] *Ibid.* The present standard norm is nine square meters per person. Sakov envisions the communist norm as fifteen to twenty square meters.

"beautiful, simple, convenient, without excesses," and furnishings will conform to the general rule that "in the apartment or room it is best to place only those pieces of furniture which are actually indispensable."[136] There will be air conditioning and machinery to take care of household chores. It is also predicted in one place that "permanent" plastic furniture will be used and that a family will be able to rearrange its assigned living space according to its particular requirements because of movable interior walls.[137] According to one speculation, there will be two types of accommodations: those for single people and for two people living together, and those for families (assuming that the children will still live with the parents). The first type of accommodation will be in "a hotel-type house" within which many of the daily services such as cleaning and laundry will be provided. Single young people will generally live in a dormitory variant of this "hotel-type" structure, while couples and older single persons will occupy a similar structure containing one- and two-room apartments.[138]

One designer claims that "project norms for living quarters that will be built after 1981 envision the discontinuation of 'little' one- and two-room apartments and the introduction of six-room apartments."[139] He provides a plan of this "apartment of the future" (see figure 1) which includes movable partitions for flexible use of the interior space, division of the space into "fully transformable, partly transformable, and stable zones," and such exotic equipment as a "mini-computer" and a "video-telephone."

We have several different portraits of the communist family commune, none of them official but all rather interesting. The following picture is presented by Strumilin, and is based upon the assumption that parents and children will, as a rule, live separately:

> In each of the palace communes with a floor space of up to 40,000 square meters all the service facilities can be located on the ground floor—the service bureau, medical office, post office, barbershop, laundry, etc., while the remaining floors could be occupied by the members of the commune. One wing of the second floor, let us say, could be used for the children's apartments. The other wing could be tenanted by the aged in need of special care and by service personnel. The third floor could consist of two- to three-room flats for married people; and the fourth floor could be made

136 M. I. Lifanov, *O byte pri kommunizme* (Moscow: Gospolitizdat, 1961), p. 12. This work is identical to the chapter entitled "Krasota novovo byta," in *O kommunizme.*

137 *Ibid.*, pp. 10, 18.

138 See A. Peremyslov, *Dom budushchevo* (Moscow: Gospolitizdat, 1962), p. 70.

139 Ya. E. Dikhter, "Kvartira budushchevo sozdaetsia segodnia," *Gorodskoe khoziaistvo moskvy,* 1974, no. 7, p. 15.

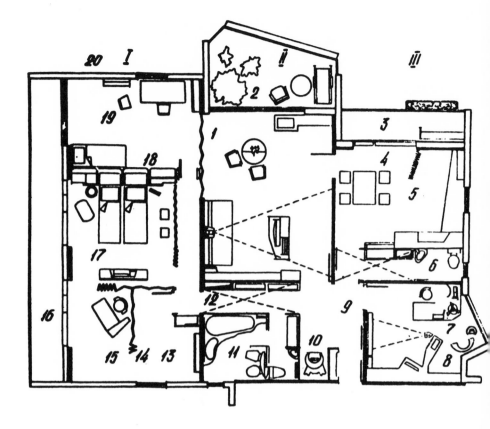

FIGURE 1. PROPOSED PLAN OF THE APARTMENT OF THE FUTURE

Zones:  I. fully transformable
II. stabilized plan
III. partly transformable

1. common room
2. garden patio
3. dining patio
4. dining area
5. transformable kitchen with all-purpose automatic appliance combination
6. additional lavatory
7–8. study with mini-computer, video-telephone, projector and other equipment
9. entrance vestibule
10. apartment console with complex apparatus for all domestic functions

11. bathroom with children's section and clothes washing-drying machine
12. air-conditioning equipment
13. room for physical exercise
14. movable partitions
15. room for young schoolchild
16. picture windows and balcony door
17. master bedroom
18. storage area
19. room for older schoolchild
20. energy source (permitting connection of appliances at any point on perimeter of walls)

up of separate rooms for working youth, students, and single people in general. According to present calculations every person can be provided with 16 to 18 square meters of living space [approximately equivalent to a twelve-by-twelve-foot room] within twenty years, and this is exclusive of floor space needed for the public dining rooms, reading rooms and other premises (for instance, the children's playroom, and the rooms for musical, choral and other amateur art activities or sports). From 8000 to 10,000 square meters of floor space may be made available for these purposes on every floor.[140]

Somewhat more authoritative, perhaps, is the proposal of the planning agency for the Moscow district (*Mosoblproekt*) which calls for "a social center, joined with a 14-story section and two eight-story buildings of the hotel type, plus several separately situated four-story nursery-kindergarten buildings and a building with apartments for the elderly."[141] The Institute of Public Buildings, under G. A. Gradov, has proposed the following model of the "home of the future":

In the primary residential group there will be 12-story buildings of the hotel type, a two-story public sector and a children's nursery and a kindergarten. All three structures will constitute a single whole.

Four types of apartment are planned on each floor of the residential buildings: one-room for one or two people, two-room for two people, and three-room. Furthermore, the two-room apartments will comprise 60 percent of the total number of apartments in the building. The entire building will house almost 1200 persons.

The apartments will be remarkably well-equipped. It is anticipated that everything will be included in them that is needed for the very best organization of daily life. Shelved room dividers will replace much of our customary furniture of today. In the bedrooms there will be convertible beds. This will make it possible to convert a bedroom into a room for rest and relaxation as desired and without particular effort. There will be no kitchens. A small electrical appliance will make possible the occasional preparation of food. A diversified set of equipment—radio-television console, electrical household appliances and many others—guarantee all conveniences to the family.

Balconies will acquire great significance. They will be required for each apartment, to join the residence with nature, with fresh air and sunshine. On the balcony, which will be enlarged, it will be possible to place a light couch, a magazine rack, a folding armchair and other compact furniture. In several residential groups it is proposed to arrange a patio. The patio will be separated from the room by a movable glass partition.

In the residential building a high-speed elevator is planned.

In the center of the lobby, behind an open counter will be the service

140 Strumilin, "Communism and the Workers' Daily Life," p. 17.
141 Peremyslov, *Dom budushchevo*, p. 79.

bureau. On both sides of the corridor extending from the building entrance to the elevators, there will be an amateur crafts shop, photographic laboratory, carriage shop, reception points for laundry and repair of footwear, a cafe with 25 seats, a buffet counter and a counter for taking out prepared food to the apartments. Here is located the electrical kitchen.

The entire second floor of the public sector is given over to the dining hall, which can simultaneously accommodate 225 diners. In the evening, the hall can be used for club activities.

The residential building is connected by heated, glass-enclosed passageways to the nursery and kindergarten arranged for the continuous occupancy of the children. It is assumed that 60 percent of all children of nursery age and 80 percent of all pre-school age children will attend nursery and kindergarten. The remaining children will be cared for by parents or elderly relatives.

The nursery-kindergarten will consist of 12 one-story buildings, connected by corridors. Each group will be established in a separate building. Near them will be well-planted plots. It is expected that an area for games, a sleeping veranda, a cloak-room and conveniences will be included in the building. A large game room for all groups will be located on the second floor of the central section.[142]

In Gradov's project, these so-called primary residential groups are included, along with boarding schools, a home for the elderly, and a park and social center, including a summer theatre and stadium, in a unit known as a *micro-raion*. The next larger unit, the "dwelling *raion*," is composed of four such *micro-raions*, plus a "cultural-educational complex," a stadium, a trade center, a hospital and clinic, a school for ninth to eleventh grades, a factory-kitchen, laundry, and automobile rental point. There will be some twenty residential groups of the type described in each dwelling *raion*.

A basically similar design has been offered by a group of architect-planners at Moscow University headed by Alexei Gutnov. The Gutnov group envisions a decentralized pattern of living, based on relatively self-contained nuclei called New Units of Settlement (NUS), surrounded by green areas.[143] Each NUS will accommodate 100,000 to 200,000 people living in high-rise buildings (from fifteen to seventeen stories) containing apartments of three basic designs: one for single individuals (with or without children), one for couples (with or without children), and one for two generations of couples (grandparents, parents, and children). The NUS would be composed of smaller, residential nuclei called "primary residential complexes," and these would be designed to

---

[142] *Ibid.*, pp. 82–83.
[143] Alexei Gutnov, A. Baburov, G. Djumenton, S. Kharitonova, I. Lezava, S. Sadovskii, *The Ideal Communist City*, trans. Renee Nen Watkins (New York: George Braziller, 1968). Figure 2 is reproduced courtesy of I Press.

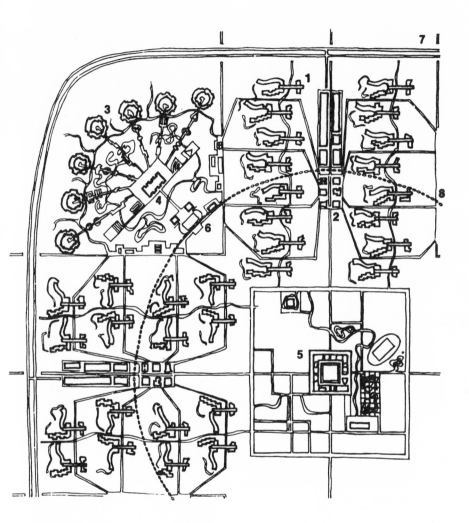

FIGURE 2. PROPOSED PLAN OF A NEW UNIT OF SETTLEMENT

1. primary residential units
2. community center for the sector
3. school community complex
4. academic center
5. community center of NUS
6. sports complex
7. highway
8. rapid transport above pedestrian level

create a feeling of functional unity in all the residential and service areas. The residential complex would contain about 1,600 to 1,700 people and would include not only apartment houses but service facilities for "articles of daily use [and] a movie theatre, pharmacy, swimming pool, ball park, local administration offices, cafe, restaurant" and an elementary school.[144] Several residential complexes are linked together with the next larger unit, the "residential sector" which includes a secondary school within easy walking distance, in addition to preschool and primary school facilities, a public transportation terminal and shopping center, and even some light industry "if desirable" in a particular instance. The total population of the sector would be about 20,000 to 35,000 people. Rapid transit would be provided to bring people to and from the industrial complex and the research complex ("a combination of laboratories, experimental projects in animal and plant cultivation, classrooms, libraries, and buildings for administrative personnel and central computers"),[145] which will be separated from the NUS. The emphasis of this plan is on avoiding the past consequences of urbanization and providing an environment which combines the advantages of urban life with the easy and constant access to nature that has heretofore been obtainable only in rural settings. The concentration of people in small units permits the development of community spirit and convenient use of service facilities, and the nuclear building-block design of the NUS allows the inclusion of many neighboring green belts in the plan.

Although these visions of the future contrast rather starkly with many features of present Soviet reality, they hardly seem so magnificently affluent when viewed from the West, particularly the United States. Furthermore, even in terms of present Soviet material conditions, the leap to communism does not seem quite so great as the previous leap from underdeveloped monarchy to superpowerful industrial state in less than forty years.

Some of the new prefabricated apartment buildings being built in the "suburban" areas of large cities in the Soviet Union have been hailed as prototypes of communist architecture, yet to a Western eye they do not seem particularly spectacular. The Soviets, nevertheless, have occasionally let their imagination run rather far afield with visions of the future city, as in the following:

> Imagine, reader, that we are walking with you down one of the streets of the future city. There are wide, well-lit thoroughfares which nowhere cross each other at the same level; hurrying automobiles, resembling

144 *Ibid.*, p. 75.
145 *Ibid.*, p. 27.

rockets, pass by us at great speed. You have noticed that they do not raise any dust, for the streets are absolutely clean; a system of drawing off dirt by suction, built directly into the roadway, solves this problem rather well. Look how freely the great buildings are placed amidst gardens and parks. Only in a section preserved from the old city like a museum rarity does there remain a few blocks of closely bunched houses. . . .

The city freely and deeply breathes with each part of its great lungs, for there is not a single corner which does not receive plenty of fresh air and life-giving sunshine.

You see around you not only the grandeur of the city and of nature, but, what is most important, the splendid people, with traits of high nobility and good breeding, proud working people of the new society, of the new life.[146]

This architect's poetic description of the future city makes it seem more like a romantic idealization of New York City than Moscow:

The city rises vaguely over gardens, grows to the sky. Facades with windows—each half-way to the heavens—dressed in white with speckles of gold or old silver in synthetic material. They blaze in the sun, shine in the moonlight. And early in the autumn evening, when the moon has not yet risen, quiet glimmers radiate and the buildings seem to be covered with gold leaves. And here we walk along the main thoroughfare—to the noise of the crowd, music, automobiles. . . . The architects have built the city out of contrasts. The towers are touched by the clouds, but below the halls embrace the earth. When the lights are turned on, the silhouette of the city reminds one of mountains. And even closer to the shape of mountains will it be at daybreak.[147]

Of course, none of this is authoritative; it merely indicates the rather wide range of physical images which exist in the minds of various present-day Soviet thinkers. There is a great difference between the grandiose design of this last bit of poetry and the prosaic austerity of Gradov's proposal.

Although there is a paucity of materials from which to draw conclusions, it is possible to surmise that there already exists a tendency toward deemphasizing the personal living quarters of the communist citizen while glorifying all types of public buildings and facilities. The things which people have in common will apparently be made grandiose, while the things they acquire individually will apparently be reduced to only those items that are "actually indispensable." This emphasis symbolizes the expectation that the communist citizen will spend a great deal more time in public pursuits, both at work and at play, than in domestic seclusion.

[146] Lifanov, *O byte pri kommunizme*, p. 3.
[147] *Ibid.*, p. 6.

In the countryside the picture will be similar. The rural settlement will offer most, if not all, of the advantages of city life, especially in terms of creature comforts. A model of the future *sovkhoz* settlement was selected from nineteen entries in a competition among seven Moscow research and planning institutes. It is depicted as follows:

> Along both sides of a wide boulevard, blocks of four-story, solidly constructed buildings stretch out. Within are apartments with all conveniences, of the kind that could only be imagined in a city. The Palace of Culture and a hotel-type residence with apartments for youths and single persons are located in the central square. Here will be the office of the *sovkhoz*, the settlement soviet, a polyclinic, communications department, social services combine and stores. Not far away, the boarding school for children of all sections of the *sovkhoz* will be built.[148]

The multi-apartment dwelling is expected to eliminate the separate family as the basic unit of rural society and draw the members of the commune into the larger collective.[149] It is generally agreed that "the future village should resemble a city in the facilities it offers," but at the same time it must "retain all the advantages of rural life" and must not "abandon nature for the skies" by building many-storied apartment houses.[150] It is expected that a certain degree of industrialization will occur in the countryside, increasing the efficiency of those industries closely connected to agriculture:

> In the country, industry will be developed all the more intensively, especially the processing of agricultural products, and also furniture, fabrics, etc. This will make it possible for people to be occupied with productive work the entire year—in summer, in the fields and gardens, and in winter, in the factories.[151]

Whether in the "agrotown" or in the city, there is no doubt that the communist citizen will be freed of all irksome household chores through the use of the multi-faceted social service organization. The rationale behind this is made quite clear in the following:

> Let us imagine a consumer setting off to the store for some goods, receiving all of his needs without charge and being given, in addition, the best quality merchandise. Very good. But then if he must waste several hours of his precious time preparing dinner and washing dishes and then occupy

[148] Peremyslov, *Dom budushchevo*, p. 102.

[149] See N. A. Aitov, "Stiranie razlichii mezhdu krest'ianstvom i rabochim klassom v bytu i kul'ture v period razvërnutovo stroitel'stva kommunizma," *Voprosy filosofii*, 1961, no. 12, p. 107.

[150] "How Should Collective Farm Villages Be Built?" *Izvestiia*, April 26, 1959 (*CDSP*, vol. 11, no. 17, p. 7).

[151] Peremyslov, *Dom budushchevo*, p. 100.

himself with scrubbing and other domestic matters, what sort of freedom does he have?

No, under communism people will not spend their time so aimlessly. A social method of satisfying social needs for nourishment and clean living quarters—this is the solution.[152]

The future citizen will be able to avail himself of a wide variety of other services in addition to social feeding and cleaning establishments, most of them not totally new but considerably expanded, and all free of charge. These include "clubs, concert halls, theatres . . . rest homes, sanatoria, socially [owned] summer homes and pioneer camps," in addition to "boarding homes . . . tourist and fishing camps, swimming and skiing stations" to be built in "picturesque suburban locations."[153] Another writer includes in this list "public dacha zones of rest with an extensive network of suburban boarding houses, restaurants, sports installations, gardens . . . [and] public garages fully supplied with up-to-date passenger cars for [temporary] personal use."[154] The communist citizen will thus be surrounded by socially provided services which will enable him to conduct his life purposefully, without becoming encumbered by the petty, mundane details of life that waste so much of the present Soviet citizen's time.

## World-Wide Communism

According to theory, communism will not be merely a phenomenon of the present Soviet Union or the "socialist camp" but a system that will eventually bind together all peoples of the world. There has never been any authoritative word on the exact form of international organization for world-wide communism, but Soviet writers generally assume that there will be some sort of world federal government, mainly concerned with problems of economic coordination. Strumilin predicts that this federation will be based on the communes:

Acting jointly as producers and consumers, the communes will be linked by a single centralized plan of action on an ascending scale—a regional, national and international scale of a world federation of countries and peoples. Such a federation is conceived by Marxists as a purely economic, non-governmental organization . . . based on the principle of democratic centralism.[155]

[152] Shakhnazarov, *Kommunizm i svoboda lichnosti*, p. 49.
[153] Sakov, *Osnovnoi printsip kommunizma*, p. 41.
[154] Ts. Stepanian, "Communism and Property," *Oktiabr'*, 1960, no. 9 (*CDSP*, vol. 12, no. 42, p. 19).
[155] Strumilin, "Communism and the Workers' Daily Life," p. 14.

Chesnokov, on the other hand, sees the future world government as arising out of some form of the present soviets: "In order to guarantee planning and coordination of all social life on a world-wide scale, a coordinating organ will be used—the Universal Soviet of Communist Society, selected at a world-wide session."[156] A third variation on this theme is proposed by Grigor'ev using the present C.M.E.A. (Council of Mutual Economic Aid) as the model for future international organization.[157]

There is widespread appreciation of the difficulty of removing national differences in culture and language, even after class differences have been eradicated forever. In the words of one Soviet writer:

> In the course of building communism the full unity of nationalities will be achieved. However, even after communism has fundamentally been built, the merger of nationalities will still not occur. This is a matter for the more distant future. . . . The eradication of national differences, particularly differences in language, is a significantly more prolonged process than the elimination of class differences.[158]

Even after politics as a means of expressing national relations and states as the instruments for this expression have both withered away, there will still be a need for some sort of regulation of relations between nations, although these relations "will lose their class-based, political imprint and will be governed by the principle of communist internationalism."[159] Nevertheless, the large scale of future undertakings (warming Antarctica has been suggested) will require the cooperation of many nations, and thus the subjugation of local to more central authorities.[160]

Eventually a single world culture and language will emerge as a result of several factors.

> In the world-wide communist system, all nations will be closely tied together by a single system of social ownership of the means of production, communist division of labor, specialization and cooperation of production, a single system of all types of transportation (including interplanetary communications), a single energy system and system of cultural institutions.[161]

---

[156] Chesnokov, *Ot gosudarstvennosti*, p. 21.

[157] Grigor'ev, *Obshchestvennaia vlast'*, p. 65.

[158] Platkovskii, "Formirovanie kommunisticheskikh obshchestvennykh otnoshenii," p. 35.

[159] Nikolaev, "O razvitii sotsialisticheskoi gosudarstvennosti," p. 26.

[160] *Ibid.*, p. 64.

[161] M. D. Kammari, "Stroitel'stvo kommunizma i dal'neishee sblizhenie natsii v SSSR," *Voprosy filosofii*, 1961, no. 9, p. 39.

Even with all these factors stimulating the assimilation of all peoples into a world-wide culture, some differences will apparently remain, for "communism does not at all mean the eradication of absolutely all the particular characteristics of populations inhabiting different parts of the earth, including those characteristics of daily life resulting from geographic surroundings."[162]

We are thus left with the rather reasonable picture—if we accept the basic doctrinal assumptions—of peoples being drawn together through the increasing use of modern communications and transportation, in addition to a shared set of basic (communist) values. Much of this theory is presented with reference to the Soviet experience as a multinational state, where gradual assimilation of the minority nationalities has been an established policy for many years. The mere technological possibility of communications between peoples does not, of course, assure an increase in mutual understanding or assimilation, but this may well be the long term effect of modern communications efficiency.[163]

Leaving aside the question of whether a single, universal culture is desirable, there is certainly little ground for disputing the statement that "one of the most important prerequisites for the future complete joining of nationalities is the creation of a single universal language as a means of communication between peoples."[164] One Soviet writer has foreseen two possible methods of developing this world language. One is the selection of an existing language already used internationally. This language, freely selected by all nations, would then be taught in all the schools and employed in the press, on the radio, and at international conferences. In time it would be augmented through use until it had adopted much of the richness of other popular languages. The other possibility would be a synthesis of all essentials in existing languages, not as in past unsuccessful attempts, but "based on a scientific, Marxist-Leninist synthesis of everything valuable in existing national languages."[165] Such a language would naturally be superior to any existing language, for it would be created scientifically rather than spontaneously.

In any case, the Soviet theorists have been careful to point out that the process of merging nationalities is a prolonged one, and that it will be brought about by objective historical forces rather than the subjective desires of one or another nation or group. Since most of this pro-

[162] *Ibid.*, p. 41.
[163] See on this point Karl W. Deutsch, *Nationalism and Social Communication* (New York: The Technology Press of The Massachusetts Institute of Technology and John Wiley & Sons, Inc., 1953), pp. 70–74.
[164] Kammari, "Stroitel'stvo kommunizma," p. 41.
[165] *Ibid.*

cess will take place during the period of full communism, when other basic social changes will already have occurred, the distinction of nationality will apparently remain as the last, dying, distinguishable mark of an otherwise homogeneous world population.

### Beyond Communism

There has been scant attention paid to the admitted fact that history will not stop on the glorious day when communism finally arrives. Just as communism developed out of socialism, something must develop from communism, even if only a refinement or a modification of the existing perfection. One obvious stimulus for this development will be the rapid pace of technological innovation. Just as technology, or rather the "forces of production," made capitalism a fetter on further progress, a new technology could conceivably make communism outmoded and ready for fundamental change. Present Soviet theory, however, rules out any such basic change in the communist social structure. It contends that "communism is a social-economic formation that knows no limit in its development [but] cannot be changed into any other formation with another economic basis."[166] The basic form of communist society is eternal, regardless of the directions in which future developments carry mankind. Within the basic shell of the communist structure, however, there will be constant change, for this is the essence of Marxism, even as it is distilled in present Soviet theory. *Eternal, but eternally changing communism* is the prospect offered by present doctrine. In the words of one of its proponents:

> Communism will develop continuously, unendingly. History cannot become petrified and cease. Development along an ascending line will continue. There can be no end to it. Material is eternal; eternal is its movement, its change, and eternal are the laws of this change. Not one of the characteristics of matter can be lost forever. This is why there will be no end to social development under communism.[167]

[166] N. D. Kolesov and K. I. Kolesova, "O razvitii i sblizhenii dvukh form sotsialisticheskoi sobstvennosti," *Voprosy filosofii*, 1960, no. 1, p. 20.
[167] Nikitin, *Chto takoe kommunizm*, p. 123.

# CHAPTER IV THE NEW COMMUNIST MAN

A perfect society deserves to be peopled by perfect men. Indeed, a perfect society requires perfect men, or at least men molded to the image of perfection which society demands. They must hold high the values which society supports, reject the values which society attacks, learn and practice a pattern of conduct of which society approves. In short, they must be perfect in their conformity to society's definition of perfection. There are as many perfect societies as there are different moral codes and conflicting ideas of right and wrong; and there are just as many varieties of ideal human beings.

One of the basic problems of all ideal societies is that they require a population composed entirely of model citizens. This is not terribly important when the ideal society is offered as an abstraction, a moral lesson, or an escape into fantasy, but when it is offered as a practical, realizable goal of an existing society, it becomes both the central problem and the crucial prerequisite.

It is not at all unfair to say that the entire success or failure of the attempt to create a particular type of ideal society in the Soviet Union in the foreseeable future rests squarely on the outcome of the drive to refashion the present Soviet citizen into the idealized model citizen of communist society. The Soviet theorists are quite aware of this, and they have faced the fact that "communist society is inconceivable without a new type of man and without a new morality."[1]

This new type of man, the "new communist man," represents, in effect, a new psychological species with a personality structure that has been clearly defined and elaborated by present Soviet theory. This theory derives from the "materialist thesis that the opinions of man change according to the influence of the conditions under which he

---

[1] I. Kon, "Communism: The Moral Factor," *New Times*, 1959, no. 16, p. 5.

lives."[2] This "materialist thesis," therefore, establishes the society as the given condition, with man's personality as the dependent variable reflecting his social environment. In order to change man's personality structure, one need only change the "objective conditions" under which he lives.[3] This, of course, gives the social engineering bent of Soviet theory unlimited horizons for manipulation of the individual personality, and the opportunity has not been overlooked. It also tends to downgrade the importance of the individual in relation to society. The individual's obligations and responsibilities to society are emphasized, while his importance, independent of society, is denied. In fact, the very possibility of his existence outside of society is questioned. For Soviet theoreticians, man is above all else a social animal. In the words of one Soviet writer:

> Man's personality must be considered in its unbroken connection with social relations which limit its existence and form their basis for its acts. . . . Man can not be considered outside of the concrete social relations of his epoch, outside of his social environment, unrelated to the character of his activities.[4]

Since man is considered a product of his environment, the most common non-Marxist criticism of the communist society, that it opposes "human nature," is considered invalid by Soviet theoreticians. They answer that there is no eternal human nature, that bourgeois critics are thinking in terms of bourgeois human nature where the rule is "Man is a wolf to man." Communist society, they affirm, will contain within it the social conditions for the "free flowering of the human personality," and it will be the *first* society in man's history able to do this.

The human personality can only reach its fullest potential, however, when society is free of all impediments to individual development. In the prevailing Soviet view, individual freedom can only be achieved

---

[2] K. V. Moroz, *Dialekticheskii materializm—ideinoe oruzhie bor'by za kommunizm* (Moscow: Izdatel'stvo VPSh i AON pri TsK KPSS, 1960), p. 44.

[3] For an explicit statement of this idea, see V. P. Tugarinov, "Kommunizm i lichnost'," *Voprosy filosofii*, 1962, no. 6, p. 14. These basic ideas are not really new to Soviet psychology. The concept of the "New Soviet Man" has been an established pillar of Soviet psychology for many years, as is clearly shown in Raymond A. Bauer, *The New Man in Soviet Psychology* (Cambridge: Harvard University Press, 1959). See especially pages 132–150.

[4] V. Zh. Kelle, *Kommunizm i gumanizm* (Moscow: Izdatel'stvo "Znanie," Vsesoiuznovo obshchestva po rasprostraneniiu politicheskikh i nauchnykh znanii, 1962), p. 13. Khrushchev asserted the same basic idea at the Twenty-first Party Congress in characteristically simple language (*CDSP*, vol. 11, no. 3, pp. 7–8): "Man is a social being; his life is inconceivable outside the group, in isolation from the society to which he is bound by the most diverse relationships."

through integration with society, for "freedom is the product of historical development and individual freedom can have no meaning outside
of society, isolated from society, without ties to society."[5] Under communism, society *gives* the individual his freedom: he need not win his
freedom *from* a society in which there is no fundamental conflict between the individual and society as a whole. But if all societies have
rules and regulations, it is only under communism that society pre-
scribes a specific code of conduct and a rigid set of values encompassing
one's entire outlook on life. The freedom to be different, eccentric,
contrary, or just plain cantankerous is nowhere mentioned. We find,
instead, a purely economic statement of freedom, reminiscent of Frank-
lin D. Roosevelt's "freedom from want":

> Freedom under communism is raised to a qualitatively new level. If under
> socialism it meant fundamentally freedom from exploitation, then under
> communism it means freedom from personal material cares. . . . Together
> with the realization of full freedom of the personality there arises the
> responsibility [of the individual personality] before society for its actions.
> Freedom without obligations and responsibility is anarchy.[6]

That this is not a sound definition of freedom is unquestionable. In a
sense, it offers the security of collective nurture as a substitute for
individual freedom of choice,[7] and it goes so far as to offer it as an
antidote to man's disquieting consciousness of his own mortality:

> Isn't it actually tragic that man should be conscious of his own death?
>     Yes, if the man does not tie in his life with the realization of social
> goals, if he becomes immersed in himself. No, if the man thoroughly gives
> himself to social matters, if he feels himself a part of a collective, if he
> sees his own happiness as the struggle for the happiness of the people.[8]

Soviet theoreticians deny that communist morality is opposed to individuality, claiming that "the formation of deep, organized ties between the personality and the collective as an affirmation of comradely
cooperation does not at all signify drowning the personality in the
collective" and that "the collective itself is interested in the development of individuality."[9] This claim cannot be taken literally, however,

---

[5] Kelle, p. 21.

[6] Tugarinov, "Kommunizm i lichnost'," p. 18.

[7] Ironically enough, this tendency in other contexts was analyzed with great
insight in Erich Fromm, *Escape from Freedom* (New York: Farrar & Rinehart,
Inc., 1941), a book that is very popular in the Soviet Union as an indictment of
the noncommunist world.

[8] Kelle, *Kommunizm i gumanizm*, p. 17.

[9] *Ibid.*, p. 19.

for the entire theory of the communist personality is one in which group interests become primary and personal interests are seen only in terms of group goals.

In any case, communist morality will become a "habit" for the new communist man. The rules of daily living will apparently remain unchanged for many centuries of communism, so instinctive observance of them will be only a matter of time. This is made clear by the statement that "people gradually will become accustomed to the observation of elementary rules, known for centuries, repeated for millenia."[10] The result of this constant repetition will be that "each worker of communist society will have an internal need to discharge [his] obligations, for this will seem to him, with all his inherent consciousness and honesty, as though it were his own law."[11] The new communist man will have totally internalized the values of his society, and will be a new version of the "inner directed" personality. This is a process that is present in any society, of course, but here again the difference lies in the scope of the social rules and values internalized, which will go far beyond those of previous societies.[12]

Communist morality, the moral code of the new communist man, has a number of components. Part of it, perhaps the chief part, is communist consciousness, generally taken to mean an understanding that personal and social interests are two aspects of the same thing. Part of it is undoubtedly "comradely discipline and voluntary observation of the rules of communist social living [*obshchezhitie*]."[13] It is also often said that "communist morality proceeds from the premise that labor is man's chief obligation and source of happiness."[14] Khrushchev has described the ethical code of communism as "devotion to communism and refusal to compromise with its enemies, a sense of social duty, active participation in work for the benefit of society, comradely mutual aid, honesty and truthfulness, and intolerance of those who violate social order."[15] Another list includes "collectivism, love of

[10] V. Platkovskii, *Politicheskaia organizatsiia obshchestva pri perekhode k kommunizmu* (Moscow: Gospolitizdat, 1962), p. 62.

[11] L. S. Iavich, *Pravo i kommunizm* (Moscow: Gosudarstvennoe izdatel'stvo iuridicheskoi literatury, 1962), p. 83.

[12] Academician G. E. Glezerman has added the qualification that not all "moral norms will become habits" but only the "elementary norms of conduct." The distinction between these two is not clear, but this does indicate that at least Glezerman's new communist man is not a compulsive "do-gooder." See V. Sukhodeev, "Problemy kommunisticheskovo vospitaniia," *Kommunist*, 1961, no. 2.

[13] P. N. Fedoseev, "Dialektika pererastaniia sotsializma v kommunizm," *Voprosy filosofii*, 1961, no. 10, p. 39.

[14] Kon, "Communism: The Moral Factor," p. 5.

[15] N. S. Khrushchev, "Kontrol'nye tsifry razvitiia narodnovo khoziaistva SSSR na 1959–1965 gody," in *Vneocherednoi XXI S" ezd Kommunisticheskoi partii*

work, consciousness of social duty, socialist internationalism and patriotism."[16]

The new communist man, as a reflection of this moral code, will be a paragon of all the communist virtues. He will be "the embodiment of harmonious mental development and physical perfection, spiritual riches and moral purity."[17] If one takes at face value the constant references to his love of work, there does seem to be a possibility that he will be a bit compulsive about his role in social production. This seems especially likely if one accepts the statement by D. I. Chesnokov that "to work and to work in an organized way . . . will be the most important need of the toilers of communist society."[18] A rather more heroic image is presented by P. I. Nikitin:

> The man of communist society is above all a fighter-builder, a creator-originator, [a man of] free, creative labor which brings him deep, moral satisfaction. Great and genuine happiness consists of this. Man by his very nature is essentially restless. To be content is death for him.[19]

Thus the new communist man will be perpetually "on the go," always striving toward a new goal. Since "communism means a society of intelligent, beautiful, strong men and women of joyful, optimistic labor,"[20] the future citizen will apparently not let his restlessness dim his positive outlook on life and society.

The attitude of the new communist man toward labor will not, it is said, be motivated by considerations of personal reward, particularly since labor will not be the yardstick by which he will receive goods from the public stores. The socialist principle of material self-interest or incentive (*zainteresovannost'*) in labor will give way to "moral self-interest" under communism.[21] This moral self-interest, or incentive, is

---

*Sovetskovo Soiza: Stenograficheskii otchet*, 2 vols. (Moscow: Gospolitizdat, 1959), 1:55.

16 S. S. Fedoseev, *Sotsialisticheskoe gosudarstvo v period razvërnutovo stroitel'stva kommunizma* (Leningrad: Obshchestvo po rasprostraneniiu politicheskikh i nauchnykh znanii RSFSR, 1959), p. 38.

17 A. Kovalev, "Kommunizm—nachalo podlinnoi istorii chelovecheskovo obshchestva," *Kommunist*, 1962, no. 3, p. 104.

18 D. I. Chesnokov, *Ot gosudarstvennosti k obshchestvennomu samoupravleniiu* (Moscow: Gospolitizdat, 1960), p. 10.

19 P. I. Nikitin, *Chto takoe kommunizm* (Moscow: Izdatel'stvo Moskovskovo Universiteta, 1961), p. 132.

20 "Report of the Y.C.L. Committee and the Young Communist League's Tasks Stemming from the Decisions of the 22nd Party Congress—Report by Comrade S. P. Pavlov, First Secretary of the Y.C.L. Central Committee," *Pravda, Izvestiia*, April 17, 1962 (*CDSP*, vol. 14, no. 16, p. 3).

21 A. P. Sertsova, "Stroitel'stvo kommunizma—internatsional'noe delo," *Voprosy filosofii*, 1961, no. 11, p. 150.

probably the same concept as that expressed by the phrases "social interest," or the "conscious interests of the entire society." Lenin's comment about communist labor is quoted in connection with this "moral" or social incentive:

> Communist labor . . . is labor without wages for the good of society, work produced not for the discharge of a definite obligation, not for the right to receive a particular product, not according to the prior establishment of a legal norm, but labor that is voluntary, outside of norms, labor given without consideration of reward due to the habit of working for the general welfare and a conscious . . . attitude toward necessary work for the general welfare, labor as the need of a healthy organism.[23]

It is this "internal need to multiply and accumulate social wealth"[24] that marks off the new communist man as almost a separate psychological species. It is not simply the idea of working for others that is so unique—people devote their lives to philanthropic causes even in the decadent West—but the thoroughgoing application of this principle to every person in every situation of social production. If the new communist man will find his greatest happiness in working for others, it follows that he will be relatively unhappy if he cannot work or if his work is not perceived to be beneficial to society. Since it is recognized in Soviet theory that not all work is equally beneficial, the individual's primary need for socially useful labor may, in itself, become a source of conflict—especially if automation creates a labor surplus and a shortened work-day. In other words, one plausible outcome could be that men would compete for the pleasure of maximizing their contribution to society.

Soviet theory, however, rejects this suggestion because maximizing pleasure is a form of ego satisfaction, and the individual ego is rejected as a potential conflicting force in society. Soviet theorists do mention communist society's concern for each individual's "free development of the personality," but this is done with the ultimate benefit of society in view; it is a bounty, part of the nurture which society offers, and hardly the same thing as conscious recognition of the ego as a legitimate, countervailing force to social interests. If a worker of communist society should receive orders to report to the coldest and most barren

[22] I. Ia. Oblomskaia, "Razvitie material'noi zainteresovannosti kak ekonomicheskoi kategorii pri perekhode k kommunizmu," *Vestnik Moskovskovo Universiteta (Filosofiia)*, 1963, no. 3, p. 6.
[23] V. I. Lenin, *Sochinenie*, XXX, 482 as quoted in V. Karpinskii, *Besedy o kommunizme*, 2nd ed. (Moscow: Gospolitizdat, 1958), p. 104.
[24] P. N. Fedoseev, *Kommunizm i filosofiia* (Moscow: Izdatel'stvo Akademii nauk SSSR, 1962), p. 246.

reaches of Siberia for five years of heavy construction work, it would be *illegitimate* for him to complain on any personal grounds. Indeed, it would be illegitimate for him to feel any pangs of disappointment. The only legitimate response would be joyous acceptance of the great trust which society had placed in him and great inner satisfaction at the prospects of devoting himself even more completely to the good of communist society. In this sense, the new communist man will be a psychological brother of the monks, mendicants, priests, and ministers of religious orders. The latter, however, choose their way of life, and we can assume some sort of complementarity between their individual psychological needs and their "decision for God." The new communist man will have no such choice in his "decision for communism."

Communist man's internalized need to work is an important requirement of communist society, because society will not have any institutional machinery to enforce work regulations and attendance at the job but nevertheless will be highly mechanized and will require careful coordination of the human work force. Thus the internalized need for work is the only way by which society can ensure the harmonious fulfillment of its production norms and schedules. This point is made clear in the following:

> It is impossible to represent communism as some sort of spontaneous and disorderly collection of people where each does "anything he pleases," and does not consider the interests of other people nor submit to any rules or regulations. Communist society . . . is a society of the greatest order, and the highest organization and discipline. But this order, this organization and discipline will not be guaranteed through the state and its administrative organs, but will be founded on the high consciousness of the members of society. Social goals, social order, obligations toward other people will achieve the highest degree of expression—*they will enter into the heart and soul of the people, becoming a living need* of the members of communist society.[25]

The idea that work will be a "living need" of each man is supported by the concept of work as a condition of life, almost as important as air and water, without which man descends to a vegetable existence. There is plenty of support for this idea both in the theory of Karl Marx and in the practical necessities of maintaining a highly industrialized, abundant society. Work is seen as the most important influence on the development of a man's character, for "in work the deepest, most well-defined

---

[25] V. I. Evdokimov, *Vozrastaiushchaia rol' partii v stroitel'stve kommunizma* (Moscow: Gospolitizdat, 1960), p. 56. (Emphasis mine.)

features of man's psychology are formed."[26] Yet we do find mention of the fact that labor is hardly its own reward:

> The process of work is hardly an end in itself. Even the transformation of work into a need does not remove its purposiveness—the result of work must be a definite quantity of material goods, which will fully satisfy people's needs.[27]

There seems to be a strong possibility that the habit of self-discipline in the work sphere may carry over into other areas of life. The "internal need" to subordinate oneself to a production plan could very well become a need to subjugate oneself to any and all collective decisions or opinions. This possibility is made quite explicit by G. C. Grigor'ev:

> The rule for people of communist society will be submission to the will of the majority without [the need for] any particular means of compulsion or, even more, punishment. *For the conscious member of society, it will be sufficient to know of a decision taken by the collective, or someone vested with its powers, for him then and there to submit to that decision.* Disagreement with the will of the collective will not serve as a basis for refusing to submit.[28]

The idea that "to know of a decision is to obey it" would certainly have a pervading influence on the psychology of the new communist man. Trained in public boarding schools, probably "from the cradle to the graduation certificate," in Strumilin's phrase, the future citizen of communism will learn to sense the direction in which the winds of social opinion are blowing and will be careful to bend with them. Of course, it may be argued, as the Soviet theoreticians have done in the past, that the citizen is free to dispute the question before the decision is taken and is bound by it only after the collective has made its will known. But in the larger and more realistic sense, every decision of public policy is provisional, subject to further modification, emendation, even reversal. Must the communist citizen consider each collective decision eternal? The tenor of current doctrine on the subject suggests that society would view with great displeasure any further agitation for the minority view after a decision has been made. The idea of submission to the collective will, therefore, implies a rather static view of social policy development. The new communist man will submit to the decision, then it will become a "habit" for him, and finally it will become hallowed, unquestioned, and unquestionable tradition.

---

[26] Moroz, *Dialekticheskii materializm*, p. 45.

[27] Oblomskaia, *Razvitie material'noi zainteresovannosti*, p. 5.

[28] G. C. Grigor'ev, *Obshchestvennaia vlast' pri kommunizme* (Perm': Permskoe knizhnoe izdatel'stvo, 1961), p. 53. (Emphasis mine.)

The emphasis on submission also spills over to the area of the new communist man's consumption patterns. From the standpoint of individual consumption, the familiar concept of superabundance has meaning only if "distribution according to needs" can be defined in some way that avoids shortages, unsatisfied needs, hoarding, favoritism, and all the other potential evils of such a system. The fundamental doctrinal concept in this area is that of "reasonable needs," as contrasted to a desire for luxuries, a desire which will be considered illegitimate and will not be satisfied. The first implication of "reasonable needs" is that the new communist man must place a rather low value on the accumulation of material goods altogether. As one Soviet writer put it:

> Communism excludes those narrow-minded people for whom the highest goal is to acquire every possible luxurious object. . . . Communism assumes wise and enlightened members of society with a developed understanding of their goals.[29]

The problem then is to distinguish rationally between reasonable needs and luxuries, a problem which is complicated by the fact that "as social wealth grows, many of those things which are now considered a luxury will be transformed into articles of common usage."[30] Here we run into the "scientific" theme of Soviet Marxism. It is made clear, first of all, that "we have in mind not the extravagant wishes, not the sick thirst for profit and personal enrichment which actually knows no bounds."[31] This enables the theorist to continue: "If we have in mind not whims and caprices but normal human needs, then their amount can always be more or less precisely determined in each historical stage of social development."[32] There are difficulties in this calculation, as we have seen in the preceding chapter, but let us assume that such calculations can be made "scientifically" to everyone's satisfaction. Distribution would still depend on the individual's own "consciousness" of the need for moderation in personal aggrandizement, as is made evident in the following:

> Individual needs of the people were not and never will be identical. Therefore, communist distribution would simply be impossible to realize according to a single standard norm of consumption.
>     Society will, of course, scientifically calculate general, fundamental

[29] G. Shakhnazarov, *Kommunizm i svoboda lichnosti* (Moscow: Izdatel'stvo TsK VLKSM, "Molodaia gvardiia," 1960), p. 48.

[30] *Ibid.*

[31] M. P. Sakov, *Osnovnoi printsip kommunizma* (Moscow: Gospolitizdat, 1961), p. 29.

[32] *Ibid.*

average norms of consumption not to force them on each individual but to plan production correctly. How much and what kind of products to take will be determined by each man depending upon his individual needs. Having different individual needs, people will not take from the social fund identical quantities of material goods according to an established norm, but rather the amount that is necessary in order to satisfy their personal requirements. Limits will themselves become a need of the people, but not through obligatory norms and external limitations.[33]

If self-determination of one's reasonable needs is to be the rule, then everything will indeed depend on the creation of a new communist man who will not set much store in physical possessions, who will be content with the absolute minimum in everything, who will, in fact, censure anyone who takes more than the minimum. But how will this minimum be determined? If it is left to the individual, will not a certain inequity enter the distribution system?

These questions go unanswered—in fact, they go unasked—by present-day theoreticians, who are content to point out that certain rational calculations of necessary food intake, clothing, and shelter can be made and conclude that the new communist man would be guided by such calculations. But the real answer to the question involves the basic image of communist man as uninterested in consumption. This gives him an economic split personality, for it turns out that he is basically *non-materialistic in consumption, but highly materialistic in production.* One might well ask how a man could be so absorbed in the process of producing things that he is not interested in using! It seems to contradict the statement quoted earlier that work will not be an end in itself for the new communist man but will be valued in terms of the goods it produces.

The conclusion that communist man will not be much concerned with consumption can be derived quite readily from the doctrine. We start with the simple fact that even superabundance cannot mean an infinite quantity of any particular consumable item. Since supplies are ultimately limited, each conscious citizen will feel bound to take only what he needs. He will calculate these needs, perhaps with the aid of some general guidelines published by society, and everything will work smoothly, *as long as he does not want something he does not need.* It is *desire*, not need, that must be eliminated from the personality of the new communist man. There must be no acquisitiveness in his personality, for if there were, this fundamentally emotional urge to acquire might extend to an object that could not be justified as needed, even with the most desperate manipulations of society's guidelines. The only

---

[33] *Ibid.*, pp. 59–60.

social solution of this psychological dilemma would be the total devaluation of personal consumption and possessions. In fact, this solution would undoubtedly be brought to bear on the unusual individual who managed to acquire more than the amount his collective considered "necessary."

Current Soviet theory denies outright the possibility that the communist man will desire anything not actually necessary for his functioning as a useful member of society. It is said that "the proposition is unwarranted that a normal man, having enough clothing, will suddenly develop the wish to have a significantly greater quantity."[34] Under full communism, such people "will be considered abnormal."[35] It is interesting to speculate on what actions society would take to "cure" this abnormality. Certainly it would have all the remedies at its disposal.

Strumilin is one of the few Soviet writers who suggests that communist man may not be totally impervious to the temptations of acquisitiveness, for he writes: "The principle 'to each according to his needs' is not the equivalent of the principle, to each will be given whatever and as much as he wants. Only reasonable demands will be satisfied."[36] Thus, Strumilin apparently foresees the possibility of the new communist man wanting more than he needs.

In a larger context, there seems to be considerable doubt among Soviet theoreticians that the proper communist morality can be developed without assuring an extremely high standard of living. This directly contradicts that body of doctrine which sees communist man as a person without particular interest in the acquisition of the products of his labor. Numerous references can be found in contemporary Soviet doctrinal literature to the idea that "communist ideals can be realized only under conditions of an abundance of society's material wealth, and only on that basis is abundance of spiritual wealth possible."[37] But, since the new communist man will have only "reasonable needs," and since the "reasonableness" of these needs will be determined ultimately by society, it does not seem particularly logical to insist on superabundance, or even a very high level of personal consumption. On the other hand, if a highly affluent society is achieved, it does not make much sense to insist on a large measure of personal austerity.

This emphasis on personal austerity in the midst of vast social wealth is one of the most striking features of contemporary theory on communism. It seems to go beyond doctrinal concern that superabundance

---

34 Nikitin, *Chto takoe kommunizm*, p. 87.

35 *Ibid.*

36 S. G. Strumilin, *Problemy sotsializma i kommunizma v SSSR* (Moscow: Izdatel'stvo ekonomicheskoi literatury, 1961), p. 361.

37 Nikitin, *Chto takoe kommunizm*, p. 115.

would be impossible if everyone were infected with the "sick craving for all luxuries." The ultimate ideal is a man who values products for their uses, who applies the utilitarian yardstick to all the material things of life. The idea of collecting things simply for the pleasure of having them must be stamped out, since the acquisitive instinct hinders the development of communist morality. For example, on the matter of clothing, M. P. Sakov writes:

> Under communism the attitude of people toward material things will change. They will acquire for personal use only enough to wear. No one will collect suits and dresses, boots and shoes, aimlessly accumulating them in his wardrobe. . . . Reasonable needs for clothing and footwear are determined by climatic conditions, time of year, age and sex, type of occupation and social activities.[38]

Another writer sees the very nature of the distribution system as responsible for the atrophy of acquisitiveness:

> Sometimes one hears the opinion that since under communism everyone will receive according to needs, then consequently everyone will accumulate many different things. This is a naive representation of communism. It is precisely due to the fact that a man will be able to acquire anything he needs at any time that in daily life he will actually surround himself with only a small quantity of absolutely necessary articles.[39]

This approach sees the instinct for possession of material things as more or less dependent on the difficulty of their attainment. This idea may have some validity, but it also has the result, when carried to the extreme of affluence, of robbing labor of its chief stimulus. It is probably correct to say that an easily obtained item is less highly valued, is less *desired*, than an item that is difficult to acquire. Communist man could, on this count, be expected to have little interest in the possession of such commonplace articles. But it is more difficult to imagine that a reasonable communist man would consider the production of these items his most essential "living need." Even under communism, a worker's attitude toward an item as a consumer product must affect his feeling about the importance of producing it.

There has been considerable comment in the Soviet literature on the activities of the new communist man during his leisure time and the educational and cultural attainments which will enrich his leisure pursuits. The point has been made by Strumilin, as by others, that despite the present emphasis on production as the key to communism, "the

---

[38] Sakov, *Osnovnoi printsip kommunizma*, p. 34.
[39] M. I. Lifanov, *O byte pri kommunizme* (Moscow: Gospolitizdat, 1961), p. 17.

purpose of [communism] is neither higher productive work, nor the shortest work day, nor complete abundance of material wealth and such . . . [but] the freedom of man from all external obstacles to the full development of all personal inclinations and abilities."[40] Communism is seen as a purifying influence that will cleanse man's soul of the moral stains brought about by the capitalist struggle for economic existence. Thus it is said that "the future communist society, built on the foundation of science and wisdom, will suppress neither individuality nor the emotional side of man's life, but, on the contrary, will develop it, freeing man's personality from the humiliating struggle for existence and man's emotions from contact with dirt."[41]

A great and totally unprecedented multiplication of creative abilities and artistic products is predicted under communism. Communist society will provide the kind of harmonious, secure, and invigorating existence that will free man's creative potential. It is stated with conviction that "only in communist society will creativity become the accomplishment of all and the genius of man create remarkable works of literature, music and art which will surpass all the best that had been created up to that time."[42] Another contemporary theoretician predicts:

> Communist society will create the most favorable conditions for the manifestation and development of talents and abilities of all people. Various forms of amateur [samodeiatel'nyi] art . . . will acquire an even more massive and multifaceted character, being raised to the level of genuine professional art.[43]

This highly idealized picture is seconded by Strumilin, who predicts that "many millions" of talented working people will be discovered because "science and all the arts will become a general accomplishment of all the people."[44] In another work, he predicts somewhat more modestly that "in their hours off work, hundreds of thousands of workers will turn to invention or reinforce the ranks of public figures, scientists and scholars, writers, inspired musicians and artists."[45]

However, not all Soviet theoreticians are convinced that masterpieces will flow from the massed ranks of the leisure-time artists. A consider-

[40] S. G. Strumilin, *Rabochii den' i kommunizm* (Moscow: Profizdat, 1959), p. 7.
[41] Kelle, *Kommunizm i gumanizm*, p. 48.
[42] Shakhnazarov, *Kommunizm i svoboda lichnosti*, p. 95.
[43] Sakov, *Osnovnoi printsip kommunizma*, p. 42.
[44] Strumilin, *Problemy sotsializma i kommunizma*, p. 354.
[45] S. G. Strumilin, "What Communism Is: Thoughts about the Future," *Oktiabr'*, 1960, no. 3 (*CDSP*, vol. 12, no. 15, p. 14).

ably more conservative viewpoint was expressed in *Kommunist*, the most authoritative theoretical journal, by another, less eminent writer:

> There is every reason to believe that the distance between the talent of the separate, most distinguished geniuses and the talents of the entire masses of members of society in the higher phase of communism will not be so great as in the past or present. . . . But the difference between professional and non-professional in art, as in any other field, will exist.[46]

This viewpoint seems more reasonable, and it is more typical of the general view. It has the advantage of offering the best of two worlds: the populist view of art as the province of the people, and the vision of individual genius still rising above the highly cultured crowd with towering works of inspiration. Communist society offers the opportunity for development of potential gifts without assuring that everyone will be able to turn out works of first-rate quality. As one Soviet writer put it: "In the future society not everyone will become a Raphael, but every person within whom resides [the genius of] Raphael will have the opportunity of freely developing his abilities."[47]

The same sort of approach is taken toward the problem of varying levels of intelligence. While it is taken for granted that those of lesser ability will not be discriminated against, there is recognition of the fact that not all new communist men will be fit for the same level of productive work or leadership. Of course, the Soviet theory of human intelligence is heavily biased toward the influence of environmental factors, and this will mean that under the standardized environment of communism the varying levels of intelligence will be brought closer together than ever before. Nevertheless, it is recognized that

> absolutely identical surroundings for all people have never existed and do not exist now. And they will not exist even in the most distant future. Therefore, one person becomes more able to do a particular thing than another; one becomes a more decisive person than another.[48]

In the same manner, the new communist man is expected to attain new levels of physical perfection, to be "beautiful," healthy, strong, and an accomplished athlete, without everyone reaching quite the same level. It is even predicted with some confidence that "in the communist society, people will live 150 years. Such is the highest possible natural age of a man as determined by present-day Soviet science."[49]

---

[46]A. Egorov, "Kommunizm i iskusstvo," *Kommunist*, 1960, no. 4, p. 85.

[47] A. F. Shishkin, "Stroitel'stvo kommunizma i nekotorye problemy marksistskoi etiki," *Voprosy filosofii*, 1959, no. 2, p. 15.

[48] Nikitin, *Chto takoe kommunizm*, p. 126.

[49] Karpinskii, *Besedy o kommunizme*, p. 112.

The new communist man is envisioned as a man of wide talents and wide interests, a man who has achieved a good appreciation of the world's culture and who is creative in both avocation and vocation. The exact scope of his "poly-specialization," as discussed earlier, is a matter for dispute between the "optimists" and "pessimists" of the Soviet philosophical scene. In fact, the main point at issue between the optimists and pessimists is their conflicting images of what the new communist man will be able to accomplish. The optimists are never more optimistic than when considering the future citizen's wide range of accomplishments, while the pessimists see only limited gains, emphasizing that new communist men will not be supermen. In any case, there is general agreement that the range of his interests and skills will considerably exceed the scope of the present Soviet worker's.

Considering the type of educational system and environmental conditioning that is planned for communist society, there is every reason to give some credence to this claim. No society of the past or present has ever given all its citizens even a reasonable approximation of equal opportunity to reach their potentials, either through uniform excellence in education or through uniform elimination of environmental barriers to full development. It is at least highly likely that a communist society, if ever established in the projected form, would be able to supply more uniformly and technically excellent education than any previous society, and great mobilization of public encouragement for achievement would certainly "inspire" the communist student to do his best.

There is a limit, however, to the results which can be achieved by education and social pressure. Against them must be weighed the onus of public opinion on the nonconformist and the tendency toward the development of the social engineer's dream of the model citizen, whose chief characteristics will be his malleability and his rather compulsive drive toward complete integration in the collective. These factors may bring about a communist society with many more *good* artists, scientists, and musicians, but many less *great* ones than ever before. There is a danger woven into the fabric of communist society that the new communist man may become a model of highly cultured and accomplished mediocrity.

There is also some question as to whether the virtually complete submergence of the self in collective values is quite the healthiest prospect for a human being, even if such a thing is possible. If men could be truly created in this image, there is every reason to suspect that they would be sorely lacking in decisiveness and self-confidence, that they would be unable to take the initiative without the assurance of collective sanction. As we have seen, the new communist man will be totally absorbed in his work for the collective, valuing it above all his other activities. This glorification of labor can be carried to rather ridiculous and mentally debilitating extremes, as exemplified in the words attributed to Alex Ulesov, a hero of socialist labor, when asked about his work:

> If you take me away from my favorite activity, from my work, I feel paralyzed, unwell, and each time I am released from work I wait [until I can return]. But if I am given an extra two or three hours of my creative labor, then I feel free and happy, and I don't notice how the time flies. This is genuine happiness—the happiness of creativity.[50]

Now such a worker—actually a compulsive worker—is held up as a model of the future communist man, and this fact, even apart from the rest of the image, leads one to suspect that the new communist man may well be not only a mediocre thinker but a highly compulsive, neurotic non-individual, an animated cog in the social machine.

The very idea of creating a model human being implies a certain uniformity, a rounding off of individual characteristics so that everyone can fit the mold. In addition, the characteristics which present theory has picked for communist man tend to increase the probability that he will emerge as a rather faceless, thoroughly socialized being with little to distinguish him from his fellows. If society is successful in creating such a person—indeed, if it is at all possible to create such an animal—he will have the inner security that is derived from having a purpose, a group to support, direct, and reward him, and the clear conscience and easy spirit that comes from an environment largely cleansed of discord and conflict. He will be wide in his interests, but narrow in his opinions and conservative in his outlook on life. He will know his communist catechism backwards and forwards, and he will apply its immortal maxims to every situation he meets in daily life.

Will the new communist man be happy? Under such ideal conditions, he probably will be, as Soviet theorists assert. Perhaps in the sphere of personal relations the possibility of some unhappiness might creep in, as one Soviet writer has cautioned:

> Of course, no one can guarantee that under communism each man will necessarily be happy. . . . Too many variables go into a man's fate and it is not within the power of the people to give to all the same pleasant course.[51]

But unhappiness will be the exception, not the rule, for the man of the future. His life will be shaped in a closed society, and his ignorance will

---

[50] *O kommunizme: Kniga dlia chteniia* (Moscow: Gospolitizdat, 1963), p. 191. In the preface this chapter is attributed to G. E. Glezerman.

[51] Shakhnazarov, *Kommunizm i svoboda lichnosti*, p. 67.

be his bliss. Doubts, anxieties, insecurity, all the psychological side effects of modern Western society will be carefully excised from the corpus of communist society. The future communist citizen will be free to be the only thing he will know how to be—a model citizen, a new communist man.

# CHAPTER V  EPILOGUE

When Nikita Khrushchev was removed from political life in 1964, Soviet utopianism lost its most powerful and energetic spokesman. Lacking further initiative from the top, Soviet ideologists continued to write about communism, but they wrote with decreasing frequency and ardor. As time went on, the subject receded from the foreground, and by 1969 it was rarely mentioned.

The new regime was determined to be more businesslike, more circumspect, more sensible. It wanted to avoid the flamboyance and theatricality of Khrushchevism and the restless, unpredictable fluidity of Khrushchev's policies. Settling down to mundane matters also meant eschewing the glitter of Khrushchev's long-run visions of communism. The new regime recognized that Khrushchev had overreached himself—and Soviet capabilities—by proclaiming in the 1961 Party Program that the "present generation of Soviet people will live under communism." Khrushchev's unbounded, irrepressible optimism was unwarranted in the eyes of Brezhnev and his colleagues. Khrushchev, in fact, left behind a number of economic and social problems which sharply contrasted with his cheerful prophecies. The new leadership group thus set about solving the problems of the here and now, leaving the vision of the future intact but choosing to emphasize more practical and pressing matters.

The new leaders also revised the priorities of the previous period, investing more rubles in military equipment, particularly advanced missile systems. The Cuban missile crisis had clearly revealed Soviet relative weakness in this area, and the new regime opted for a policy of detente through strength. The rubles for defense hardware were necessarily diverted from those civilian industries that were to build the "material-technical base" of communism. In addition, the new regime announced, in March 1965, a program of increased investments in agriculture which was intended to eliminate the chronic lag in agricultural productivity. Even though investments never reached the predicted level, this program also implied the diversion of rubles from those industries that were supposed to provide the Soviet consumer with an increasingly affluent standard of living.

In contrast to Khrushchev's style, the Brezhnev regime has characteristically preferred an incremental, relatively cautious and conservative approach to solving problems. Proposed solutions have been tested experimentally, on a limited scale, and gradually expanded when experience indicated success. Thus the long-run goal has been divided into a succession of short-run, relatively pragmatic policies. The glow of communism can still be seen over the horizon, but the regime has preferred to look for firm footing before taking its next step. Faced with this changed atmosphere, Soviet ideologists have modified their approach to the subject of communist society. Two main trends can be discerned, in their writings on the subject in the decade since Khrushchev's removal: (1) decreased frequency of writing on the subject of communism and the transition to communism; (2) relatively greater attention to defining the present transitional stage and less emphasis on future stages of development.

The Khrushchevian theory of communism has not been directly attacked, and indeed most of his definitions remain intact, but the more optimistic forecasts and the specific timetable for development to the communist stage have been ignored. Khrushchev's assertion that the dictatorship of the proletariat had been replaced in the Soviet Union by the "state of the whole people" was reconfirmed (although mentioned less often), along with its ostensible features of increased participatory democracy for Soviet citizens and the decreasing role of "compulsion" and increasing importance of "persuasion" in observance of socialist norms of behavior. But the timetable of communist construction was stretched and left far vaguer than in Khrushchev's formulation; and the phrase "rapid building of communism" (*razvernutoe stroitel'stvo kommunizma*) was eventually dropped as a description of the present Soviet historical stage of development—to be replaced by the simple phrase "building communism." D. I. Chesnokov, an ideologist possessing remarkable sensitivity to changing ideological currents, indicated the shift in emphasis in an article that appeared just a year after Khrushchev's fall:

Undoubtedly, the socialist state is neither eliminated nor abolished—it withers away. However, speaking about the withering away of the state, V. I. Lenin first emphasized the "extended period [required for] this process, its dependence on the rapidity of development of the highest phase of communism," and second, pointed out that this process would be both gradual and natural. If one takes a long-run perspective, then the process of withering away of the state can be divided into a whole set of stages. . . . To the extent that economic conditions of socialist society develop, its gradual transition to communism creates the conditions for the gradual withering away of the state.[1]

Such mentions of communism as did appear in the next several years consistently mentioned the prolonged and gradual nature of the transition process. This trend was enhanced by developments in China. Ironically, it was the Chinese "great leap forward" campaign in 1958 that had been the immediate stimulus for Khrushchev's sponsorship of imminent communism in the Soviet Union. The Chinese Cultural Revolution of the mid-sixties, however, evoked the opposite reaction from the Brezhnev leadership: instead of emulating the Chinese and "going one up" by claiming priority in social progress, as Khrushchev had done, the post-Khrushchev regime stressed the dangers of hasty "unscientific" efforts to restructure society. The conservative Soviet reaction to the Cultural Revolution had the effect of pushing communist society further into the Soviet future. The following is typical of Soviet reaction:

> The creation of communism is a *natural historical process* accomplished through objective laws. This means that economic and social relations in the process of communist construction are not created through an act of will, but rather in accordance with the achieved level of productive forces; it means that each successive stage of social development emerges from the preceding stage and that it is impossible, through human will, to skip through incomplete stages of development. Society, for example, has not the power now to move forward to the communist principle of distribution according to needs, since it has not yet achieved the level of development of productive forces required for that stage.[2]

There can be no doubt that the Chinese Cultural Revolution, with its attack on the established power structure of Chinese society (and particularly the Chinese Communist party), was viewed with great alarm by the Soviet leaders. Similarly, the liberal reforms announced by the Dubcek regime in Czechoslovakia during the spring of 1968 were viewed as a threat (because of their potential for domestic emulation) by Brezhnev and his colleagues. The effects of external events were noticeable in the ideological sphere. Most evident was the return to "Leninism" as a universally applicable theory of existence. This in itself

---

[1] D. I. Chesnokov, "Razvitie sovetskoi sotsialisticheskoi gosudarstvennosti," *Kommunist*, 1965, no. 17, p. 20.

[2] V. Afanas'ev, "Stroitel'stvo kommunizma—nauchno upravliaemyi protsess," *Kommunist*, 1967, no. 14, p. 65.

was an indication of the regime's desire to emphasize its ties with the past both as an argument against dangerous innovation and a symbol of its solidity. During 1969, and in the aftermath of the intervention in Czechoslovakia, there was practically no mention of the transition to communist society, although the phrase "building communism" was still occasionally used, without elaboration.

From what appeared to be a passing remark by Leonid Brezhnev in his Central Committee Report to the Twenty-fourth Party Congress (March 1971), Soviet ideologists began to write of a new historical stage which the Soviet Union had reached on the way to communism: the stage of "developed socialist society." Because Brezhnev did not mention the time when this stage had been reached and did not define its characteristics, there has since been some confusion in ideological circles over both questions. Brezhnev merely remarked that "through their own labors the Soviet people have built a developed socialist society, of which Lenin spoke in 1918 as our country's future."[3]

The resolutions adopted by that Party congress also used the phrase without any descriptive comment, and the words quickly became a standard part of the ideological repertoire. Because theorists lacked authoritative guidance, the meaning of "developed" or "fully developed" socialist society—as distinct from the socialist society that had existed since 1936, by Soviet definition—became just as quickly a matter of dispute. The specifics of this debate are not particularly noteworthy, but to some extent the entire exercise has generated renewed attention to the theoretical questions of building communism. Brezhnev opened the door to this trend by connecting the completion of the "developed socialist society" to the process of building communism.[4] The stage of developed socialist society was in due course adopted by other countries in the Soviet orbit as an immediate objective, once again affirming Soviet leadership.

Although the phrase is now widely used, Brezhnev has not elaborated on its meaning and, as always in the absence of authoritative definitions, the bulk of commentary has been rather cautious. Naturally, the phrase primarily describes the present condition of Soviet society and there has been relatively little mention of how this stage will eventually move toward the "fully developed" communist society. Nevertheless, there has been an increasing tendency to return to the themes of the Khrushchev era since the nadir of utopianism in 1969. An example of this is the prediction by one ideologist (in May 1973) that "class

---

[3] L. I. Brezhnev, "Otchetnyi doklad TsK KPSS XXIV S'ezdu KPSS," *Kommunist*, 1971, no. 5, p. 31.
[4] *Ibid.*

differences between workers and peasants will disappear earlier than
will other complex problems of building communism, such as building
the material-technical base of communism, overcoming the differences
between mental and physical workers . . . and the change to distribution
according to need."[5] Even the old "pessimists vs. optimists" debate of
the Khrushchev years, concerning the nature of the division of labor
under full communism, has been renewed.[6]

Another development which has stimulated interest in the periodization of the present stage of development was Brezhnev's announcement
in December 1972 that a new constitution would be drafted, after more
than a decade of such announcements and subsequent silences. Even
without a single published excerpt of the new draft constitution, it is
clear that the new text is meant to define a new historical stage and will
perforce contain definitions of Soviet stages of progress toward the
building of a full communist society. This process of defining historical
stages inevitably leads to further utopian speculation, linking the
present stage to the communist future. Thus the whole process of writing a new constitution for "developed socialist society," with its "state
of the whole people," engenders the kind of philosophical utopianism
that characterized the Khrushchev era. The utopianism of the Brezhnev
era has not reached—and may never reach—the level of the earlier
period, but it does demonstrate a central and absolutely decisive point:
*there can be no Soviet system of government, with its legitimate one-
party monopoly of power, without a continuing, viable mission of building communism as its justification.*

Like a moth circling a flame, the Soviet regime is drawn by its very
nature closer to its all-consuming end. It cannot fly away, for that
would deny its nature, nor can it stay at a safe distance forever. The
goal is part of the Party's essence, yet the goal, when reached, means
the Party's disappearance. The conservatism of the current regime and
even its suppression of dissident voices in Soviet society are only means
to the self-destructive end. As long as there is a one-party state in the
Soviet Union, and as long as Marxism-Leninism is its legitimizing
ideology, there will be a utopian goal known as communist society to
justify it and all its acts.

Will the moth ever fly too close to the flame? Can it defy nature and
declare its own survival even then? Or will it eventually become exhausted through endless orbits of barely decreasing radius? These seem

[5] A. Pashkov, "Ob etapakh ekonomicheskovo razvitiia sotsialisticheskovo obshchestva," *Kommunist*, 1973, no. 8, p. 38.
[6] See A. Yegorov, "Partiia nauchnovo kommunizma," *Kommunist*, 1973, no. 2
(*CDSP*, vol. 25, no. 13, pp. 8–11, 20).

to be the only alternatives open to the Soviet regime, unless it changes its character. If it continues to keep a safe distance indefinitely, it must eventually eschew the utopian goal and evolve into a more conservative and more repressive regime. In such a situation, the military and police forces would undoubtedly play a larger role; in Soviet parlance, the role of "compulsion" would inevitably grow as the role of "persuasion" necessarily declined in the absence of persuasive utopian goals. While this might prove to be a viable alternative to the present dilemma, it seems more likely that such a mutation of the Soviet regime would be destabilizing and would lead to increased dissident activities. The utopianism of the Soviet regime has always in the past tended to thwart dissenters even more effectively than the K.G.B.; and a regime which depended on the K.G.B. alone—without putting dissenters in the shameful position of opposing brotherhood and equality and prosperity —would be in serious difficulty. How much easier it would be to attack a frankly authoritarian, semimilitary regime without any utopian pretensions! Without "ideals," without the messaianic mission that has long fascinated Russian intellectuals, the regime would not only be open to attack from without—it would also suffer decay from within. Throughout Soviet history, the Communist party has always been most effective when confronted with its greatest challenges. Like an army, it suffers demoralization in times of relative peace. Then it becomes a slothful, self-serving, and somewhat disoriented giant. Like the pre-Revolutionary intelligentsia, it suffers from "Oblomovism"—the plight of the "superfluous men" whose inactivity and privileged social position made them guilty.

Thus the goal of communist society, bequeathed to the Party by Karl Marx, Frederick Engels, and Vladimir Ilyitch Lenin, has become a paradoxical legacy for their heirs. Within the next century, Soviet leaders will have to resolve the paradox. One suspects that the solution that they find will preserve their power and privilege, but beyond that the ideological consequences are difficult to imagine. The Soviet dissident Andrei Amalrik has asked whether the Soviet Union will survive until 1984. Despite his predictions, the answer seems to be an unqualified affirmative. But, considering the utopian paradox of this regime, one is entitled to wonder whether it can survive and maintain its forward momentum until 2084, or whether its own professed ideals will consume it.

# INDEX

on capitalism, 44–46
on communist man, 38–39
definition of freedom of, 35–36
on division of labor, 36–38, 132–33
on education, 44
on equality, 45–46
on the family, 41–42
on historical materialism, 44–45
on politics, 39
on production, 40–41
on the proletariat, 48
on property, 36–37
on representative democracy, 44
on the sexes, 41–42
on transition to communism, 34–35, 43
view of utopia of, 28–31
on work, 45, 71–72
Marxian utopia, 24
Marxism-Leninism
on historical inevitability, 60
moral values of, 12–13
as "science," 23–24, 173–74
utopian goals of 13–14
view of the future of, 2
Material desires, 176–77
Material self-interest, 71
"Material superabundance," 7, 95, 123–28, 173, 175
Material-technical base of communism, 85–86, 94–95, 98–99
Messianic tradition, 1
Mobilization through utopianism, 17–19
Model citizen, 180
Molotov, Viacheslav, 3
Money, elimination of, 124–26
Morality
according to Marx, 68
modern Soviet view of, 68–69, 73
More, Sir Thomas, 26–27, 32, 34, 101
Morris, William, 31–32

National income, 95
Nationalities, 86, 162–64
New Units of Settlement (NUS), 156–58
Nikitin, P. I., 169
Nonconformity, 151
Novoselov, N. S., 142

Oblomovism, 187
Orwell, George, 33, 114
Ostrovitianov, K. S., 126

Parenthood under communism, 103–6
Paris Commune, 44

Party Program (1961), 5, 64
on material goals, 93–95
Periodization of history, 61, 97, 185–86
Personality cult, 3
Personal property, 130–31
Personal wealth, 15
Planning, 120
Plato, 32, 34, 41
Politburo, as ideological authority, 22
Political consciousness, 109–10
Political socialization, 23
Politics under communism, 109–10
Property, 129–31
Public organizations, 67, 115–16
Public policy, 172

Religion and ideology, 12
Residential planning, 152–59
Rukovodstvo, 59, 141
Rural settlements, 160

Samizdat, 20
Scientific communism, 99
Scientific Soviet Marxism, 23–24, 73–74
Self-rule, 117–18
Sergeev, Kim, 143–44
Shklar, Judith, 27
Siniavskii, Andrei [pseud. Abram Tertz], 16
Sino-Soviet rivalry, 4–7
Skinner, B. F., 31, 33
Social consciousness, 90
Socialist revolution, 43, 47
Social rules, 111
Social services, 160–61
Soviet cadres, 5
Soviet ideology, effects of, 12–13
Soviets, 64–66, 116–17
Soviet society, diversity of, 18–20
Soviet Union as center of world communism, 5, 7
Sovkhoz, 83, 160
Sovnarkhoz, 116–18
Stages of history, 61, 97, 185–86
Stalin, Josef, 2, 15
personality cult of, 3
Standard of living, 128–29
State, future of, 63–64
Strumilin, S. G., 103–5, 111, 125, 141–42, 175, 177
Superabundance, 7, 95, 123–28, 173, 175

Technical-economic intelligentsia, 119
Tertz, Abram. See Siniavskii, Andrei

**Library of Congress Cataloging in Publication Data**

Gilison, Jerome M      1935–
    The Soviet image of utopia.

    Includes bibliographical references and index.
    1.  Communism—Russia.  2.  Utopias.  I.  Title.
HX313.5.G55          335.43          74-24388
ISBN 0-8018-1696-3